RELATING NARRATIVES

'Cavarero's text is one of the most brilliant, nuanced, inspiring, and erudite studies in philosophy and literature to be produced by a feminist scholar in recent years. This text is a pure pleasure to read as it confounds our understanding of autobiography, revealing the fundamental dependency of the one who might narrate his or her own life on the "you" to whom he or she turns in order to become a narratable subject. Cavarero moves with imagination and acute intelligence, with Arendt and Benjamin as her philosophers, through classical and modern works of literature to show us how the one to whom we speak constitutes the possibility of our own life-stories. Her conclusions reverberate with significance for thinking through the relation between ethics and narration, where telling, living, and loving come to life through the insuperability of the "you".'

Judith Butler, University of California, Berkeley

'*Relating Narratives* combines the insights of a philosopher and a storyteller in ways that command our fullest attention. Drawing on the thought of Hannah Arendt, Adriana Cavarero, Italy's most important feminist philosopher, offers us here an innovative ontology and politics of uniqueness. Remarkable in its range, the book powerfully addresses the crises of philosophy and feminist, literary and cultural theory today. It is a book that should not be ignored.'

Christine Battersby, University of Warwick

'Adriana Cavarero's book is a challenge to Anglo-American debates about the question of identity ... one hopes that the English speaking world will give her challenge the attention it deserves.'

Women's Philosophy Review

WARWICK STUDIES IN EUROPEAN PHILOSOPHY

Andrew Benjamin

Professor of Philosophy, University of Warwick

This series presents the best and most original work being done within the European philosophical tradition. The books included in the series seek not only to reflect what is taking place within European philosophy, they will also contribute to the growth and development of that plural tradition. Works written in English, as well as translations into English, are included, engaging the tradition at all levels – whether by introductions that show the contemporary philosophical power of certain works, or in collections that explore an important thinker or topic, as well as significant contributions that call for their own critical evaluations.

Also available in Warwick Studies in European Philosophy:

RELATING NARRATIVES

Storytelling and Selfhood

Adriana Cavarero

Translated and with an introduction by
Paul A. Kottman

London and New York

First published 1997, in Italian, as *Tu che mi guardi, tu che mi racconti*
by Giagiacomo Feltrinelli Editore
via Andegari, 20121 Milano, Italy

English translation first published 2000
by Routledge
2 Park Square, Milton Park, Abingdon, Oxon, OX14 4RN

Simultaneously published in the USA and Canada
by Routledge
270 Madison Ave, New York NY 10016

Routledge is an imprint of the Taylor & Francis Group

Transferred to Digital Printing 2006

Typeset in Perpetua by Taylor & Francis Books Ltd

British Library Cataloguing in Publication Data
A catalogue record for this book is available from the British Library

Library of Congress Cataloging in Publication Data
Cavarero, Adriana.
[Tu che mi guardi, tu che mi racconti. English]
Relating narratives: storytelling and selfhood / Adriana Cavarero;
translated with an introduction by Paul A. Kottman.
(Warwick studies in European philosophy)
Includes bibliographical references and index.
1. Narration (Rhetoric). 2. Literature–Philosophy.
3. Self in literature. 4. Self (Philosophy). 5. Autobiography.
6. Storytelling. 7. Self. I. Title. II. Series.
PN212.C38 2000
809'.93384–dc21   99-046437

ISBN 0–415–20057–1 (hbk)
ISBN 0–415–20058–X (pbk)

Publisher's Note

The publisher has gone to great lengths to ensure
the quality of this reprint but points out that some
imperfections in the original may be apparent

CONTENTS

CONTENTS

TRANSLATOR'S INTRODUCTION

Paul A. Kottman

> By a name
> I know not how to tell thee who I am
>
> (*Romeo and Juliet*)

Romeo's problem is, first of all, one of 'introduction.' How to introduce himself, his body, to Juliet; and how to avoid doing so through his father's name, which he, tragically, inherits.[1] His desire, the desire of all lovers, is that Juliet should recognize *who* he is, beyond his name.

To name *who* someone is, without being led astray into naming *what* he/she is, has long been something that the philosophical discourse(s) of metaphysics seem incapable of doing – for *who* someone is eludes philosophical knowledge. Hannah Arendt – whose thoughts provide an indispensable point of departure for Adriana Cavarero's work – notes that philosophy sets out to define or determine Man by establishing 'what' Man is, by enumerating qualities that 'he could possibly share with other living beings.'[2] Philosophical discourse is therefore unable to determine in words the individual *uniqueness* of a human being. As far as philosophy is concerned, remarks Arendt, 'who' someone is, in all of his or her singularity, 'retains a curious intangibility that confounds all efforts toward unequivocal verbal expression.' Put another way, 'the moment we want to say *who* someone is, our very vocabulary leads us astray into saying *what* he is.'[3] 'Who' someone is, therefore, marks a limit of philosophical language, a limit of conceptual definition – a limit that would then appear to make 'who' someone is into something ineffable.

And yet, this is not Arendt's point. 'Who' someone is remains inexpressible in philosophical terms – not because the term 'who' designates something that is absolutely unnameable or 'outside' language – but rather because each person reveals that he or she is absolutely unique and singular. It is this *uniqueness*, this oneness, which philosophy fails to express. Moreover, for Arendt, 'who' someone is is not ineffable at all, but rather is revealed and made manifest through that person's actions and speech – words and deeds which, *ex post facto*, form the unique life-story of that person. Arendt writes: '*Who* somebody is or was we can know only by knowing the story of which he is himself the hero – his biography, in other words.'[4] 'Who' someone is, therefore, remains inexpressible within the language of philosophy; but does not, as a result, remain utterly ineffable.[5] Rather, 'who' someone is can be 'known' (although this is not epistemological knowledge) through the narration of the life-story of which that person is the protagonist.

This is an important starting point for Cavarero's work.[6] When it comes to knowing 'who' someone is, the language of philosophy reveals its shortcomings and limitations, but in a way that shows how the bounds of philosophy do not also limit what is sayable or tellable. Importantly, philosophy is not the only discourse in which we know how to engage; it does not devour all of our language(s). Indeed, words are spoken and tales are told – tales that could never belong fully to philosophical discourse. Cavarero expresses this as follows:

> We could define it as the confrontation between two discursive regis-
> ters, which manifest opposite characteristics. One, that of philosophy,
> has the form of a definite knowledge which regards the universality of
> Man. The other, that of narration, has the form of a biographical
> knowledge which regards the unrepeatable identity of someone. The
> questions which sustain the two discursive styles are equally diverse.
> The first asks '*what* is Man?' The second asks instead of someone '*who* he
> or she is.' (p. 13 of this volume)

One could imagine the following objection: how would this 'confrontation' between 'philosophy' and 'narration' differ from the old alternative *logos/mythos*? Would not this 'confrontation' between 'philosophy' and 'narration' simply be an old philosophical 'confrontation,' one that relies upon familiar, unquestioned genres, registers, figures and so forth? And yet, I would suggest by way of introduction, that by offering itself as something 'other than philosophy,' the narration, according to Cavarero, also points towards what Jacques Derrida has called 'a genre beyond genre.'[7] That is to say, the narration here exceeds the opposition *myth/logos*, in so far as it takes on a sense, or reveals a latent potency, that is unforeseen by this opposition, and that cannot be contained by it. This question becomes even more pertinent when we consider that Cavarero suggests narration might be considered as a 'feminine art.'[8] Again, one could pose an analogous objection: 'if narration is said to be the feminine other of phallogo-centric philosophy, is this not simply to *figure* narration as feminine and philosophy as masculine, in a way that falls back upon the same old binaries and figures?' Yet, when Cavarero calls narration a 'feminine art,' she is implying that the feminine cannot be reduced to any one of its figurations within the male/female binary.[9] In this sense, narration – all the more so as something feminine – would designate a set of possibilities that exceed any philosophical opposition that would claim to contain it.[10] Here, these possibilities have precisely to do with the disclosure of an absolutely unique existent, the tale of *who* someone is.

Importantly, immediately after Arendt writes of the 'curious intangibility' of 'who' someone is for philosophical discourse, she links philosophy's inability to determine 'who' someone is to '*politics*.'[11] Philosophy's failure to name 'who' someone uniquely is, in other words, also signals a failure of traditional Western politics. It indicates, for instance, the extent to which traditional philosophy and politics respond to universals, rather than to unique persons and their interaction. As a result, the link between narration, and the revelation of 'who' someone is through that narration, offer – for Arendt, and for Cavarero – a new sense of politics, an alternative way of understanding human interaction, as the interaction of unique existents.[12] I will try to outline some implications of this in what follows.

For both Arendt and Cavarero, the uniqueness of each life does not indicate a life lived in isolation, but rather 'the togetherness and intercourse' of these single existents. It is important to understand that what Cavarero has in mind by 'unique existent' here is not the same as the 'individual' championed by modern political doctrines. Political doctrines, from Aristotle to Hobbes, notes Cavarero, all 'respond, in different ways, to the same question: what is Man? This insistence on the *what* to the detriment of the *who* is symptomatically even truer when the "individualist theory" refuses to emphasize the competitive nature of the single, or "dissolves" it into the political principle of equality.'[13] Indeed, Cavarero criticizes the tradition of 'individualist thought' for the way in which it flattens out the uniqueness of the individual, in favor of a set of universal rights for the individual, which are 'equal,' or 'equivalent.'[14] The 'unique existent' in Cavarero's sense – contrary to the 'individual' invoked in modern and contemporary doctrines of 'individual rights' – is in a constitutive relation with the other, with *others*. Like Arendt, Cavarero begins from the simple fact that the first consideration for any politics is that human beings live together, and are constitutively exposed to each other through the bodily senses.[15] To this, Cavarero adds the fact that each of us is *narratable* by the other; that is, we are dependent upon the other for the narration of our own life-story, which begins from birth. To Arendt's notion of the constitutive exposure of the self, Cavarero thus adds the *narratability* of that self. The 'narratable self' – one of the central notions introduced in *Relating Narratives* – is a self, which, following Arendt, is exposed from birth within the interactive scene of the world (which Arendt calls 'political'). Through this constitutive exhibition, the 'self' comes to desire the tale of his or her own life-story from the mouth (or pen) of another.

The narration of a life-story, therefore, offers an alternative sense to politics, not only because it deals with unique persons, but because it illustrates the *interaction* of unique people. Arendt suggests that the fact 'that every individual life can eventually be told as a story with a beginning and end *is the prepolitical and prehistorical condition* of history.'[16] And Cavarero goes one step further and formulates this 'prepolitical and prehistorical condition' as the 'narratability' of every person, which is in a sense prior to whatever particular story or history that person then lives and leaves behind; prior to politics and history in the conventional sense. The narration of another's life-story, therefore, takes on the revealing and expositive sense that Arendt gives to politics. Cavarero provides a striking instance of this in *Relating Narratives*, through a compelling interpretation of Italian feminist practices of storytelling.[17] The reciprocal narrations of 'consciousness-raising groups' are one scene in which the self is constitutively exposed to the other – an exposure that makes this a *political* scene. In short, narration is political for Cavarero and Arendt first of all because it is *relational*. Furthermore, whereas philosophical discourse functions politically only through the question of 'what' men and women are – their qualities, or qualifications as individuals, citizens and so forth – narration reveals, in a way that totally refocuses the political, *who* someone actually is. Narration, writes Cavarero, is the 'verbal response' to this 'who' – a response which, remarkably, can take on the meaning of a political action.

When Cavarero speaks of a 'narratable self,' therefore, she is not speaking of the classical 'subject,' or about 'subject-formation.' What makes a narration a political act is not simply that this narration invokes the struggle of a collective subjectivity, but rather that it makes clear the fragility of the unique. The uniqueness and the unity of a self, which is disclosed through that self's actions and words, and which is then narrated as a unique and unified life-story, does not display any of the general characteristics of traditional subjectivity: interiority, psychology, agency, self-presence, mastery and so forth. Rather, the 'narratable self' is a unique *existent*, 'who' someone is. Also this 'narratable self' is constitutively *in relation* with others.[18] In this sense, Cavarero's work might be read alongside what Jean-Luc Nancy outlines in his own critique of subjectivity. Nancy remarks that the 'subject' has traditionally called up 'essence' or 'being,' but that this subject also 'designates and delivers an entirely different thought: that of *one* and that of some *one*, of the singular existent that the subject announces, promises, and at the same time conceals.'[19] Nancy, too, uses the pronoun 'who' to indicate an 'existent (and not the existence *of* the existent).' He also adds that this 'who' is indeed what is finally 'called forth' by the traditional philosophical question of essence.[20] To put it in Arendt's and

Cavarero's terms, the question of 'what' someone is, which asks after the 'essence' of Man, at the same time calls for the 'who' of the existent in response.

In all of these ways, the priority of the classical subject is displaced, in Cavarero's work, in favor of a self that is narratable. I emphasize this point in order to distinguish Cavarero's thinking from contemporary Anglo-American theories that endeavor to articulate the social, or psychic, or discursive 'formation of the subject.' (To be sure, the phrase 'Anglo–American theories' does not have a fixed referent, but, nevertheless, I trust that the English-speaking reader will allow that, without referring to a homogeneous unity, I might still introduce Cavarero's work as a 'translation,' that is, as something new that is entering an already living discursive environment.) Indeed, in my view, Cavarero's work offers a unique challenge, and thus an opportunity, for a contemporary Anglo-American thought that deals with subject-formation, or for a politics that relies upon revisiting the question of the 'subject.'

In order to better understand some points of comparison and divergence, I will imagine briefly an encounter between Cavarero's work and that of Judith Butler. Butler's work is especially helpful here – *not* because she is representative of Anglo-American theories of subject-formation[21] (on the contrary, while her work no doubt resonates with larger debates in the United States and elsewhere, and it is exemplary for its insightful innovation and philosophical rigor – not to mention its influence) – rather, Butler's work seems helpful in the context of this introduction, first because her work may offer a familiar point of departure for the English-speaking reader of this book, and second because it shares a number of concerns with Cavarero's work. Beyond the generalities – the fact that both have made significant contributions to feminism, that both are trained in philosophy, and work within a certain tradition of continental thought – I will try to outline some compatibilities and a number of divergences. My aim is not to take sides when discussing these two authors, for this does not seem to me to be a productive way to proceed.[22] I would rather, hopefully, create a space for a discussion that would include other voices as well, by indicating where and how Cavarero's work might effectively intervene in – by radically re-orienting – contemporary debates in the English-speaking world.

Butler's work is characterized by a trenchant articulation of the formation of the subject (as well as an articulation of the limits of that very articulation). Taking up Foucault, she understands the 'subject' to be constituted through an 'exclusionary matrix,' which also outlines 'the domain of that subject;' and thus which also produces 'those who are not yet 'subjects.' The subject, in so far as one can trace its formation, emerges through a matrix of power that forms subjects through a process of exclusion: by producing 'a constitutive outside to the subject.' As a result, the subject is understood to be formed through its unavoidable relationship to what becomes excluded in the process of its own formation 'as subject.'[23] Reminiscent of Hegel's account of the slave's march towards freedom and his fall back into 'unhappy consciousness,' Butler sees the subject as being constituted through 'a repudiation [of an abject outside] without which the subject cannot emerge.'[24] In this sense, Butler's articulation of subject-formation, or 'subjection,' emphasizes that one cannot speak of a 'subject' whose 'inside' is not always, already, in some sense inhabited and constituted by its 'outside.' In Butler's account, the repudiated 'outside' returns as a 'threatening spectre,' which reveals itself to be a kind of 'necessary outside' for 'the self-grounding presumptions of the subject' – an 'outside' that turns out, disturbingly, to be 'inside.'[25]

One might be tempted to see in this articulation a kind of affinity with Cavarero's assertion that, for the 'narratable self,' there is always a *necessary other*.[26] In other words, one might be tempted to see an affinity between the extent to which – for Butler – the 'subject' emerges through an inevitable relation with what is excluded as 'outside' the subject, and the way in which – for Cavarero – the narratable self is constitutively related to others. And yet, upon closer inspection, a number of important distinctions become clear – distinctions that open up a host of divergences between the two thinkers.

An initial difference between the 'abject outside,' which is, in Butler's terms, necessary for the emergence of the 'subject,' – and what Cavarero has in mind by 'the necessary other' – is the following. For Cavarero, the 'necessary other' is above all another person, an existent, a unique being. What Cavarero calls the 'necessary other' is therefore not an 'abject outside' that threatens the stability of the narratable self – but is rather simply *an other* narratable self. The relation between the 'narratable self,' as a unique individual, and the necessary other, as an equally unique existent, is above all a relation between singular persons. Moreover, the relation between 'narratable selves' in Cavarero's thinking need not be a threatening, or violent, relationship at all. Indeed, in this book, these relations often take the form of friendships or love affairs.[27] In the context of their narrative relation, neither 'narratable self' is reducible to an essence; nor could they be absolutely located in the 'domain of abject beings,' for instance.[28] This is one reason why Cavarero insists that the self is *narratable* and not *narrated*. It is an existence that has not been reduced to an essence, a 'who' that has not been distilled into the 'what.' In short, for Cavarero it is the unique, individual existent – who is in constitutive relation with other existents, and who is not yet, or no longer, a subject – who takes 'priority,' so to speak.

Butler's work, too, relies upon a working distinction between 'individuals' or 'persons,' and 'subjects.'[29] However, unlike Cavarero, she relies upon this distinction in order to revisit the paradox of subject-formation. Here the difference between 'persons' and 'subjects' is invoked in a way that gives 'priority' to the subject or subjection. Butler begins by asserting that 'subjection' is the very condition for the intelligibility of individual persons. In order to become 'intelligible' as individuals, she argues, it is first necessary that one become a 'subject,' or undergo subjection. Distinguishing the subject from the 'person' or the 'individual,' in order to treat the 'subject' as something distinct, she writes:

> 'The subject' is sometimes bandied about as if it were interchangeable with 'the person' or 'the individual.' The genealogy of the subject as a critical category, however, suggests that the subject, rather than be identified strictly with the individual, ought to be designated as a linguistic category, a place-holder, a structure in formation. Individuals come to occupy the site of the subject (the subject simultaneously emerges as a 'site'), and they enjoy intelligibility only to the extent that they are, as it were, first established in language. The subject is the linguistic occasion for the individual to achieve and reproduce intelligibility, the linguistic condition of its existence and agency. No individual becomes a subject without first becoming subjected or undergoing 'subjectivation' ... It makes little sense to treat 'the individual' as an intelligible term if individuals are said to acquire their intelligibility by becoming subjects.[30]

In this account, subjection is the condition of intelligibility, which in turn is the condition for speaking of 'individuals.' In other words, the 'individual' person acquires the only intelligibility he/she can have – a *linguistic* one – by becoming a subject. Without the linguistic category of the 'subject' to inhabit, the individual remains unintelligible, unsayable. In this sense, Butler's work would operate within that philosophical framework whose dominance Cavarero, following Arendt, seeks to undermine, precisely by illuminating the extent to which 'subjectivation' is not the only 'linguistic occasion' through which the individual can be revealed in language. Indeed, to presume moreover that unique beings can become 'intelligible' only through the 'critical category' of the subject is, for Cavarero, part of a philosophical legacy which seeks to efface the unique, the particular.[31] By contrast, Cavarero argues that uniqueness, the absolutely particular existent, has a meaning that is revealed through the narration of that person's life-story, precisely in so far as this person is *not* already 'subjected' to philosophical definition, or to the circular paradox of subjection. For Cavarero, as for Arendt, the intelligibility of the unique existent is not 'first established in language,' but rather he/she is a flesh and blood existent whose unique identity is revealed *ex post facto* through the words of his or her life-story.

Interestingly, Butler too refers to a certain relation between the formation of the subject and storytelling or auto-narration. Immediately after the passage I cited at length above, she writes:

> The story by which subjection is told is, inevitably, circular, presupposing the very subject for which it seeks to give an account. On the one hand, the subject can refer to its own genesis only by taking a third-person perspective on itself, that is, by dispossessing its own perspective in the act of narrating its genesis. On the other hand, the narration of how the subject is constituted presupposes that the constitution has already taken place, and thus arrives after the fact. The subject loses itself to tell the story of itself, but in telling the story of itself seeks to give an account of what the narration has already made plain.[32]

Here Butler too offers 'storytelling' or 'narration' as a way to understand the constitution of the subject. And as with Cavarero, there is a certain circularity to this account, but with some crucial differences.[33] First, Butler notes that the 'subject can only refer to its own genesis by taking a third-person perspective on itself, that is, by dispossessing its own perspective in the act of narrating its genesis.' (I would add that, in so far as the 'subject' in question is a 'linguistic category' and not an 'individual' or 'person,' the 'genesis' in question would not be birth. Nonetheless, like the person who cannot tell the story of his/her birth, the subject cannot account for its own genesis.) In Butler's account the subject does not rely upon another to tell him/her this story – but rather *takes* a third-person perspective upon his or her own subjectivity, and tells the story of the very genesis, which, as the subject of that story, he/she ought not to be able to know. The subject goes outside of itself in order to tell its own story ('loses itself to tell the story of itself'). This, remarks Cavarero, is the 'pretense' involved in the tradition of classical autobiography (which parallels the genealogy of the philosophical 'subject'). It is, Cavarero writes, 'the strange pretense of a self which makes himself an other in order to be able to tell his own story ... The *other* is here the fantasmatic product of a doubling, the supplement of an absence, the parody of a relation.'[34] Rather than repeat this classical strategy, Cavarero challenges the autonomy of philosophical autobiography by insisting upon 'an other who really is *an* other.'[35]

Moreover, Cavarero, in contrast to Butler, makes clear that the 'narratable self' cannot tell the story of his or her own genesis – which is, for Cavarero, not a discursive 'genesis,' but rather springs from birth. The 'narratable self' does not possess this appropriating power of the 'subject,' which can take the perspective of the third-person.[36] The narratable self, unlike the subject, does not make of him/herself a third-person, does not go from 'I' to 's/he,' but rather *desires this story, this story of birth, from the mouth of another*. For Cavarero, this desire is a fundamental feature of every 'narratable self.' (More on this desire in a moment.)

On the other hand, in the above passage Butler notes that 'the narration of how the subject is constituted presupposes that the constitution has already taken place, and thus arrives after the fact.' Here, the subject tells the tale of its own constitution, but in order to tell that tale the subject must already be fully constituted. This side of the paradox, which Butler outlines, in other words, arises from the temporal impossibility of the subject making itself into its own narratable 'object.' The subject, impossibly, *reflects* back upon itself in order to tell of its own formation. (Again, that we are talking about 'the subject' in the context of Butler's text in no way assures us that we are discussing a unique person. Rather, the 'story' in question here appears to be the story of the philosophical subject, the 'linguistic category,' or 'place-holder.' Hence, this 'story' would not be a personal life-story, but rather a 'genealogy.')[37]

Cavarero suggests that in personal experience, too, the 'narratable self is at once the transcendental *subject* and the elusive *object* of all autobiographical exercises of memory.' But Cavarero insists that this experience of memory is not the same as the 'reflecting' or reflexive structure, which characterizes the constitution of the subject.[38] While it is true that the narratable self functions as both 'subject and object' in Cavarero's account, the unreflective, inactive working of memory in the narratable self renders the universality of these terms 'subject/object' irremediably ambiguous. For indeed, in personal experience, the 'terms' *subject and object of the story* lose their generality, and function instead as expressions of the unique self's sense of familiarity within the context of auto-narration. Indeed, *narration* works here to displace philosophically intelligible discourse as the only possibility for speaking of 'individuals' (and, for that matter, of speaking about 'subjects or objects'). Moreover, in the autobiographical exercise of memory, as Cavarero outlines the matter, it is not a question of the self becoming 'intelligible' – but rather the experience that the self has of being narratable, and therefore *familiar*. When formulating what she means by the 'narratable self,' Cavarero does not use the terms 'intelligibility' or 'knowledge,' but rather she insists upon the 'familiar sense' of every self.[39] The 'narratable self' does not *make* him or herself into the object of his/her own narration – for instance, by *taking* the third-person perspective – but rather, as Cavarero puts it, '*lives him or herself* as his/her own story, without being able to distinguish the *I* who narrates from the *self* who gets narrated.'[40] Put simply, each of us is familiar with the experience of memory's auto-narration, which continually – and involuntarily – 'tells us our own personal story.' 'The narratable self,' writes Cavarero, 'finds its home, not simply in a conscious exercise of remembering, but in the spontaneous narrating structure of memory itself.'[41] This is not a temporally reflexive structure, but rather the temporality of a life-span – 'the temporal extension of a life-story which is this and not another.'[42]

In this way, the narratable self has the innate sense – which springs from having been born a unique being – that his or her life-story is unique and belongs to him or her alone. The 'story' of the birth of each narratable self would thus – contrary to the genesis of the subject – be equally unique and unrepeatable. Furthermore, Cavarero adds that this 'sense' extends towards our perception of others. Just as each of us has the sense that our life-story is unique, so too 'each of us knows that who we meet always has a unique story [storia]. And this is true even if we meet them for the first time without knowing their story at all.'[43] What is important, therefore, is not a *knowledge* of this story, or a knowledge of its contents or details. *What* the life-story says is not, finally, at issue. The 'intelligibility' of the person that we meet is, likewise, not at stake – for even in the absence of such intelligibility we know that the other is a unique person, with a unique story. We know this, moreover, without regard to whatever category or social place that person may occupy. Even the amnesiac, Cavarero points out, has the *sense* that he or she has a unique life-story – even without being able to recall it.[44] It is this *sense* of being narratable – quite apart from the content of the narration itself – and the accompanying sense that others are also narratable selves with unique stories, which is essential to the self, and which makes it possible to speak of a unique being that is not simply a 'subject.'

What is more, the 'narratable self' cannot be said to be a *product* of his or her life-story, or an effect of that story's performative force, but 'coincides rather with the uncontrollable narrative impulse of memory which produces the text [of this story].'[45] This is not to deny that stories have a performative or rhetorical force; rather, it is to suggest that this force is not essential to the 'narratable self.' While the 'narratable self' is not fully distinguishable from his or her life-story, neither is he or she reducible to the *contents* of this story. In other words, *what* this story tells about the person whose life it recounts does not, finally, *produce* or reveal the identity of that person – even if this person depends upon this life-story recounting *something*. 'Put simply,' writes Cavarero, 'through the unreflecting knowledge of my sense of self [dell'assporarmi], I know that I have a story and that I consist in this story … I could nevertheless not know myself to be narratable unless I was not always already interwoven into the autobiographical text of this story. Such an interweaving is indeed irreparable, and comes to the self as a reifying experience.'[46] Thus, Cavarero presents us with a narratable self whose identity – while interwoven with *what* his or her life-story recounts – consists in the unreflective sense that this life-story belongs to him or her alone, and that it therefore reveals *who* he or she uniquely is.

Cavarero goes a step further, and claims that this sense of self that results from 'knowing' oneself to be narratable is accompanied by a *desire* for this narration. Again, what one desires in the tale of his or her life-story is not simply the 'information' which that narration tells – for the contents alone do not confer identity. Rather, Cavarero argues that, knowing him or herself to be *unique* and therefore narratable, the self desires 'the *unity* ... which this tale confers to identity.' Everyone, asserts Cavarero, is born both unique and one. However, this unity, which is there at the moment of birth, is lost with the passage of time – a loss that feeds the desire for this lost unity, in the form of the tale of the life-story. If the unity that is there at birth is what is desired, then this tale must logically include the story of birth and early childhood – which, of course, cannot be told autobiographically. As Cavarero demonstrates through an innovative rereading of the *Oedipus* myth, this unity, which the tale of one's life-story confers, can only come from the mouth of another. The desire for this narration, therefore, implies that each of us is exposed to, and narratable by, another. And it implies that each of us entrusts his or her 'unity' and identity to another's tale.

Here again, this desire leads to a constitutive exposition of the self to the others, for we can only come to know our life-story by being exposed to others. And this 'exposition,' following Arendt, is above all *political* (again in Arendt's anomalous sense). Here one might perhaps see a certain compatibility between this constitutive exposure and Butler's provocative notion of 'passionate attachments.' In the course of her articulation of the 'ambivalent' formation of the subject in *The Psychic Life of Power*, Butler offers an interesting thesis about adult–child relations, in which the child's 'primary dependency' upon the adult is offered as one way of understanding how 'this situation of primary dependency conditions the *political* formation and regulation of subjects.'[47] Although, as Butler points out, the child's dependency upon adults 'is not *political* subordination is any usual sense,' she suggests that the child's vulnerability to subordination, violence, and even death, is a condition for that child's becoming a subject – and thus conditions his or her 'political formation' as well.[48] Here one might recognize in Butler's formulation a fleeting affinity with Cavarero's sense that the absolute exposure of the newborn prefigures, or *is*, political exposure of a different kind.[49] Indeed, by attributing *some* sense of politics (even if not 'in any usual sense') to this fundamental dependency of the child upon the adult – a dependency that is a condition of, and thus in some sense *prior to*, the child's becoming a 'subject' – Butler leaves open the possibility of an utterly *different*, *un*usual, politics; indeed, a politics that would not yet beg the question of subjects, subjection, or the ambivalence of agency – the questions that occupy the bulk of her text.[50] Although Butler devotes only a moment to this child–adult relation, it seems to me that this moment is one place in which the possibility of a new dialogue, or a new sense, of politics might present itself – one which is founded upon the exposition and vulnerability inherent in each of our entrances into the world.

This moment of compatibility, however, also marks a point of divergence – for the direction for thinking proposed by Cavarero in this present work is radically different from the one proposed by Butler and others interested in revisiting the problem of subject-formation.

Butler's argument goes in one direction, shifting from the vulnerability inherent in every child–adult relation to a more general 'power' upon which one is dependent for one's formation as an adult-subject.[51] In the larger context of Butler's argument in *The Psychic Life of Power*, the child–adult relationship described earlier appears to end up metonymically figuring the way in which 'power acts on the subject ... as what makes the subject possible ... its formative occasion ... ' (p. 14 of Butler's book).[52] In addition to this Foucauldian notion of 'power,' which Butler draws upon and reworks, she also develops her political work in large part through the Althusserian notion of 'interpellation,' and Austin's notion of 'performativity' (especially through Derrida's radical reformulation of Austin).[53] That these notions are developed so thoroughly in Butler's texts is an indication of the important role that a rethinking of the relation between the 'subject' and *language* plays in her political thinking. Butler, for instance, continually problematizes the neat separation of the subject from language, in order to illuminate the extent to which the agency of the subject is bound up with the agency of language. Althusser proves helpful in this regard, for 'interpellation' helps us to understand that the 'subject's capacity to address appears to be derived from having been addressed.' Moreover, we come to understand that we cannot even 'imagine [the subject] ... apart from the constitutive possibility of addressing others and being addressed by others ... without this linguistic bearing toward one another.'[54] Butler understands that the condition for the 'social existence' of the subject is that one enter into 'linguistic life,' that one be called something by *another* – even if the subject then acquires some sense of agency by miming the language through which one gains this linguistic life.[55] Here, Butler emphasizes – in a manner not inconsistent with Arendt's or Cavarero's sense that the 'self' is exposed from the start to others – that subjects are constitutively *exposed* ('vulnerable') to one another linguistically; and that this 'linguistic vulnerability ... is one of the primary forms' of social relation.[56] Just as Arendt emphasizes that 'to be alive means to live in a world that preceded one's own arrival and will survive one's own departure,' Butler's notion of 'vulnerability' implies that we inherit a language that precedes us and which we do not own.[57] And yet, it seems to me that the constitutive exposure of the 'narratable self,' as described by Cavarero in the present text, offers a quite different understanding of the valences and possibilities inherent in this 'vulnerability.'

Allow me to pause for a moment on this point, which seems to me an important point of productive divergence between Cavarero's work and other theories that treat the problem of language in relation to the formation of the subject, or the self (of which there are, of course, many). Now, the reader of Cavarero's work will of course note that Cavarero, too, is interested in developing a notion of a 'narratable self' that is constitutively *exposed* to others in a manner that is likewise linguistic – namely, her sense that each of us is narratable by another.[58] Each of us is constitutively exposed to the others' narration of our life-story – an exposure that is a condition for social and political life. What is important for Cavarero, however, is that this *exposure* reveals *who* one is; a 'who' that is in turn disclosed through the tale of a life-story.

However, for Butler, the crucial point is that the 'ongoing interpellations of social life' deal with '*what* I have been called.'[59] That is to say, interpellation names someone in a way that produces that person's 'social existence' by impacting *what* form that person's social existence will take. In fact, one of the defining features of interpellation is that it works with *indifference* with regard to the one *who* is named. Butler takes note of this alienating effect of interpellation, which often results in a person being confronted with a set of terms or names that do not seem to correspond at all with *who* he or she considers him/herself to be:

> Indeed, one may well imagine oneself in ways that are quite to the contrary of how one is socially constituted; one may, as it were, meet that socially constituted self by surprise, with alarm or pleasure, or even shock. And such an encounter underscores the way in which the name wields a linguistic power of constitution *in ways that are indifferent to the one who bears the name*.[60]

Again, interpellation works in relation to the constitutive linguistic vulnerability of the subject, but in a way is indifferent to *who* is being 'constituted.' It is, moreover, this indifferent and alienating effect of interpellation or name-calling that accounts for much of its (often) hurtful or violent impact. This is the case with hate-speech, although this is not exactly the account that Butler goes on to provide. Indeed, by shifting the emphasis on to the fact that a '*who*,' so to speak, is at stake, we can begin to imagine an account of hate-speech and linguistic vulnerability quite different from the one that Butler ends up offering. For the pain caused by the word comes not simply from the fact that one is called a hurtful name, or not solely from the sedimented history or semantics of that name; but moreover from the feeling that *who* one is, is *not* being addressed, and indeed has no place in the name-calling scene at all. In other words, the pain of hate-speech comes not solely from *what* one is being called, but from the fact that one's singularity, a singularity that exceeds any 'what,' is utterly and violently ignored, excluded from these semantics. Put quite simply, it is the total disregard for *who* one is that makes hate-speech so painful.

In addition, in so far as this disregard prevails, to varying degrees, in *all* scenes of interpellation, one could not hope to *radically* counteract hate-speech without also offering alternative versions of social existence that do *not* rely chiefly upon 'interpellation' as the model for the formation of linguistically vulnerable beings. On this point, perhaps, Cavarero's thinking might offer just such an alternative.

Indeed, it seems to me that Cavarero's work might offer an entirely different perspective from which to understand name-calling, 'interpellation,' or 'linguistic vulnerability' more generally. It is no doubt true, as Butler asserts, that language can hurt us because it also forms us, that the wounding power of words is in large part a consequence of our constitutive linguistic vulnerability, and a consequence of our vulnerability to the interpellative effects of discourse. And yet, there are perhaps other ways of understanding this vulnerability, ways that take into account the uniqueness of the one that is vulnerable. We might begin, following Cavarero and Arendt, to understand this vulnerability as something which exposes each of us, uniquely, to each other. Each of us is open, and therefore vulnerable, to what others tell or call us. But this is a vulnerability that, beyond being a condition for social existence in a general sense, also belongs to *who* each of us is; for we are all uniquely vulnerable, in different ways, to different words, at different times. 'Linguistic vulnerability,' recast in the light of Cavarero's thinking, is thus a constitutive feature of our *uniqueness*. Put simply, this vulnerability – by opening us to be hurt, or affected, by 'what' we are called – might even be that which gives us the sense, through the pain or shock we feel, that *what* we are called does not correspond with *who* we feel ourselves to be.

It should be recalled that Butler's account does not end with interpellation, and that one of the conclusions which Butler draws is that the terms by which one is addressed can be put to (potentially) new uses, 'one whose future is partially open.'[61] This is no doubt true; and in and of itself this claim would be recognizable in much of Cavarero's previous work.[62] And yet – although Cavarero would hardly disagree with Butler's sense of the subversive possibilities inherent in repetition – in *Relating Narratives* Cavarero offers a whole other perspective on the disjunction between discourse and life.

'Discourse is not life; its time is not yours.' Butler often refers to this axiom of Foucault.[63] For Butler, the disjunction between discourse and the life of the subject is precisely what opens a space for resignification, for subversive citation and so forth. Again, Butler suggests that the subject might gain some sense of individual agency by appropriating, and reworking, the terms by which he or she is addressed. This implies, of course, that there is a fundamental disjunction between the terms through which one is constituted and one's 'life.' One can redeploy the discursive terms through which one is constituted, precisely because these terms are, by definition, indifferent to *who* one is — they pre-date the subject's life, and have a potential life beyond that subject's death. As Butler indicates, it is this very disjunction between discourse and life ('its time is not yours'), which makes 'the speaking time of the subject' possible. But this temporal disjunction, Butler underscores, also opens a risk. For when we redeploy the terms by which we are addressed (for example, in an effort to resist or resignify that address), we take the risk that these words will come to signify in ways we never envisioned. The fact that the terms of language are appropriatable — in other words — means that they belong to no one.

Discourse is not life; its time is not yours.[64]

How many ways are there of understanding this disjunction of life and discourse? Might the relation between 'narration' and 'life,' as Cavarero outlines it in *Relating Narratives*, offer us a different perspective on this disjunction?

Cavarero, of course, does not refer so much to the relation between 'life' and 'discourse,' as focus upon the relation between a life and the story or tale of that life. Whereas Butler emphasizes, or offers a new theory of, the relation between the individual and discourse *vis-à-vis* the disjunction between 'discourse and life,' Cavarero focuses instead upon the relation between the self and the narration of his/her life-story. Now obviously, a 'narration' takes shape discursively; it unfolds in a given language, with a given style, employs certain terms, and draws upon relatively determined conventions — historical and otherwise. Moreover, to be sure, the 'time' of a life-story is not reducible to the 'time' of that life. As Cavarero admits, in reference to Ulysses or Achilles for instance, the life-story of a hero belongs to a temporality different from the life-span of that hero. The 'story' that Homer recounts in *The Iliad* or *The Odyssey* (whether orally or in writing) has a life that is incommensurate with the lives and actions of Achilles or Ulysses. Indeed, Achilles and Ulysses are able to overcome death, in a way, through the immortality of Homer's verse. In this sense, the relation between a life and his/her story is fleeting — we could say that this 'life' becomes a 'character,' one which is open to infinite interpretation or resignification in precisely the ways upon which literary criticism thrives.

However, Cavarero's approach is attentive to a different perspective. Again, in her view, *the text* (whether oral or written) or the *script* of this life-story, is not the most important thing. Indeed, *what* the life-story contains — its discursive manifestation, its contents, its style, even its particular language or idiom — is, from her perspective, 'inessential.'[65] Instead, Cavarero describes the relation between one's life and his/her life-story, in terms of the *desire* that he/she has for that narration. It is the desire to hear, or to read, the tale of one's life, which leads Cavarero toward a different understanding of the relation between 'life' and the tale that designs a unity for that life, or gives it a figure. (Again, the life-story reveals not only the uniqueness, but also the *unity* of the life from which it results.) It is this unity that is desired by the narratable self, a unity that only the tale of his/her life-story can provide. Now, to say that the self has a 'unity' is not to say that it has 'at its center a compact and coherent identity.' On the contrary, lives are disjointed and fragmentary – nonetheless, Cavarero understands that a certain fleeting, 'unstable and insubstantial unity' can be provided by the tale of one's life-story.[66] And it is the *desire* for this unity or form that manifests itself in the relation between life and narration or storytelling.

Importantly, this *desire* creates a scene where the relation between a life and the tale of that life is *not* a disjunction, but rather a relation of 'tension' (Cavarero's word). In such a scene, Foucault's axiom is suspended, for the desire that binds the narration of a life to that life does not have a 'time' that pre-exists or post-dates that life-span. The 'tension' of the desire that binds one's life to the tale of that life's story has no other time than what passes between birth and death. The self desires to hear his/her story *while he/she is alive*. Put another way, by introducing *desire* into the scene of narrative relations, Cavarero is able to describe the relation between a 'life,' and the words that reveal the sense of that life, in a way that is not a disjunction. In such a scene, since the self is a *desiring* self, he or she is also 'linguistically vulnerable' – although not solely to an interpellative discourse that forms him or her, while remaining indifferent to his or her lifetime. Rather, the self desires, and is open to, the tale of a life-story that unfolds *in* his or her lifetime in a way that uniquely reveals *who* that person is. Unlike 'interpellation,' the tale is not 'indifferent' to the one whose life it reveals; on the contrary, the tale is *for* that unique existent. This is why Cavarero focuses not so much on the 'immortalizing verse,' (or its style or content), but rather upon the desire which a person shows to hear the tale of his/her life, *while they are alive*.

All of this, importantly, indicates to Cavarero some latent possibilities for reconfiguring politics in a more radical sense. Indeed, it is here precisely the possibility of *suspending* the disjunction between 'discourse and life' that orients our attention towards this desire that binds unique lives to narration, and that may open a new relation between the narrative scene and politics. Butler's account, like other Foucaultian or post-Foucaultian theories, makes use of the space opened up by the incommensurability of discourse and life in order to illuminate some possibilities and risks involved in the subject attaining a relatively 'autonomous' agency or voice.[67] However, Cavarero focuses instead upon those moments when the disjunction between discourse and life is *suspended* through narration, and suggests that narrative relations, which see the desire for narration encounter its tale, can themselves be a political action. This happens, for instance, when one tells another the tale of his or her life; revealing that they recognize *who* that person is. If one understands 'politics' in Arendt's sense, argues Cavarero – that is, as a 'plural and interactive space of exhibition' – then the scene of narration, of telling each other life-stories, takes on the character of political action.[68] Moreover, through such a suspension of the disjunction between discourse and life, it becomes possible to imagine a relational politics that is attentive to *who* one is, rather than to *what* one is. For within the context of telling someone the story of his/her life, within the scene of a narrative relation, the focus is shifted from the generalizable qualities of those involved, to the unique existents with whom the tales correspond.

The story of Romeo and Juliet is also a story of 'interpellation,' of the disjunction between discourse and life – the tragedy of the name; or, of having been vulnerable to it. Romeo and Juliet's unique, singular story, *their* tragedy, would not be what it is without this 'other' tragedy of the name, which surfaces whenever *anyone* is named. Therefore, the singular, tragic story that belongs only to Romeo and Juliet, and their desire (in all of its retellings before and after Shakespeare) *also* tells the story of a tragedy that is not *only* theirs. For the tragedy of the name (and this is what is tragic about *Romeo and Juliet*) is that it is *indifferent* to the one who is named. This indifference is again the pain, even the death, that name-calling carries with it. ('As if that name,/Shot from the deadly level of a gun,/Did murder her, as that name's cursed hand/Murder'd her kinsman' (III. iii. 101–4)). The name carries death for the one who bears it, because the name has no regard for the life of its bearer: it is destined to survive that life, and thus announces its death. I recall *Romeo and Juliet* in conclusion here first of all because of this double tragedy. It is, on the one hand, a tragedy that is theirs alone, a story through which we come to know *who* Romeo and Juliet were. On the other hand, *their* tragedy is inseparable from the 'other' tragedy of the name, which is lethally indifferent to *who* they were.

In Shakespeare's retelling, Romeo and Juliet themselves seem to understand that *their* story, what is happening uniquely to them, is also this 'other' tragedy of the name that is not only theirs. Romeo and Juliet analyze their predicament in precisely this way – moving from *their* names to naming in general, from 'Montague' to 'rose,' from 'Romeo' to 'love' ('Call me but love, and I'll be new baptis'd: Henceforth I never will be Romeo' (II. ii. 50–1)). The name 'Romeo' is, Juliet knows, not *who* she desires – it names nothing of his body, nothing 'belonging to a man;' she loves not his name, which she says is her 'enemy,' but rather desires *who* he is. We 'know' this, just as Juliet knows that *who* Romeo is, his body, is separable from his name – for the latter is 'hateful,' while the former is loved. Indeed, her love is made possible by – or perhaps itself is the occasion of – the separation of 'who' Romeo is from his name, from his genealogy.[69] For his part, Romeo comes to hate his name only when he is loved by Juliet; that is, he only begins to imagine himself to be separable from his name at the moment in which he realizes he is desired by an*other*. It is this loving relation with the other, we might say, which makes possible the disjunction between 'who' one is and 'what' one is called.

But this is a tragic love. The tragedy of the name is not, in other words, a tragedy that simply *befalls* Romeo and Juliet, or happens 'to' them – for *who* Romeo and Juliet are, as their story reveals, is bound up with the tragedy of the name. Romeo and Juliet would not be *who* they are without this 'other' tragedy of name-calling, which is indifferent to who they are. A proper name ('Romeo,' 'Capulet') does not designate anything human – and yet, a unique 'who' is unique only through his/her vulnerability to this name.[70] On the one hand, only a unique existent is loved, or desired, beyond his/her name – and yet, only a unique existent is so *vulnerable* to this name, a vulnerability that is a part of *who* he/she is.[71] Only a human being bears this paradoxical relation to the name, to 'what' is so indifferent to 'who' he/she is. For while the name 'Romeo' does not name him as a unique 'existent,' it is nonetheless inseparable from his essence; he could not *be* who he is without it. Juliet recognizes this when she asks 'Wherefore *art thou* Romeo?' Romeo's 'being,' she laments, is inseparable from the 'you' ('thou') that bears the name 'Romeo.' Unlike the 'rose,' a thing that would retain its sensuous essence without the name 'rose,' Romeo's being, as a human, is not fully separable from his name.[72] The tragedy of Romeo and Juliet, therefore, is not – as we might imagine – simply the lethal indifference of the name to the unique 'who.' Rather, the tragedy lies more deeply in the relation the unique 'who' maintains with this lethal indifference of the name. Romeo and Juliet would not be *who* they are – that is, their story would be different – without this vulnerability to 'what' they are called. Their unique story would not be what it is without the 'other' story of the name.

And yet, in speaking of this 'other' story or tragedy of the name, it is important to recall that a story is not reducible to a name; just as a tale does not work like 'interpellation.' Telling someone a story, in short, is not the same as calling them a name. For while the names 'Capulet' and 'Montague' are lethally indifferent to who Romeo and Juliet are, their story is not indifferent to this 'who' – indeed, their story is *theirs*. Shakespeare's *Romeo and Juliet* ends by invoking the 'story' *of* Romeo and Juliet, as that which belongs to them ('For never was a story of more woe/Than this of Juliet and her Romeo' (V. iii. 308–9)).[73] One might claim that this is the 'story' of their names, 'of Juliet and her Romeo.' And yet, these names now conjure a singular story – one that we are instructed to repeat ('Go hence to have more talk of these sad things' (V. iii.

306)). In other words, the names 'Romeo and Juliet,' and their tragic effect, give way to the story of Romeo and Juliet. While this is a story that bears their names as its title, it nonetheless tells of 'who' they were beyond their names. If their names, 'Romeo' and 'Juliet,' have a life beyond the life of the protagonists – it is equally true that these names also survive *thanks to* this story, thanks to its singularity. The very names 'Romeo' and 'Juliet,' which were so indifferent to *who* they were while they lived, curiously end up surviving in the title of the story that uniquely reveals *who* they were. Thus, if *Romeo and Juliet* says something about the indifference of the name to the unique life that bears it, it also serves to remind us of the power of the singular story to suspend this indifference.

Indeed, the survival of the story of Romeo and Juliet – infinitely revised, interpreted, restaged, with names and places changed, in different languages – says something about *our* desire for their story as well. In other words, the survival of a story beyond the 'life' of which it tells – unlike the survival of a 'name' – indicates a continuing desire *for* this story, for its singularity. While names survive without regard for the ones who bear them, the survival of a life-story depends upon a desire for the singularity of that story, of that life. Following Cavarero, we might say that the desire for the story of Romeo and Juliet is more than just the desire for Shakespeare's *Romeo and Juliet*. Of course, we might doubt that the story of Romeo and Juliet would have survived without Shakespeare (or, for that matter, without Bandello or da Porto). And yet, Shakespeare's text, or his language, is not itself the object of our desire, even if it serves to heighten it. The text is, as Cavarero teaches us, inessential where this desire is concerned. Like the lovers themselves, we desire Romeo and Juliet for 'who' they are *through* their story, beyond the form that story takes.

In *Relating Narratives*, Cavarero indeed connects the desire for a lover to the desire for one's story, taking note of the way in which lovers engage in reciprocal narrations, alternating love-making with storytelling.[74] The desire for one's story is bound up, especially in the case of lovers, with a desire for another. Of course, we do not know what stories Romeo and Juliet told each other. Shakespeare does not give us this any more than he gives us the form their love-making took. For we do not need to know 'what' narrative exchanges took place between Romeo and Juliet. While Romeo and Juliet are independent beings, each with their own unique life-story, for us the tale of these independent stories is not important. For us it is *their* story, the story of their love, which we desire. It is *their* story, *their* tragedy, which survives in our desire for its singularity.

NOTES

1 William Shakespeare, *Romeo and Juliet* (II. ii. 53–4), from the Arden edition, edited by Brian Gibbons (New York, 1980). All further citations from the play are taken from this edition.

2 Hannah Arendt, *The Human Condition* (Chicago: University of Chicago Press, 1957), p. 181.

3 *Ibid.*

4 *Ibid.*, p. 186.

5 Cavarero puts it this way: '... one of the centuries-old problems of philosophy becomes superfluous; namely, the unsayability of the individual, already decreed by Aristotle ... within the expositive horizon of the *who*, the individual is not ineffable at all' (this volume, p. 89).

6 Since there is already an excellent introduction in English to Cavarero's work in general by Rosi Braidotti, I will focus instead upon questions pertaining to *Relating Narratives*. Cf. 'Foreword' to *In Spite of Plato* (New York: Routledge, 1995), pp. vii–xix.

7 Cf. Jacques Derrida, 'Khora,' in *On the Name* (Stanford: Stanford University Press, 1993), p. 90.

8 See, for example, Cavarero's discussion of *The Arabian Nights* in Part IV, Chapter 11 of this volume.

9 Here one can recognize the strong influence that Luce Irigaray's work has had upon Cavarero's thinking. Irigaray, of course, was the first to argue that the feminine cannot be reduced to its figuration – especially in her *Speculum of the Other Woman*, trans. Gillian C. Gill (Ithaca, NY: Cornell University Press, 1985), and *This Sex Which is Not One*, trans. Catherine Porter and Carolyn Burke (Ithaca, NY: Cornell University Press, 1985). Cavarero has invoked Irigaray in this regard on a number of occasions, see for instance her essay 'Towards a Theory of Sexual Difference,' in *The Lonely Mirror*, edited by Sandra Kemp and Paola Bono (New York: Routledge, 1993); see also Rosi Braidotti's introduction to *In Spite of Plato*, pp. xiv–xv, xvi.

10 Cavarero writes, moreover, that the very split between narration and philosophy, between *logos/mythos*, is itself an effect of masculine, phallocentrism '... the tragedy of the originary scission between the ... discursive order of philosophy and that of narration – is an entirely masculine tragedy' (p. 53 of this volume).

11 Arendt writes: '... the impossibility, as it were, to solidify in words the living essence of the person as it shows itself in the flux of actions and speech, has great bearing upon the whole realm of human affairs ... [and] is a basic factor in the equally notorious uncertainty not only of all political matters, but of all affairs that go on between men directly ...' *The Human Condition*, pp. 181–2.

12 As Cavarero indicates in this volume, what Arendt means by 'politics' is something completely different from the traditional usage of that term. I am not able to unpack here the anomalous sense that Arendt gives to that word, and I would like to refer the reader to Cavarero's comments throughout this text, and to the notes that she provides.

13 Cavarero, p. 88 of this volume. See also Cavarero's discussion of Hobbes' *Leviathan* in her *Figures of the Body: Philosophy and Politics* (forthcoming, University of Michigan Press).

14 Cavarero, p. 88 of this volume.

15 Arendt, *The Life of Mind* (New York: Harcourt Brace, 1977), pp. 26–9.

16 Arendt, *The Human Condition*, p. 184 (my italics).

17 See Section II, Chapter 5 of this volume.

18 This is why, in choosing an English title for the book, I wanted to include the term 'relation,' which is at once narrative and interpersonal. The Italian title, which was

chosen by the publisher Feltrinelli (not by Adriana Cavarero), does not contain this term. I would like to thank Olivia Guaraldo for her advice.

19 *Who Comes After the Subject?* edited by Jean-Luc Nancy, Eduardo Cadava and Peter Conner (New York: Routledge, 1991), p. 4. See also Cavarero, p. 38 of this volume.

20 '... the question of essence – "What, existence?" – calls forth a "who" in response.' *Who Comes After the Subject*, p. 7.

21 Indeed, while Butler is no doubt concerned with accounting for the forming of the subject or with subjectivity, this concern simultaneously unfolds as the articulation of the limits of any such an account. 'Perhaps ... we are no longer in the business of "giving an account of the formation of the subject." We are, rather, confronted with the tropological presumption made by any such explanation, one that facilitates the explanation but also marks its limits.' Judith Butler, *The Psychic Life of Power* (Stanford: Stanford University Press, 1997), p. 4.

22 I would like to add that I have been fortunate enough to have studied with both Butler and Cavarero, and that the two have a professed, mutual admiration. Cavarero wrote the Foreword to the Italian translation of *Bodies that Matter*, and Butler in turn has been instrumental in introducing Cavarero's work to American publishers.

23 The reader might look at the first pages of *Bodies that Matter*, following the occurrences of the word 'subject.' For instance, '... the subject is constituted through the force of exclusion and abjection, one which produces a constitutive outside to the subject, and abjected outside, which is, after all, "inside" the subject as its own founding repudiation.' Judith Butler, *Bodies that Matter* (New York: Routledge, 1993), p. 3.

24 *Ibid.* In *The Psychic Life of Power*, in the context of a different argument, Butler names Hegel in this regard: 'the question of how the subject is formed in subordination, preoccupies the section of Hegel's *Phenomenology of the Spirit* that traces the slave's approach to freedom and his disappointing fall into the "unhappy consciousness." The master, who at first appears to be "external" to the slave, re-emerges as the slave's own conscience' (p. 3). For more on Butler's use of Hegel, see Christine Battersby's remarks in *The Phenomenal Woman* (Cambridge: Polity Press, 1998), pp. 120–4.

25 Butler, *Bodies that Matter*, p. 3.

26 See Part III, Chapter 7 of this volume.

27 Which is not, of course, to say that friendships or love-affairs are free from violence. However, the scenes that Cavarero chooses in order to sketch her theory are characteristically different from those chosen by Hegel in the *Phenomenology of Spirit*, or by Butler. The relation between narrative selves is not invasive – and does not necessarily beg the question of penetration in the manner that is so central to *Bodies that Matter*.

28 This would be different from Butler's claim that the 'exclusionary matrix through which subjects are formed thus requires the simultaneous production of a domain of abject beings.' *Bodies that Matter*, p. 3.

29 Butler, *The Psychic Life of Power*, p. 10 and *passim*. It is clear from the context that by 'individuals,' Butler does not mean the 'individual' of individualist political theories, like that of Hobbes, for instance, but rather an individual person, more akin to what Cavarero or Nancy call the unique 'existent.'

30 Butler, *The Psychic Life of Power*, pp. 10–11

31 Cavarero writes in this volume: '... to erase the miracle of finitude ... from Plato onwards, has been the mission that philosophy, seduced by the universal, originally

decided to take upon itself: to redeem, to save, to rescue the particular from its finitude, and uniqueness from its scandal. This task of redemption, however, logically transformed itself into an act of erasure. As Hegel admits … "philosophical contemplation has no other intention than to abolish the accidental." ' (p. 53 of this volume).

32 Butler, *The Psychic Life of Power*, p. 11.

33 The paradoxes that Butler articulates are not the same paradoxes that Cavarero outlines in her theory of the 'narratable self' – I am thinking first of all of what Cavarero calls 'The Paradox of Ulysses.' See Chapter 2 of this volume.

34 Cavarero, p. 84 of this volume.

35 See Cavarero's reading of Gertrude Stein's radical autobiography, in this volume, Part III, Chapter 7.

36 Of course, as Cavarero points out, within a certain, classical, autobiographical tradition, there are instances of 'selves' that *presume* to tell the story of their own birth; Cavarero remarks, however, that this is the same mistake that Oedipus made – with tragic consequences.

37 There would be a lot more to say, of course, about the relation between 'story,' narration and 'genealogy,' through Nietzsche, Foucault, Irigaray and others. I might recall briefly that, at least etymologically, a 'genealogy' would imply the subsumption of the unique being into a lineage that privileges the social or collective over the individual existent. I take this from Emile Benveniste's observation that the root word *gen*, which appears in *genus* or *genealogy*, implies a notion of birth as a *social* event, and refers to the 'reproduction' of citizens, free males and so forth. A genealogy of the subject, considered from this perspective, works contrary to the notion of uniqueness and birth that Cavarero strives to recover in her writing. In this sense too, Cavarero's work is closely aligned with what Luce Irigaray has to say about genealogy, and the exclusion of the feminine (the daughter). Cf. Emile Benveniste, *Le vocabulaire des institutions indo-européennes*, 2 vols (Paris: Minuit, 1969), Livre 2, 'Le vocabulaire de la parenté,' pp. 203–76; and Luce Irigaray, 'Une chance de vivre,' in *Sexes and Genealogies* (New York: Columbia Press, 1993).

38 For an excellent summary of 'reflection' as a characteristic of philosophical discourse, see Rodolphe Gasché, *The Tain of the Mirror: Derrida and the Philosophy of Reflection* (Cambridge: Harvard University Press, 1986), pp. 13–80.

39 'Sense' is my English translation for an effectively untranslatable set of Italian terms that Cavarero uses to express this 'non-knowledgeable' familiarity. She refers to a *sapore* – literally, a 'taste' or 'flavour,' but which could also mean a 'scent,' a 'tang', a 'zest,' and she uses the verb *assaporarsi*, which means to 'have a taste of oneself,' or 'to recognize one's own scent or flavour.' The word *sapore* is phonetically close to *sapere* [knowledge], but the emphasis falls, instead, on an experience that one has of being familiar with oneself *bodily* rather than intellectually. One *senses* oneself to be oneself unreflectively, rather than knowing oneself to be oneself through reflection.

40 Cavarero, p. 34 of this volume.

41 *Ibid.*

42 *Ibid.*, p. 35.

43 *Ibid.*

44 On this point, I might take the liberty, as a translator, to pose a question or two regarding the *language* in which the amnesiac senses him/herself to be narratable. For without the possibility of a trace, for example, of some language in which to say 'I,' how could the amnesiac 'I' *sense* itself to be narratable? (I am thinking, for instance, of

what Jacques Derrida says regarding autobiography in *Monolingualism of the Other*, where he writes: '... in whatever manner one invents the story of a construction of the *self*, the *autos*, or the *ipse*, it is always *imagined* that the one who writes should know how to say *I*.' *Monolingualism of the Other*, trans. Patrick Mensah (Stanford: Stanford University Press, 1998), p. 28.) What is the relation between Cavarero's notion of this '*familiar sense*,' which even the amnesiac possesses, and language? Does this sense function without regard to any trace of a language? Or is this 'familiar sense' also linguistic, even apart from memory? Are memory and language separable? What might it mean to retain the memory of a language without the memory of one's story?

45 *Ibid.*, p. 35 of this volume.

46 *Ibid.*

47 Butler, *The Psychic Life of Power*, p. 7 (my italics).

48 *Ibid.*

49 However, surely this exposure or vulnerability takes on a number of different valences in each of their accounts. Again, the word 'political' ought to be understood in Arendt's sense of a unique exposure – not as designating the emergence of a free, individual subject or heir. Cavarero has written elsewhere, at greater length, on the relation between birth [*physis*] and politics [*polis*]. See especially the chapter on 'Demeter,' in *In Spite of Plato*, and the section on Antigone in the forthcoming *Figures of the Body: Philosophy and Politics*.

50 It may well be that I am reading a lot into these few sentences in Butler's book (*The Psychic Life of Power* (Stanford: Stanford University Press, 1997)) for it is difficult to ascertain from the context of her argument the extent to which the child is more than a *figure* for the subject-in-formation. And yet, my reading seems plausible, given what Butler says about the 'child's love [which] is prior to judgment and decision;' namely, that 'there is no possibility of not loving, where love is bound up with the require- ments for life' (p. 8 of Butler's book). Here, the child's love is the necessary condi- tion for life, and for physically continuing in its body – in Cavarero's terms, for continuing as a unique existent. Thus it appears to be something *other* than its emer- gence as a subject; even though, for Butler, this loving is immediately bound up with the subject's emergence. (The next sentence of Butler's text makes this link.) This is, I confess, a point of confusion for me in Butler's text. Does the child's love, and thus its vulnerability and exposability from birth, present to us (as it does to Cavarero and Arendt) a politics that does not immediately fall back into that of the 'subject,' however ambiguous that subject may now be?

51 *Ibid.* On the page immediately following the one that I have just discussed, Butler shifts immediately from the 'child' to the 'subject.' Drawing upon her discussion of 'passionate attachments,' she writes that 'to desire the conditions of one's own subordination is thus required to persist as oneself ... one is dependent upon power for one's very formation, [and] that formation is impossible without dependency.' From the context it appears that for Butler this 'formation' and 'existence' is the 'formation' or 'existence' of an adult *subject*. (*Ibid.*, p. 9.)

52 *Ibid.* Butler, of course, sees power not only as 'formative' in a Foucauldian sense, but also 'as what is taken up and reiterated in the subject's "own" acting' (*Ibid.*, p. 14). She has provided numerous articulations of the various ways in which this reiterative power works in relation to the 'formative' one.

53 The subtitle for her recent *Excitable Speech*, for instance, is 'A Politics of the Performative.' Since Butler's notion of 'performativity,' not to mention that of Austin or Derrida, has already been the topic of numerous critical works, I will not discuss it here.

54 *Excitable Speech*, p. 30 and *passim*.

55 'Because I have been called something, I have been entered into linguistic life, refer to myself through the language given by the Other, but perhaps never quite in the same terms that my language mimes.' *Excitable Speech*, p. 38.

56 In a footnote to this passage, Butler reminds the reader that this is 'a fundamentally Heideggerian point,' which could account for the compatibility that I am seeing between her position here and Arendt's, who also draws upon Heidegger in this regard.

57 Hannah Arendt, *The Life of Mind* (New York: Harcourt Brace, 1971), p. 20. Of course, Arendt's sense of 'appearance' is somewhat different from the sort of social interaction that Butler articulates in her work.

58 Cavarero (this volume) indeed notes that 'the word' is often the 'privileged vehicle' through which we are exposed to one another (p. 59).

59 *Excitable Speech*, p. 38.

60 *Ibid.*, p. 31 (my italics).

61 *Ibid.*, p. 38. Butler has, again, offered a number of different articulations of this notion of subversive repetition. See, to begin with, the last chapter of *Bodies that Matter*; or the concluding sections of *Gender Trouble* (New York: Routledge Press, 1990), or the last pages of *Excitable Speech*.

62 In fact, Cavarero's previous publications, *In Spite of Plato* and the forthcoming *Figures of the Body: Philosophy and Politics*, often employ an analogous strategy – they find subversive possibilities through radical refigurations and redeployments of the traditional figures of femininity that characterize our philosophical and cultural inheritance. Both Cavarero and Butler refer to Luce Irigaray as an important influence in this regard.

63 This axiom serves as the epigraph for the last chapter of *Bodies that Matter*, and resurfaces in *Excitable Speech: a Politics of the Performative* (New York: Routledge, 1997), where Butler offers the following interpretation. 'By this statement, Foucault appears to mean that one's life is not reducible to the discourse that one speaks or to the sphere of discourse that animates one's life. What he fails to emphasize, however, is that the time of discourse, even in its radical incommensurability with the time of the subject, *makes possible* the speaking time of the subject.' p. 28. Also cf. Michel Foucault, 'Politics and the Study of Discourse,' in *The Foucault Effect: Studies in Governmentality*, ed. Graham Burchell, Colin Gordon and Peter Miller (Chicago: University of Chicago Press, 1991), p. 71.

64 When Adriana Cavarero presented part of *Relating Narratives* as a lecture at UC Berkeley in October, 1997, Judith Butler was one of the respondents. I remember quite vividly Butler's citation of this phrase as the thrust of her response to Cavarero's paper. At the time, I understood Butler's point to be a critique of Cavarero's notion of the bond between a narratable self and that self's life-story. My intention here is not to restage that response, but rather perhaps to imagine a different way of positioning it.

65 This is not to say that they are utterly insignificant, or without consequence; rather to suggest that they are not essential to the alternative perspective that Cavarero is proposing (Cavarero, p. 35 of this volume).

66 *Ibid.*, p. 34.

67 *Excitable Speech*, p. 28.

68 Cavarero (this volume) notes, as a salient instance, the way in which feminist 'consciousness-raising groups' have been characterized by the act of reciprocal narration. See Part II, Chapter 4.

69 Cavarero (this volume) says as much, that one loves *who* the other is, in spite of what he/she is (p. 112).

70 Cavarero does not say this, although this might be one way of understanding that interpellation describes not only the general formation of the 'subject,' but pertains uniquely to each one of us.

71 Cavarero (this volume) herself notes that only a human being can have a proper name 'as a sort of vocative unity of his/her uniqueness.' (p. 18). In other words, the proper name, while itself something inhuman ('not belonging to a man'), happens only to humans.

72 I take my cue here from Jacques Derrida's remarks in his essay 'Aphorism countertime,' in *Acts of Literature*, edited by Derek Attridge (New York: Routledge Press, 1991), especially pp. 427–8.

73 As many critics of Shakespeare have noted, Romeo and Juliet disdain their first names as if they were inseparable from their family names, 'Montague' and 'Capulet,' but it is their first names that survive as the title of *their* story – and that have a singularity that exceeds the story of their respective families.

74 See Part III (entitled 'Lovers') in this volume.

TRANSLATOR'S NOTE

I have, on occasion, translated some ambiguously gendered Italian pronouns into English as either he or she, depending upon the context. In general, wherever the pronoun designated a unique existent, I used the feminine. I did this according to Adriana Cavarero's suggestion, since she did not want to use the neutral English 'it' to refer to a person. Also, I have generally translated the Italian 'storia' as 'story,' rather than 'history,' following Cavarero's wishes. Where English translations of passages cited by Cavarero were not readily available, I have translated them myself. I would like to thank Adriana Cavarero, Olivia Guaraldo and Chica Preda for their kind assistance with this translation.

A STORK FOR AN INTRODUCTION

Karen Blixen recounts a story that she was told as a child. A man, who lived by a pond, was awakened one night by a great noise. He went out into the night and headed for the pond, but in the darkness, running up and down, back and forth, guided only by the noise, he stumbled and fell repeatedly. At last, he found a leak in the dike, from which water and fish were escaping. He set to work plugging the leak and only when he had finished went back to bed. The next morning, looking out of the window, he saw with surprise that his footprints had traced the figure of a stork on the ground.

At this point Karen Blixen asks herself: 'When the design of my life is complete, will I see, or will others see a stork?'[1] We might add: does the course of every life allow itself be looked upon in the end like a design that has a meaning?

Apparently we are not dealing with a design that has been foreseen; it is not projected or controlled. On the contrary, the poor man, called to action by external circumstances, runs and stumbles into the darkness. He works hard, and only when the disaster is under control does he return home. He never loses sight of his purpose, he never abandons the aim of his course; rather, he brings it to completion. His journey mixes intention with accident. While he is subjected to many trials and tribulations, his steps nonetheless leave behind a design; or, rather, a design results from his journey – one that has the unity of a figure. The significance of the story lies precisely in the figural *unity* of the design, and in this simple '*resulting*,' which does not follow from any projected plan. In other words, the design – which does not consist simply of confused marks, but has the unity of a figure – is not one that guides the course of a life from the beginning. Rather the design is what that life, without ever being able to predict or even imagine it, leaves behind. The stork is only seen at the end, when whoever has drawn it with his life – or when *other* spectators, looking from above – see the prints *left* on the ground.

Blixen's text bears the printed design of the stork on the same page as the story. When she was a child, the person who told her the story traced for her the

1

development of the design that sustains the narration. Rather than simply being an effective, didactic device, it was a gesture that grasped a fundamental truth of the fable. Precisely because the design *is* the story, rather than just accompanying the story or illustrating it, the design coincides with it perfectly – in the sense that the pattern that every human being leaves behind is nothing but their life-story. 'All sorrows can be borne if you put them into a story or tell a story about them,' writes Blixen; and Hannah Arendt comments: 'the story reveals the meaning of what would otherwise remain an intolerable sequence of events.'[2]

For the man in the fable, the meaning is represented by the stork. It could obviously be another animal, tree or object. The meaning that saves each life from being a mere sequence of events does not consist in a determined figure; but rather consists precisely in leaving behind a figure, or something from which the unity of a design can be discerned in the telling of the story. Like the design, the story comes after the events and the actions from which it results. Like the design – which is seen only at sunrise from the perspective of whoever looks at the ground from above without treading on it – the story can only be narrated from the posthumous perspective of someone who does not participate in the events. 'When the design of my life is completed, will I see, or will others see, a stork?' The figural unity of the design, the unifying meaning of the story, can only be posed, by the one who lives it, in the form of a question. Or, perhaps, in the form of a desire.

It is not by chance that the child's story, animated by the movement of the design, narrates a stork. The stork – protagonist of a folklore, which, in the West, has no boundaries – brings babies and narrates them fables.[3] No one knows where the migrating stork, with her long wings and benign face of mystery, comes from; or from whence come the babies which she brings or the fables that she tells. The stork does not 'make,' but rather brings, transports and hands down. She is a narrator, not an author. Like Karen Blixen, she is a *storyteller*: she tells stories.[4]

In any case, the design traced by the life of Karen Blixen could never be the same stork that the man in the fable saw at sunrise. Every human being is unique, an unrepeatable existence, which – however much they run disoriented in the dark, mixing accidents with intentions – neither follows in the footsteps of another life, nor repeats the very same course, nor leaves behind the same story. This is also why life-stories are told and listened to with interest; because they are similar and yet new, insubstitutable and unexpected, from beginning to end. They are always 'anecdotes of destiny.'[5]

According to Hannah Arendt, Blixen's 'philosophy' suggests that 'no one has a life worthy of consideration about which a story cannot be told.' It does not follow, however, 'that life could be or rather should be lived like a story, that what must be done in life must be done in such a way that a story comes after it.'[6] Life cannot be lived like a story, because the story always comes afterwards, it results; it is unforeseeable and uncontrollable, just like life. If the man of the fable had voluntarily run through the night in order to trace the design of a stork, he would not have fulfilled the story. A different story would have resulted from his actions: the strange tale of a man who spent the night tracing a stork with his footsteps.

The man of the story is, of course, privileged. The magic of the fable, which is capable of concentrating an entire life into a single night, allows him to see the design on the following morning. Doubting that she will enjoy the same privilege, Karen Blixen cautiously asks herself if, instead, there will be *others* who will be able to see a stork when the design of her life is complete. If life is a 'run-around' that responds to events without being able to transcend them; if it consists simply of acting and reacting without prefiguring its own traces, then this is probably the case. In other words, the one who walks on the ground cannot see the figure that his/her footsteps leave behind, and so he/she needs *another* perspective. It is no accident that the one who understands the meaning of the story is above all the narrator, who, tracing the stork on the page, accompanies the story with the design.

Narration, as is well known, is a delicate art – narration 'reveals the meaning without committing the error of defining it.'[7] Unlike philosophy, which for millennia has persisted in capturing the universal in the trap of definition, narration reveals the finite in its fragile uniqueness, and sings its glory. Karen Blixen knows this well, and, like a modern Scheherazade, she entrusts her existence to the passion of telling stories – the stories of others, like Esa, her African chef; or invented stories, stories which branch off into thousands of other stories. 'No one could have told her life-story as she herself would have told it,' observes Hannah Arendt.[8] The fact remains that she never told it as a design, not even in the semi-autobiographical pages of *Out of Africa*. Evidently Karen Blixen knew that she could not see with her own eyes the design of her life. She knew that, outside of the child's tale, it is always another who sees the stork.

As the fable teaches, the design lasted only for one morning. The footprints on the wet ground will disappear with the first rain or, perhaps, will lose their form under the trampling of other shoes. The stork is fragile; it is the fleeting mark of a unity that is only glimpsed. It is the gift of a moment in the mirage of desire.

There is an ethic of the gift in the pleasure of the narrator. The one who narrates not only entertains and enchants, like Scheherazade, but gives to the protagonists of his/her story their own stork. If leaving behind a design, a 'destiny,' an unrepeatable figure of our existence, 'is the only aspiration deserving of the fact that life was given us,' then nothing responds to the human desire more than the telling of our story.[9] Even before revealing the meaning of a life, a biography therefore recognizes the desire for it.

According to Karen Blixen, the question: 'who am I?' flows indeed, sooner or later, from the beating of every heart. It is a question that only a unique being can sensibly pronounce. Its response, as all narrators know, lies in the *classic rule of storytelling*.[10]

NOTES

1 Karen Blixen, *Out of Africa* (New York: Random House, 1938), p. 201.
2 Hannah Arendt, 'Isak Dinesen: (1885–1962)', *Daguerrotypes* (Chicago: University of Chicago Press, 1979), p. xx.
3 Cf. Marina Warner, *From the Beast to the Blonde* (London: Vintage, 1995), pp. 58–65.
4 [TN: 'Storyteller' is in English in the original.]
5 [TN: *Anecdotes of Destiny* is the title of a work by Karen Blixen (New York: Vintage Books, 1985).]
6 Arendt, 'Isak Dinesen (1885–1962),' p. 170.
7 *Ibid.*, p. 169.
8 *Ibid.*, p. 165.
9 *Ibid.*, p. 169.
10 Karen Blixen, 'The Cardinal's Tale,' in *Last Tales* (New York: Vintage Press, 1975).

Part I

HEROES

1

THE STORY OF OEDIPUS

The mythological Sphinx will rise, and Oedipus will suddenly find himself facing her: confronted with her question, to which he wisely responds, but without realizing that this response of his would do no good for anyone, without realizing that his knowledge was only good for something general – 'Man,' he responded, as we know – when the point was to know himself, he himself, in the hiddenness of his being. He was indeed hidden – until, totally defenseless, he was exposed into the world – just born, barely awake.

Maria Zambano, Chiari del Bosco

'Now, Oedipus great and glorious, we seek your help again. Find some deliverance for us by any way that god or man can show,' says the Priest in *Oedipus the King*.[1] He has solved the riddle of the Sphinx, freeing Thebes. He answered the monster's question regarding which animal walks first with four legs, then with two, and finally with three: 'Man.' Oedipus knows, therefore, 'what' man is. The knowledge that he shares with the monstrous riddler consists in a definition of the *universal*.

It goes without saying that there is a correspondence between Oedipus' response and the form of Platonic discourse. What is 'the just,' the 'beautiful,' the 'good' and, of course, 'what is man?' are, for Plato, the genuine questions of the universal, which solicit a definition in response.[2] It is, in short, the very form of philosophy. Might we therefore say that, faced with the Sphinx, Oedipus reveals himself to be a philosopher? It would seem so. His knowledge says that: man is an animal that as a child walks on four legs, as an adult on two, and in old age – leaning against a cane – on three. Certainly, the scarcity of the enunciation can, at first sight, astonish us if compared with the famous Aristotelian formula that defines man as a rational and political animal – showing itself in this way to be decidedly in keeping with the speculative tones of philosophical language.

Then again, Plato himself, in one of his most enjoyable exercises on the art of definition, defines man as a two-footed animal, featherless and without horns.[3] The joke is obvious, but the *structure* of the discourse is the same. Philosophy asks after man as a universal. (For this reason, we will now write Man, so that the upper-case carries the weight of universality.) The definition, which functions as a necessary response to this question, can be more or less refined, and is almost always inadequate or even wrong, but the *correct* approach to the problem, its epistemic form, does not change.

Oedipus' response – evidently in keeping with the philosophical school of the Theban monster – is nevertheless the right one. The fearful creature annihilates itself: Thebes is freed from the monster. In exchange, Oedipus will have the throne and the Queen Iocasta. Looking closely, with respect to the Platonic canon, the Sphinx has, however, composed a philosophical discourse in reverse. First came the definition in the interrogative form – then its object, as a response. Thus, the logic of the riddle, which always goes backwards from the interrogative definition to the discovery of what it meant, imposes itself. This is a logic, which, on the other hand, is rather dreadful since the answer is in any case linked with an effect of death. The challenge, of course, is deadly: as is typical of ancient Greece, 'the riddle flows from the cruelty of a god, from malevolence towards men.'[4] Either Oedipus or the Sphinx must die; he to be devoured by the monster, she to be cast into the abyss. No one gets out alive from the ancient game that stages the extraordinary 'contrast between the banality, in the form and the content, of these riddles and the tragedy of their outcome.'[5] It is the secret of her knowledge of Man that keeps the monster alive. The one who reveals this secret is saved, but we begin to suspect that he risks living with this monstrous knowledge.

Indeed, the definition itself is not the fearful or deadly side of the formula. The Thebans knew this harmless definition, which speaks of the number of legs, by heart. What decides who lives and who dies is, rather, the response, the *definiendum* – namely, Man. The Sphinx obviously knows this already: her knowledge is complete. By guessing the answer and putting it together with the question, Oedipus takes possession of that knowledge. And yet, in this transition from the secret of the monster to the human word, the deadly effect is not lost. It would therefore seem that there is something constitutively monstrous about the knowledge of Man. It is almost as though it is the attribution of universality itself that makes a monster of Man. The legacy of the Sphinx is burdensome. Philosophy in Thebes, despite the relief of the city, seems to be born under a bad omen.

Perhaps the riddle is to blame – what with its reversed logic and its lethal effect. Indeed, normally philosophers neither make riddles nor put themselves at risk in the deadly game of the riddle. Rather, philosophers quickly and peacefully determine what it is about the universal Man that should be questioned regarding 'reality,' and they then proceed to the answer by means of a definition. In this way, having unwisely accepted the crucial aspect of the monstrous, philosophers shift the problem on to the 'definition.' And yet the definition, rather than being a problem – as the Sphinx understood all too well, evidenced by the banal tone of her riddle – is nothing but child's play, a game of variously assemblable formulas (after all, even old Plato had fun with such formulas!).

The true mark of the monster lies, rather, in Man, as Oedipus had the occasion to learn. 'Man' is a universal that applies to everyone precisely because it is no one. It disincarnates itself from the living singularity of each one, while claiming to substantiate it. It is at once masculine and neuter, a hybrid creature generated by thought, a fantastic universal produced by the mind. It is invisible and intangible, while nevertheless declaring itself to be the only thing 'sayable' in true discourse. It lives on its noetic status, even though it never leaves behind any life-story, and impedes language with the many philosophic progeny of its abstract conception.

If the Sphinx's riddle concealed a philosophical monster, then it seems that Oedipus has had the chance to glimpse its face.

A famous vase-painting shows Oedipus facing the Sphinx, in the act of solving the riddle. He does not speak, he points at himself with his finger. The answer is not verbal and does not name Man, but rather consists in the tacit word 'I/me.' The situation is truly paradoxical. At a time when he has yet to learn who he himself is, Oedipus recognizes himself in the definition of Man. In the discovery of the object of this definition, he indicates *himself*. More than simply being a paradox, this seems once again to be the monster's umpteenth cruel game; since it is precisely the extent to which Oedipus does not know *who* he is, that he can identify himself in the Man that concerns the definition. Philosophers themselves – servants of the universal – are the ones who teach us that the knowledge of Man requires that the particularity of each one, the uniqueness of human existence, be unknowable.[6] Knowledge of the universal, which excludes embodied uniqueness from its epistemology, attains its maximum perfection by presupposing the absence of such a uniqueness. *What* Man is can be known and defined, as Aristotle assures us; *who* Socrates is, instead, eludes the parameters of knowledge as science, it eludes the truth of the *episteme*.

In this way we can understand more exactly how the monster's last lethal game works. Since Oedipus does not know at all *who* he is; or, rather, he believes that he knows, but is mistaken – there, where the universal stakes its claim to reality by neglecting 'uniqueness' – he is already in a vulnerable position.

The deadly alternative of the challenge, between the Sphinx and Oedipus, is therefore also a deadly alternative between abstract Man and concrete uniqueness. In the sentence, 'I, Man,' it is the reality of the 'I' that dies. The ancient painting is a tremendous warning.

Thus, it seems to follow that, faced with the Sphinx and the philosophical strength of the riddle, Oedipus does not yet know *who* he himself is. Within the context of the Sophoclean play, all the same, the situation is rather complex, since, on the other hand, Sophocles, the Athenian public and, obviously, we too, know very well who Oedipus is. Indeed, we know who he is in detail. The play presupposes a knowledge of the *mythos*; that is, a detailed knowledge of the tale, which, from time immemorial, has recounted the entire story of Oedipus. The story is therefore known by all, except for the protagonists on stage. The theatrical play consists in bringing the plot of events back to the ambiguity that sustains them and thus renders them narratable by the protagonists themselves. In this way, duplicate narrations intersect: the internal, ambiguous one of the actors, and the external, omniscient one of the myth, which comprehends the first and puts it to work. The myth is capable of narrating at once – and this is its power – the 'true' story of Oedipus, the story of *who* he is, and the false story that leads him to be ignorant of 'who' he is. It is, moreover, this ignorance that allows the two stories to emerge from the same act. The death of Laius, at the fatal crossroads, is at once the murder of a stranger and a parricide. The union with Iocasta is both a legitimate marriage, and an act of incest. What governs the double narration – the ambiguous duplication that makes Oedipus an enigmatic mask of duplicity – is his birth, the truth of which he is ignorant, and whose truth the myth knows.[7]

This birth ends up being decisive in more than one sense. As a driving force of the plot, it is loaded first of all by a prophesied parricide that determines the protagonists' exchange of identity. The myth is well known. Oedipus is born of Iocasta under a prophecy that destines him to slay Laius, his father. Oedipus, however, escapes the infanticidal command of his parent – a good man took pity on him and took him to Corinth, where Polybus raised him as if he were his son. The story is familiar. Oedipus kills his father, believing him to be a stranger, and, not knowing her to be his mother, marries Iocasta. That Oedipus is ignorant of *who* he is, because he is ignorant of his birth, is therefore part of the story. Only by knowing his birth can he know *his* story.

Indeed, within the scene of *Oedipus the King*, it is precisely the enigma of this birth which catches up with him, making him discover who he is. He does not come across the truth of his birth by accident – like many protagonists of modern novels – but rather looks for it. The spread of the plague, the new evil that afflicts Thebes after the horror of the Sphinx, gives him the chance. The oracle says that the plague is the effect of the ancient unpunished guilt of the murderer of Laius who, remaining unknown, contaminates the city with his presence. So, who better than Oedipus, King of Thebes – who already solved the riddle of the

Sphinx – to track down the guilty party and free Thebes once more from the curse? Thus, Oedipus sets about looking into the identity of the unknown; that is, the identity, unknown to him, of himself.

Being the subject and object of the investigation – as though the philosophical guise fit him like a glove – Oedipus therefore seems to unknowingly obey the Delphic command, so dear to the philosopher: *gnothi se auton* ('know thy self'). For now, we will not follow this train of thought. Here philosophy does not matter; on the contrary, we will go in the opposite direction. In the 'know yourself,' of Oedipus, it is indeed his unrepeatable identity that is found, and not, as with Socrates, a principle of universal value: the famous 'knowledge of not knowing.' Furthermore, Oedipus does not embark on any introspective journey into the *interior* of his self, but rather comes to know his identity from the *outside*, through the story that others tell him. While Oedipus may have been a philosopher in front of the Sphinx, now he is no longer one. The philosophical undertaking concluded with the monster. For Oedipus, the adventure of the narration has just begun.

As we know, this is an adventure with an unhappy outcome. From the narration of another, Oedipus comes to know of his true birth, and thus his true story: an awful story that makes him incestuous and parricidal. Yet, however awful the outcome of such a narration may be, the *drama* of the Sophoclean scene is nonetheless rather simple. Oedipus does not know who he is because he is ignorant of his birth. Therefore, only the story of his birth can reveal the story of which he is the protagonist. For Oedipus, in other words, knowing himself means knowing his birth, because that is where his story began. That this story is unfortunate, like the birth from which it begins, is of course part of the tragedy; but this does not affect the truth of a general principle. The story of one's life always begins where that person's life begins. We are not speaking of Man in his disembodied and universal substance, but rather of a particular man, a unique being who bears the name of Oedipus. Since he exists, he was born of a mother. The uniqueness of his identity, his *daimon*, has its origin in the event of this birth. Oedipus has no doubts regarding this:

> *She* is my mother; my sisters are the Seasons;
> My rising and my falling march with theirs.
> Born thus, I ask to be no other man
> Than that I am, and *will know who I am*[8]

The link between personal identity and birth, according to Oedipus, is as materially founded as it is indubitable. His *daimon* is rooted in being born of a mother, *this* and not another; a mother who, by giving birth to him, has generated the 'seasons' of his entire existence, *this* existence and not another. By being ignorant of the factual truth of his birth, he has been able to believe himself to be another; but he was never able to become another. He became exactly who he was and is – in the very times that his uniqueness lived through, perhaps under a false genealogy, but not under a false *daimon*.

In so far as the Oedipus myth is so awful – and so full of symbolic references, as well as a remarkable history of interpretation – it speaks, therefore, in its elementary structure, of a *daimon* that is rooted in the birth of the protagonist, and who is revealed in all of his actions … even though he is ignorant of their meaning while he performs them. From the myth's omniscient point of view, such a *daimon* can thus be read as a prophecy brought inexorably to fulfillment. From the point of view of Oedipus on stage, this is rather the uniqueness of his personal identity, which is revealed through the actions that he has performed. Such a revelation – which is always and in every way unmasterable for the one who is being revealed – is, in Oedipus' case, simply made even more invisible and unknowable to him. His *daimon* is indeed hidden by an initial misunderstanding that changes the effective relations of the context. In other words, Oedipus is ignorant of the relationships that bind him to those he meets. Nevertheless, as proof of the fact that the meaning of a given action escapes every agent – as Hannah Arendt would say – a story *results* from Oedipus' actions, which harbors the meaning of his identity.[9]

The Sophoclean text is thus able to suggest an initial thesis: what Man is, is said by a definitory knowledge of philosophical assonance – who Oedipus is, is said by the narration of his story. To complete the thesis, however, we must add a qualification: it is *others* who tell him *his* story.

Indeed, for Oedipus, *who* he is, is the result of the life-story that others tell him. This is a polyphonic tale, as it comes from the narrative fragments that Iocasta, the pastor, and the messenger from Corinth recite on stage in a dramatic assembly.

In the end, the whole story becomes clear anyway, and even the misunderstandings that sustained it re-enter the story coherently. The actions that Oedipus has performed are still the same – a murder, a marriage – but their meaning has changed. If at first Oedipus believed himself to be someone else, then now he knows who he is, having finally learned from the tale of his life-story. The Oedipal form of *gnothi se auton* does not consist in an exercise of introspection, but rather in soliciting the external tale of his own life-story.

Discovering in this the truth of his birth, the son of Iocasta is thus born into his identity, which is rendered tangible by the story; that is to say, he is reborn through the *daimon* of his own origin. 'This day will give you life and it will destroy you,' Teiresias had predicted.[10] On the very same day on which he is once again given life through the story of his birth, the *other* Oedipus – the man of Corinth and the happy King of Thebes – is destroyed. The result is, obviously, the revelation of the enormous misfortune that the omniscience of the myth had made known to us from the start. Oedipus is *who* was born. Oedipus is who he was and had always been – from beginning to end in the unity of a self now rendered palpable by the story – never having been able to become someone else. Moreover, being able to believe himself to be another was in fact part of his unique, and unfortunate, story. The mixture of intentions and circumstances was indeed too unbalanced in favor of unlucky combinations. The unforeseeable outcome of actions became for him something terrible.

Rivers of critics' ink, and a century of psychoanalysis, free us from the task of reflecting further upon the meaning of this blameless misfortune. What is certain is that, even in the search for his own identity, the monstrous catches up with Oedipus. We will skip the reasons for this, and will follow another way of reading, which concerns that already announced self-differentiation of philosophy from narration, which seems to lead again to the mask of Oedipus. We could define it as the confrontation between two discursive registers that manifest opposite characteristics. One, that of philosophy, has the form of a definitory knowledge that regards the universality of Man. The other, that of narration, has the form of a biographical knowledge that regards the unrepeatable identity of someone. The questions that sustain the two discursive styles are equally diverse. The first asks '*what* is Man?' The second asks instead of someone '*who* he or she is.' Oedipus is implicated in both questions, but it is obviously above all the latter that occupies the scene of *Oedipus the King*.

In this scene, one of the narrators is blind: Teiresias, the soothsayer, whose figure personifies the omniscience of the myth itself. The soothsayer, Teiresias, like the myth, knows the whole story in minute detail. Like us – the spectators, the readers – he is omniscient. And yet, unlike us, he is on stage. He knows what has happened, what is happening and what will happen, because the times of the story are already condensed into the present of his soothsayer's memory. Unlike the spectators, who are there to watch, he is blind. Indeed, Teiresias does not see the things as they happen, he does not participate in the performance of the events. Instead, he conserves the story in the present of a memory where everything has already happened. For him 'the *factum infectum fieri nequit* is applied, even to the future event.'[11] If the telling of every story cannot help concerning what has already been done, and cannot be undone, then the omniscient myth, which is embodied in the mask of the soothsayer Teiresias, implicates the future as well in this rule.

The particularity of Teiresias lies therefore in being on stage *while* things happen, and in being able to tell stories about them as though they had already happened. Like the spectator who knows the myth, he is powerless; that is, he cannot act in a way that interferes in the events. And yet, contrary to the spectator who watches, he cannot see them because, as a narrator, he has already seen them happen. In any case, how could he undo that which, in the story of the myth, has already been done? How could he intervene in a future that is already past? In so far as his role as soothsayer links him to the future, the gaze of Teiresias, like that of every narrator, is always retrospective.[12] The singular, staged duplication of the myth, which he narrates, is a story of which neither he nor anyone else is the author. As an odd, staged reduplication of the biographical story, which others, in unison, make of Oedipus, he is the only one who can narrate a biography in which even that polyphonic story, with everything that follows, already comes back.

What is more, when Oedipus has heard the whole story, he too goes blind. The recognition of the narratable status of his identity, or, the explicit desire to know his story, whatever it is, produces for Oedipus a tragic self-confinement in the solipsistic sphere of personal memory. In other words, Oedipus is now blind because he sees, replayed in his memory, what he had never seen before. He was the first, autobiographical narrator of his false story – the story that concealed rather than revealed *who* he is, the radical model of the unreliability of every autobiography. Now that he has been told his real story, the terrible significance of his identity holds him bound to this story. Blind to the present, like his memory, he will continue to live without existing in the present, carrying only his story with him. Oedipus has learned at great cost that existence, in its embodied uniqueness, is narratable. And yet, it would seem that there is nothing in the world for which he would give up this narration.

Although many believe that the parricide and incest sustain the Oedipal desire, it seems plausible that the desire in Oedipus to be born into his 'real' identity, through others' tales of his life-story, is equally strong. With what seems at first sight to be an analogous approach, Roland Barthes wonders: 'Does not every tale lead back to Oedipus? Is not storytelling always the search for one's own origin, to tell of one's own troubles with the Law, to enter into a dialectic with emotion and hate?' Again, what Barthes himself defines as '*le monument psychoanalytique*' enters into play, as does the discounted phallocentric mark that links the story to Oedipal pleasure: '(denuding, knowing, being familiar with the beginning and the end), if it is true that every tale (every revelation of truth) is a *mise-en-scène* of the Father (absent, hidden, hypothesized).'[13] Contrary to Barthes – and in contrast to *le monument psychoanalytique*, which has held sway over the Oedipus myth for too long – we are trying to underscore the way in which the Oedipal desire turns stubbornly towards the life-story that reveals to him *who* he is, as he was born of his mother. In short, we are reading Sophocles, not Freud. Hannah Arendt, denouncing the disappearance of the custom of telling stories in contemporary times, wonders if this disappearance is the result of 'this curious neurotic concern with the self which in analysis was shown to have nothing to tell but variations of identical experiences – the Oedipus complex, as distinguished from the tale Sophocles had to tell –?'[14]

Taking into account Barthes' suggestion, which focalizes 'the nexus between the tale and Oedipus, between desire and narration,' we therefore affirm that what the Sophoclean Oedipus manifests is first of all a desire *for* narration, or the desire for the telling of his story. This story is, importantly, biographical, not autobiographical. It comes tragically to Oedipus from others' narrations, at the very moment at which he mistakenly claims to be telling it. 'Doomed man! O never to live to learn the truth of who you are!'[15] cried a piteous Iocasta, hoping that the autobiographical exercise of her son would leave no room for the eruption of the biographical storm.

Unfortunately, however, *who* else could ever be the Oedipus whose identity we know and whose name we remember, if not the protagonist of his story? And what does this story teach if not Oedipus' looking-for-himself, as he is 'this and not another'? – if not his 'considering himself to be a destiny, and not wanting to be otherwise.'[16]

NOTES

1 Sophocles, *Oedipus the King*, translated by E. F. Watling (Baltimore: Penguin Books, 1947), p. 26.
2 Plato, *Parmenides*, 130b–c. See, *Plato: The Complete Works*, edited by John Cooper (Indianapolis: Hackett Publishing, 1997).
3 Plato, *Statesman*, 265b.
4 Giorgio Colli, *La nascita della filosofia* (Milan: Adelphi, 1981), p. 50. [TN: Translation is mine.]
5 *Ibid.*, p. 52.
6 Cf. Luce Irigaray, *Sexes and Genealogies*, trans. Gillian Gill (New York: Columbia, 1993).
7 Cf. Jean-Pierre Vernant, *Myth and Tragedy in Ancient Greece*, trans. Janet Lloyd (Sussex: Brighton Press, 1981), p. 92; and Umberto Curi, *Endiadi*, (Milan: Feltrinelli, 1995), p. 34 and *passim*.
8 Sophocles, *Oedipus the King*, p. 55.
9 Hannah Arendt, *The Human Condition* (Chicago: University of Chicago Press, 1958), p. 184.
10 Sophocles, *Oedipus the King*, p. 38.
11 Giuseppe Serra, *Edipo e la peste* (Venice: Marsilio, 1994), p. 41. I owe much more than this citation to this magnificent book by Serra.
12 Arendt, *The Human Condition*, p. 184.
13 Roland Barthes, *The Pleasure of the Text*, trans. Richard Miller (New York: Hill and Wang, 1975), pp. 20, 74 and 92.
14 Arendt, 'Letter to Mary McCarthy, May 28–31, 1971', from *Between Friends* (New York: Harcourt and Brace, 1995), p. 295.

15 Sophocles, *Oedipus the King*, p. 55.
16 Friedrich Nietzsche, *Ecce Homo*, trans. Walter Kaufmann (New York: Vintage, 1967), pp. 327–35.

2

THE PARADOX OF ULYSSES

Octavio seemed upset. 'And we?' – he asked, his voice trembled slightly, 'We have a story?'

As I hesitated to respond, he began to weep uncontrollably.

'We have a story,' he repeated between sobs, as though he had just learned that he belonged to a new rung on the ladder of beings.

Adele bent over to caress him, 'Do not cry,' she murmured, 'we all have a story. However we cannot know our own, but only those of others.'

Paola Capriolo, *Il gigante*

Among ancient characters, Oedipus is a truly special case. There is, however, another equally famous hero, who, while not ignorant of his birth, does not seem to know who he is, until he meets up with himself through the tale of his story. His name is Ulysses.

In one of the most beautiful scenes of the *Odyssey*, Ulysses is seated as a guest in the court of the Phaecians, incognito. A blind rhapsod entertains those gathered with his song. He sings, 'the famous deeds of men, that song whose renown had already reached the wide sky.'[1] He sings of the Trojan war, and tells of Ulysses and his undertakings. And Ulysses, hiding himself in a great purple tunic, weeps. 'He has never wept before,' comments Hannah Arendt, 'and certainly not when what he is now hearing actually happened. Only when he hears the story does he becomes fully aware of its significance.'[2]

We will call this scene *the paradox of Ulysses*. As we saw with Oedipus, this consists in the situation for which someone receives his own story from another's narration. And so it happens to Ulysses at the court of the Phaecians. He weeps because he fully realizes the meaning of the story. But what exactly does the story *signify*? – neither the action itself nor the agent, suggests Arendt, but rather the story that the agent, through his actions, left behind him: that is, his life-story. In hearing his story, then, Ulysses is moved to tears. Not only because the narrated events are painful, but because when he had lived them directly he had not understood their meaning. It is as if, while acting, he had been immersed in the contextuality of the events. It is as if, each time, he were captured in the present of the action that cuts off the temporal series of before and after. But now, in the tale of the rhapsod, the discontinuous times of that happening come together in a story. Now Ulysses comes to recognize himself as the hero of this story. By fully realizing the meaning of his narrated story, he also gains a notion of *who* is its protagonist. Therefore, before hearing his story, Ulysses did not yet know *who* he was: the story of the rhapsod, the story told by an 'other,' finally revealed his own identity. And he, dressed in his magnificent purple tunic, breaks down and cries.

Unlike Oedipus, Ulysses is not ignorant of his birth. If Ulysses is *who* was born, 'this and not another,' he is not mistaken at all about the noble parents who engendered him. He should therefore have no reason to be ignorant of *who* he is; or, at least, he should not have the same reasons as Oedipus. In fact, when the King of the Phaecians, moved by Ulysses' crying, asks him who he is, he responds: 'I am Odysseus, son of Laertes,' and then proceeds with a long, autobiographical tale. The way in which the questions of the nobleman were formulated furnishes us, however, with a valuable indication. 'Tell me the name you go by at home – what your mother and father and countrymen call you. For no one in the world is nameless, however mean or noble, since parents give names to all the children they have.'[3]

There is here, obviously, also an ironic game being played by Homer, since No One was the name chosen by Ulysses to mislead Polyphemus. (Is it perhaps the case that the hero, discovering how his name already has immortal fame, now weeps out of relief for being released from the cruel joke of calling himself No One?) In any case, this is not the final point. The point lies in the gravity of the question posed to the unknown guest.

By posing this question, the King of the Phaecians underscores that every human being, from the time of his or her birth, has a proper name, as a sort of 'vocative' unity of his or her uniqueness. Only a human being has such a proper name. This is even more true in the case of Ulysses – because among the Homeric characters he is the only one to hear this proper name. Still, it is not this absolute, onomastic originality that makes a name into a sign of uniqueness. The uniqueness lies rather in the paradoxical fact that everyone responds immediately to the question '*who* are you?' by pronouncing the proper name, even if a thousand others can respond with the same name. Notwithstanding the fact that it is shared with many others, the proper name is the strange, verbal synthesis of a uniqueness that is exposed to its own question; moreover, there is no further knowledge that corresponds with it. As Walter Benjamin notes, the names that parents give a child 'do not correspond – in a metaphysical rather than etymological sense – to any knowledge, for they name newborn children.'[4] The name announces the uniqueness, in its inaugural appearing to the world, even before someone can know who the newborn is; or, *who* he or she will turn out to be in the course of their life. A unique being is without any quality at its beginning, and yet it *already* has a name. The newborn does not choose this name, but is given it by another, just as every human being does not choose how to be. The uniqueness which pertains to the *proper* is always a *given*, a *gift*.

Of course, it is not always the parents who name children. This is the case of orphans, to whose names there corresponds a valuable truth.[5] Names like Donato and Benedetto suggestively disclose that whoever is born and abandoned by the mother is still an existent offered by her as a gift [*donato/dono*] to the world and blessed [*benedetta*] by it. The infant, though found in solitude, finds in this solitude only a disgraceful and extraordinary state of affairs. Indeed, the absence of the mother is immediately perceptible in the question that is inevitable but is destined to remain unanswered: 'who gave birth to this creature?' With this question, the language of the existent reveals its symptomatic opposition to the language of philosophers. The latter, looking to the existent in general, asks 'from where' the newborn came, and is therefore required to confine its explanation to the alternative, as solemn as it is empty, between *being* and *nothingness*. But the question that is addressed to the unique, newborn being is precisely that which asks 'from *whom*' the newborn came. And common parlance answers 'from God' – thereby bequeathing to the infant the surname Diodato ('God-given') – or, looking ahead – Diotallevi ('may God raise you'). And yet, God himself, besides being the Creator of us all, is called upon to make up for the absence of a mother because every existent, from its birth, is *exposed*; that is, brought into appearance as someone who is abandoned. This exposure is, in the case of the orphan, simply more fragile. The mother, who embodies the *ex-* of *existent*, despite having been there at the origin of the child's existence, is now no longer there. Existence as exposure becomes, in this case, the perceptible truth of every existent, made more acute by the immediate loss of one's own origin.

'I am Odysseus, son of Laertes,' responds Ulysses instead, ignoring the maternal origin of existence (as is typical not only of heroes). The name thus works like a glue between the story that the blind rhapsod has told up until this point, and the rest of the story which Ulysses sets about recounting. The proper name, as a phonetic seal of the hero's identity, works like a glue between the biographical story and the autobiographical one. And yet, this is precisely where the heart of the paradox lies. How was Ulysses able to weep over the revelatory effect of the biographical tale if he himself is capable of narrating his autobiography? Why – as already happened with Oedipus and whatever may be the circumstances of his birth – is the meaning of identity *always* entrusted to others' telling of one's own life-story?

Hannah Arendt would have no trouble unpacking this strange paradox. For her, it follows from the fact that the category of personal identity postulates an*other* as necessary. Even before another can render tangible the identity of someone by telling him/her his/her story, many others have indeed been spectators of the constitutive exposure of the very same identity to their gaze. In other words a human being, in so far as he/she is unique and shows him- or herself to be such from the time of his or her birth, is *exposed*. This is why identity corresponds with the *who* 'of the question posed to every newcomer: "who are you?" '[6] 'The urge toward self-display by which living things fit themselves into a world of appearances' makes of identity an in-born [*in-nato*] exposure of the *who* to the gaze and to others' questions.[7]

Of course, this self-showing and reciprocal exhibition does not only concern human beings. 'The world in which men are born contains many things, natural and artificial, alive and dead, all of which have in common that fact that they *appear*, and are therefore destined to be seen, touched, tasted, smelled, to be perceived by sensing creatures.'[8] In a similar way, María Zambrano writes that: 'everything is correlated, in life: seeing is correlated to being seen, speaking to listening, asking to giving.'[9] Only in Arendt does this cosmic feast of reciprocity marry with radical phenomenology, which for her is concentrated in the formula for which '*Being and Appearing coincide*.'[10] Such an appearing has 'an ontological, and not simply phenomenological, bearing.'[11] In the general exhibitionist spectacle which Arendt gives us, appearing is indeed not the *superficial* phenomenon of a more intimate and true 'essence.' Appearing is the *whole* of being, understood as a plural finitude of existing. This goes above all for human beings, who have the privilege of appearing to one another, distinguishing *themselves* in their in-born [*in-nata*] uniqueness, such that, in this reciprocal exhibition, a *who* is shown to appear, entirely as it is. As Jean-Luc Nancy also emphasizes, 'for the one who exists, what matters is existence, not essence';[12] that is, at stake is a uniqueness of personal identity, which, far from being a substance, is of a totally expositive and relational character. From birth, everyone, as a unique existent, shows *who* he or she is to others.

The expositive and the relational character of identity are thus indistinguishable. One always appears to someone. One cannot appear if there is no one else there. It follows, to say it again with Nancy, that 'the un-exposable is the non-existent';[13] that is, existing consists in disclosing oneself within a scene of plurality where everyone, by appearing to one another, is shown to be unique. They appear to each other reciprocally – first of all in their corporeal materiality and as creatures endowed with sensory organs. Put another way, the language of the existent assumes the bodily condition of 'this and not another' in all of its perceptible concreteness. Starting from birth, from the 'naked reality of our originary physical appearance,' each of us is *who* appears to others uniquely and distinctly.[14]

Besides being she from whom the existent comes, the mother is also the *other* to whom the existent first appears, although Arendt does not say this. This physical identity continues to appear to others throughout life 'in the unique form of a body and sound of voice.'[15] The primacy of appearance constitutes, through the others' gaze, the fundamental corporal aspect of identity. In other words, already on the corporeal level, in so far as a unique being is concerned, identity depends upon the presence of others. Appearing, always and everywhere, is the only principle of reality: 'the "sensation" of reality, of sheer thereness relates to the *context* in which single objects appear as well as the context in which we ourselves as appearances exist among other appearing creatures.'[16]

The distinction between a corporeal level and, so to speak, a 'spiritual' level of identity, nonetheless has its justification only within the polemical limits to which the dichotomic obsession of philosophy restricts us.[17] Philosophy, of course, loves to separate – within the subject – the body from the soul. In spite of philosophy, appearance – and the primacy of the visible with which it embraces phenomena – are nonetheless always and everywhere rooted in the materiality of the context. Even the newborn creature is already a unique existent that exhibits his/her body and spirit to others as inseparable. As Oedipus knew all too well, uniqueness is an embodied uniqueness – this and not another, all his life, until *who* is born dies. The primacy of the visible thus has the merit of exemplifying the reason for which an identity constitutively exposed to others is also unmasterable. Indeed, the one who is exposed cannot know *who* is exposing because he/she does not see him- or herself. It is therefore, argues Arendt, quite likely 'that the "who" which appears so clearly and unmistakably to others remains hidden to the person himself; like the *daimon* in Greek religion, which accompanies each man throughout his life, looking over his shoulder from behind and thus visible only to those he encounters.'[18]

To appear to others simply because one encounters them, and to actively show them *who* one is, are nevertheless two different things for Arendt. Simply put, this difference concerns the mere appearing physical identities and their *active* self-disclosure. This is not a difference between mere materiality and a lofty spirituality, or between body and soul. Rather, it is a difference of scene. The scene upon which 'human beings appear to one another not as physical objects, but *as* men' is indeed that which sees them *acting* with words and deeds.[19] Going against the traditional, canonical lexicon, Arendt gives this scene of interactive exhibition the name of *politics*.[20]

As the direct descendant of the natal impulse toward self-exhibition, the human faculty of action bears indeed, in Arendt's view, the task of actively revealing the uniqueness of personal identity. Actively revealing oneself to others, with words and deeds, grants a plural space and therefore a political space to identity – confirming its exhibitive, relational and contextual nature. Put another way, *who* each one is, is revealed to others when he or she acts in their presence in an interactive theater where each is, at the same time, *actor and spectator*. In this world, where already 'there exists nothing and no one who does not presuppose a *spectator*,' not even the actor of the specifically human theater of politics knows, as yet, *who* he reveals.[21] Following his impulse to self-revelation, he limits himself to showing *who* he is to others, distinguishing himself actively in the horizon of the 'paradoxical plurality of unique beings' that characterizes the human condition.[22] For him it is as unmasterable and invisible as the *daimon*; his identity remains as yet unknown. Even on the active level of the properly human (or political) revelation, the meaning of the identity remains patrimony of an other.

With a nod to the *daimon*, we are thus ready to return to Greece in order to recover Homer's Ulysses from our paradox.

However, we cannot avoid recalling that, from Arendt's point of view, Ulysses – while being unique like every human being – has a particular feature. He is a *hero*, a champion of action in whom the impulse to self-revelation is *heightened*.[23] Arendt, by the way, is not particularly original in having this conviction: the emphasis on the self-revelatory character of heroic action has been well noted by the critical tradition. Hegel, for example, emphasizes that for the hero 'action is the clearest illumination of the individual.' Maurice Blanchot develops this even more explicitly, when he writes that heroism is the 'revelation, the dazzling exploit of the act, in which being and appearing are united [...] while the hero who does not act is nothing.'[24] Affirming that the hero who does not act is nothing, Blanchot therefore comes to focus the emphasis on heroic action at a crucial point. His sentence indeed means that the *whole* hero lies in the action that reveals him.

What is absolutely unique to Arendt, however, is the political genealogy which she sees forming from the heroic figure. Indeed, for Arendt, the hero becomes the prototype of action for ancient Greece – that same exhibitive action that comes to characterize the agonistic spirit of the democratic *polis*. The passage from the Homeric hero to the citizen of the *polis* is coherent and direct. A self-exhibiting impulse is shown in both; one which finds, or rather creates, adequate space – interactive space – for its own expression. For the hero, such a space is the plain of Troy, where he shows to his peers *who* he is with words and actions. For the citizen, on the other hand, this is the *agora*: the central square of the *polis*. On the Trojan plain, the heroes have 'the opportunity to show themselves as they really are, to reveal themselves in their real appearance and therefore to become fully real.'[25] In the *agora*, the citizens likewise construct the only status of *reality* allowed to the human existent as a unique existent upon interaction and upon a plural network of gazes. In this way, we can easily understand why, for Arendt, action is synonymous with *politics* – modeled on the heroic action of the Homeric epic, it acquires in the *polis* its more famous scenario.

Heightening the impulse to self-disclosure that pertains to acting, heroic action thus has the merit of highlighting the constitutive coinciding of *being* and *appearing* that defines the totally exhibitive character of identity. This is an identity that, far from corresponding with a substance, is entirely expressive. Blanchot too, finally, suggests that beneath this identity, before it or beyond it, there is nothing else. Arendt makes clear that identity does not express (that is, press out) something internal, the deep and intimate identity of the self. Identity expresses nothing other than 'itself and what is shown or exhibited.'[26] Commenting on the Arendtian notion of acting, Bonnie Honig affirms that 'identity is not the expressive condition or the essence of action, but rather its product.'[27] It is important to underline that this is nonetheless a producing that does not follow a temporality of before and after, or of cause and effect, but rather actively shows that which from the beginning – from birth – consists in its self-showing.

To be sure, by emphasizing heroic action, the constitutive unmasterability [*impadroneggiabilità*] of the '*who*' is made hugely evident. No one can know, master or decide upon identity. Each one of us is only capable of exhibiting it, of exhibiting that unrepeatable uniqueness which he is, as he appears to others in the actual context of his exhibition. Our Ulysses, who interacts with his peers on the Trojan plain, is thus not an extraordinary case at all. As happens not only with heroes, but also with all of the other *actors*, he does not know who he is because he could in no way know it. The one who is revealed never knows *whom* he reveals. Given that everyone's identity lies completely in the exhibitive character of this *who* – *who* the agent reveals is, by definition, unknown to the agent himself.

On Arendt's suggestion, we have therefore finally solved one side of the paradox; namely, that enigma by which, at the court of the Phaecians and before listening to his story, Ulysses shows that he does not know *who* he is. In this ignorance of his own identity, he is not a special case. And yet, the fact that he is a hero is still not an incidental feature, for the hero is not limited to acting among his peers. By heightening the impulse to self-revelation, he spontaneously performs *great* deeds. He performs actions worthy of fame; he performs *memorable* actions. The story that results from such actions is thus already characterized by an intrinsic memorability. The narrator, in telling of them, simply puts them into words.

We are therefore approaching the second side of the paradox. In Arendt's terms, the crucial aspect consists in recognizing that the story of Ulysses, like every story, has no author. It simply results from Ulysses' actions. Indeed, 'the real story in which we are engaged as long as we live has no visible or invisible maker, because it is not made.'[28] Even though, for the one who acts, 'the meaningfulness of his act is not in the story that follows,' nevertheless a story always *results* from the succession of his active revelations – *his* life-story.[29] He is not its author; he is, however, the protagonist. The story that results from his actions is, in this sense, an impalpable plot that goes in search of its tale, of its narrator.

Even if a life-story never has an author, it always has a protagonist – a hero as we say, not by chance – and, sometimes, a narrator. Indeed, if we want to continue following Arendt, only an invented story reveals an artifice that can rightly be defined as its author. A life-story, on the contrary, turns its narrator into a simple biographer. He is limited to comprehending the story that the actor left behind, and to putting it into words. The personal identity of the actor, who is revealed intangibly through his actions, thus becomes tangible at the end of the narration: '*who* somebody is or was we can know only by knowing the story of which he is himself the hero – the biography, in other words.'[30] Socrates left behind nothing written; and yet, through his story written by others, we know who he was much more fully than we know who 'Plato and Aristotle were, about whose opinions we are so much better informed.'[31] The works that Plato and Aristotle have left to us tell us not *who* but *what* they were. We know that they were philosophers. But this, for Arendt, only indicates one of their qualities; certainly a notable talent, but one that they nonetheless share with many others. In this alone, they do not reveal themselves to be unique at all.

Plato is therefore lacking a biographer. (Evidently the autobiographical character of the *Seventh Letter* does not count for Arendt.) The autobiography would figure, in Arendt's view, as an absurd exercise, since the identity revealed by its actions is the very thing that the agent does not master and does not know. Thus, it will be even more difficult for him to be able to know and master the story that such actions leave behind. 'Autobiographical data are worth retelling only if they are felt be unique, to possess some unique unrepeatable value,' writes Arendt in one of the rare pages that allow a sense of autobiography.[32] The fact remains that the *meaning* of a life-story is for her always entrusted to biography, to the tale of another.

The relational status of identity indeed always postulates *an other* as necessary – whether this other is embodied by a plurality of spectators who see the self-revelatory actions of the actor, or whether this other is embodied by the narrator who tells the story from which these actions result. Unlike the spectator, the narrator is still not present at the events, and thus, like the historian, gazes upon them retrospectively. He knows better than the others what happened, precisely because he does not participate directly in the context of the actions from which the story results. Indeed, the eventual reports by the actors can become at most 'useful sources' at the disposal of the narrator. But, for the meaning and the truth of the story, it is imperative that the one who tells the tale is not involved in the action of its protagonist.

At the court of the Phaecians, the relationship between Ulysses and the rhapsod is thus perfect. The obvious double of Homer, the rhapsod, as happens also with Teiresias, is blind. He sees neither the action nor the agent, because he is not present at the scene where the action takes place and where the agent is exposed to the spectator. Rather, he sees, with his blind eyes, the story that results from these actions – because this story is present to him in the invisible form of memory. The blindness of the narrator, the blindness of Homer, of the rhapsod and of Teiresias, contrasts with the gaze of the spectator – and underscores the essential difference between action and narration. Both appertain to the meaning [significarsi] of identity. But, while on the level of action this meaningfulness is rooted in the fragility and the unmasterability of the context, on the level of narration the meaning pertains rather to a story that is as immutable as the past. The fleeting and discontinuous present is opposed to the immutability, and the duration, of the past. The fundamental difference between action and narration lies in this: the revelatory power of action expires in the moment of its occurring, the story conserves the identity of its hero in time – and every so often for *all* time – if it has the fortune of finding a great narrator. After all these millennia, thanks to Homer, are we not still concerned with Ulysses?

Ulysses-the-hero is indeed above all paradigmatic for the intrinsic memorability of his actions. Foreseeing the inevitable death that sooner or later awaits him, he performs great actions, trusting in their memorable effect. 'To save human deeds from oblivion,' is indeed, in Greece, the task of the narrator who passes them on through the memory of those who follow.[33] Importantly, according to Arendt, this immortalizing role of narrating concerns both poet and historian – Homer as much as Herodotus. They can 'bestow mortal fame upon word and deed to make them outlast not only the futile moment of speech and action but even the mortal life of their agent.'[34] As the true greatness of man, as a measure of his being-human, acting is indeed fragile. It appears, and consumes itself in the very moment of its appearing. Only the poet and the historian can save it from oblivion. They share the same task, since individual stories (like History, a 'book of the tales of humanity'[35]) are constituted by their interlacing. They result from human actions.

Both the poet and the historian, therefore, appeal to the unrepeatability of the unique, not to the universal and the general. They have neither theses to demonstrate, nor historical 'laws' to discover. They are impartial, they simply recount that which happened one day in the shared space of appearance. Homer, the inspiration to Herodotus, is at the same time the first poet and the first historian. Arendt can thus say that, 'impartiality, and with it all true historiography, came into the world when Homer decided to sing the deeds of the Trojans no less than those of the Achaeans, and to praise the glory of Hector no less than the greatness of Achilles.'[36] The result, of course, is a multi-perspective narration that brings together the different stories in a plot rich with digressions and suspensions. To this extent, the epic style could be defined as anticipating post-modernity in its narrative model, even as it is also the faithful tradition of the unmasterable crossing of diverse stories that result from different actions. Indeed, for Arendt, Homer is the archetypal figure of the *storyteller* – the narrator of stories who concentrates both the art of the historian and the art of the poet in his work. In other words, he is the blind poet; the one who, by recounting stories, saves the reciprocal exhibitions of the actors from that fragile actuality of the present to which they belong.[37]

'Homeric impartiality rested upon the assumption that great things are self-evident, shine by themselves' says Arendt.[38] Like every hero, Ulysses is surely convinced of this. He performs great actions precisely because their splendor imposes itself upon the poet, earning the hero the tale. While he does not control the story that results from his actions, it can nonetheless be affirmed that Ulysses is able to 'produce' their narratability. This is not, however, a 'producing' in the usual sense of the term, which implies a capacity to project and control the 'product,' but rather in the sense of the memorability and thus the narratability that is guaranteed to the intrinsic brilliance of great actions. The hero indeed explicitly seeks an *immortal* fame, namely the narratability of a story that is passed down through the generations. Ulysses' descendants know *who* he was, well beyond his death. The same etymological root that links fame, *kleos*, to the name pronounced out loud, *kledon*, brings together in the hero the uniqueness of the proper name, and that which assures him the posthumous fame of his own story.[39]

At the court of the Phaecians, when Ulysses happens upon the tale of his story, while having the honor of becoming 'paradigmatic for both history and poetry,' he is nevertheless still alive and kicking.[40] We will leave him, therefore, to his quite human tears, in order to turn to another hero; one who – even though he too weeps unabashedly, as is typical of heroes – was able to fully plan the memorable effect of his death. Of course, I'm talking about Achilles.

Already extraordinary by birth, as he is the son of the divine Thetis and the mortal Peleus, Achilles is indeed able to choose his destiny. Rather than opt for a long and obscure life, he chooses a brief and glorious one instead. This is why we see him weep on the seashore and lament that the young Briseis, the coveted spoil of war and deserved prize for his valor, has already been given to another. 'Mother! You gave me life, short as that life will be, so at least Olympian Zeus, thundering up on high, should give me honor,' complains Achilles.[41] That his life would be both glorious and brief was in fact part of the pact of his choice. His life had to be brief, precisely because the mark of glory was clear, and on account of the immortal fame that gave it its meaning. His wrath for the offense, like his complaining prayer, therefore has its reasons. Moreover, it serves as the motivation for even greater actions in the conclusive battle on the Trojan plain. Thus, in the end, everything comes back. Achilles dies young, at the culmination of a great action and in that full and deserved glory which, in fact, gave him immortal fame. The *daimon* of Achilles, frozen in the Homeric tale of his life-story, became *eudaimon*.

According to Hannah Arendt, we have lost the meaning of the ancient saying that no one can be called *eudaimon* before dying. We translate *eudaimon* as happy or blessed, but the term *eudaimonia* indicates neither happiness nor blessedness. The word indicates rather 'blessedness, but without any religious overtones, and means literally something like the well-being of the *daimon* who accompanies every man throughout life, who is his distinct identity, but appears and is visible only to others.'[42] It indicates a sort of 'well-being' of identity, or that the identity endures; that is, it designates a state in which the identity is no longer subject to changes. It is a state that is, of course, impossible in life – but after death, after the revelatory actions come to a definitive end, it becomes possible in the form of a story. The essence of *who* someone is 'can come into being only when the life departs, leaving behind nothing but a story.'[43] This 'unchangeable identity of the person' that only death rescues from change, renders anyone *eudaimon*, by giving them their story.

Achilles is thus an extraordinary hero because he is able not only to earn, but also to control, his narration. By choosing a brief and glorious life, he is in fact sure to act in a manner that is close to an imminent death. He is *eudaimon* therefore because he chooses to obtain a lasting state of identity through his death. Summing up his whole life 'in a single deed, so that the story of the act comes to an end together with the life itself,'[44] Achilles consigns to the narrator a personal identity that is already immutably configured as an *essence* of his *who*. Of course, even he needs Homer and, therefore, he depends on the narrator. But, among the heroes, he is the one who gets closest to that paradoxical situation in which the protagonist of a life-story is also its author.

It therefore seems that, in the example of Achilles, the hero re-enters at the very end – if not in the philosophical mode of 'thinking for death,' at least in that of 'acting for death.' All of this appertains to the epic – to the pact that Homer makes with *Mnemosyne*, Memory, in order to respond to death, which brings forgetting. As Benjamin writes, 'only by virtue of a comprehensive memory can epic writing absorb the course of events on the one hand and, with the passing of these, make its peace with the power of death on the other.'[45] In spite of this tradition, the homage that heroic actions concede to death in order to earn an imperishable memory is, within Arendt's speculative horizon, quite astonishing.

The remarkable anomaly of Arendt's political thought depends in fact upon a radical change of perspective that consists in looking at the category of birth rather than of death. 'Since action is the political activity *par excellence*, natality, and not mortality, may be the central category of political, as distinguished from metaphysical, thought' she proclaims in a famous passage.[46] She elaborates: 'speaking in terms of existential modalities, the difference between, or the opposition of, Politics and Philosophy, is equivalent to the difference between, or the opposition of, Birth and Death; or in conceptual terms, to the opposition between Natality and Mortality. Natality is the fundamental condition of every living-together and thus of every politics; Mortality is the fundamental condition of thought, in so far as thought refers itself to something that is as it is and is for itself.'[47] The exhibitive quality of acting is rooted in this same theoretical horizon. It makes birth into a phenomenal scene capable of conferring upon identity its expressive, contextual and relational status. In this way, birth, action and narration become the scenes of an identity that always postulates the presence of an *other*.

Indeed, it is precisely the centrality of birth that produces the tight link between action and narration. Explicitly recalling Aristotle's *Poetics*, Arendt repeatedly emphasizes how the protagonist of the narrated story is *who* was shown in the actions from which the story itself resulted. To put it in the lexicon of Roland Barthes, 'the character is always the agent of an action,' dependent upon it and subordinated to it.[48] Unlike how it appears in the modern novel – where the character embodies a psychological essence and becomes a 'persona,' or 'a fully formed being, even when he/she does nothing, even before acting' – the hero of a story, according to Arendt, is necessarily the one who, with words and deeds, is revealed *to others*, leaving behind the story. The story is subordinated to the revelatory action. A story can be told because there was first an actor on the world stage.

The story is therefore distinct from the narration. It has, so to speak, a reality all of its own, which follows the action and precedes the narration. All actors leave behind a story [*storia*], even if nothing guarantees that this story will later get told. Simply put, according to Arendt, although there can never be a tale without a story, there can nonetheless be stories without a tale. The hero's story finds its origin in his actions, not in the epic narration. The story [*la storia*] is a series of events, not a text. The hero's story is a series of events, which, thanks to their greatness, expose themselves to the immortalizing work of the text.

28

The problematic side of our approach lies precisely in this immortalizing function. However valuable the Arendtian idea of narration may be, its heroes, like Achilles, continue to astonish us – if not trouble us – by their love of death. This emphasis on a desire (which is, in truth, rather virile) that combines the challenge of death with a fame that survives it, sounds much like a homage to the patriarchal tradition. To this we can add the autobiographical tale of Ulysses, which captivated the ears of the Phaecians for four books of the *Odyssey*. The hero is *excessive* in all of his actions. He places emphasis on both action and autobiographical narration.

But if this is the way that things are, what reasons do we have for privileging the biographical tale of the blind rhapsod, and for neglecting the relationship between the identity of Ulysses and the emphatic autobiographical exercise of his narrating memory? Have we been too moved by his emotion? Have we missed something in the hero's weeping?

NOTES

1 Homer, *The Odyssey*, trans. Ennis Rees (New York: Modern Library, 1960), p. 119: Book viii, vv. 72–4.
2 Hannah Arendt, *The Life of Mind* (New York: Harcourt and Brace, 1971), p. 132.
3 Homer, *The Odyssey*, p. 134: Book viii, vv. 550–4.
4 Walter Benjamin, 'On language as such,' in *Selected Writings, Vol. 1* (Cambridge: Harvard University Press, 1996), p. 69.
5 [TN: These next few paragraphs have already appeared in English as part of the article 'Birth, love, politics,' *Radical Philosophy*, **86** (1997), pp. 19–23, translated by Isabella Bertoletti and Miguel Vatter. I have made use of their translation, with a few minor changes where necessary.]
6 Arendt, *The Human Condition*, p. 183.
7 Arendt, *The Life of Mind*, p. 34.
8 *Ibid.*, p. 32.
9 María Zambrano, *I Beati* (Milano: Feltrinelli, 1992), p. 116. [TN: My translation.]
10 Arendt, *The Life of Mind*, p. 19.
11 Roberto Esposito, *L'Origine Della Politica* (Rome: Donzelli, 1996), p. 48. [TN: My translation.]
12 Jean-Luc Nancy, *The Inoperative Community* (Minneapolis: University of Minnesota Press, 1991), pp. 1–43.
13 *Ibid.*
14 Arendt, *The Human Condition*, p. 176.
15 *Ibid.*, p. 177.
16 Arendt, *The Life of Mind*, p. 51.
17 Cf. Arendt, *The Life of Mind*, pp. 30–3.
18 Arendt, *The Human Condition*, p. 179–80.
19 *Ibid.*, p. 177.
20 Here I am confined to synthesizing, in the space of a few lines, a political thought that is totally original and anomalous, whose complexity makes me refer the reader to the

excellent, and well-documented, book by Simona Forti, *'Vita Della Mente' e Tempo Della Polis* (Milan: Franco Angeli, 1994). [TN: English readers might see M. Canovan, *Hannah Arendt: A Reinterpretation of her Political Thought* (Cambridge: Cambridge University Press, 1992).]

21 Arendt, *The Life of Mind*, p. 28.

22 Arendt, *The Human Condition*, p. 130.

23 *Ibid.*, p. 126.

24 Cf. Georg Wilhelm Friedrich Hegel, *Aesthetics* (Oxford: Clarendon Press, 1975), p. 247; Maurice Blanchot, *The Infinite Conversation* (Minneapolis: University of Minnesota Press, 1993), pp. 74–8; see also, Franco Moretti, *Modern Epic: The World-System from Goethe to Garcia Marquez*, translated by Quintin Hoare (New York: Verso, 1996), p. 14.

25 Arendt, *The Human Condition*, p. 95. Notice the repetition of the word 'reality.' Even more explicitly in the same text, Arendt writes that 'for us, what appears – what is seen and felt by others as by ourselves – constitutes reality' (*ibid.*, p. 85), 'the reality of the public sphere is founded on the simultaneous presence of innumerable perspectives' (*ibid.*, p. 90).

26 Arendt, *The Life of Mind*, p. 35. In a similar way, and still focused on *discourse*, we read in Heidegger: 'In speaking, Being-there expresses itself – not because it is encapsulated in an "inside" which is opposed to an outside, but rather because this, as being-in-the-world, is already "outside." What gets expressed is precisely this being outside.' Martin Heidegger, *Being and Time*, translated by Macquarrie and Robinson (New York: Harper and Row, 1962), p. 289.

27 Bonnie Honig, 'Towards an agonistic feminism: Hannah Arendt and the politics of identity' in *Feminists Theorize the Political*, edited by Judith Butler and Jean Scott (New York: Routledge Press, 1992), p. 220.

28 Arendt, *The Human Condition*, p. 186.

29 *Ibid.*, p. 192.

30 *Ibid.*, p. 186.

31 *Ibid.*

32 Hannah Arendt, *The Jew as Pariah* (New York: Grove Press, 1978), p. 101.

33 Hannah Arendt, *Between Past and Future* (New York: Penguin, 1961), p. 43.

34 *Ibid.*, p. 46.

35 Hannah Arendt, *The Human Condition*, p. 186. For the importance of this idea of the link between History and narration, which anticipates the theories of Hayden White and Paul Veyne, see Simona Forti, *'Vita della mente' e tempo della polis*, pp. 238–41.

36 Arendt, *Between Past and Future*, p. 51.

37 In Arendtian terms, the blind poet – modelled on Homer – indicates the figure of the *storyteller*. The *storyteller* does not, however, encompass the whole arena of poeticizing. Arendt, who has been interested in poets for the whole of her life, cites them continuously and co-signs with her first husband, Gunther Stern, an essay on Rilke. She appreciates the intensity of Auden, and considers Benjamin to be a writer who 'without being a poet, *thought poetically.*'

38 Arendt, *Between Past and Future*, p. 52.

39 Cf. Marcel Detienne, *La scrittura di Orfeo* (Rome: Laterza, 1990), p. 137.

40 Arendt, *Between Past and Future*, p. 45.

41 *The Iliad*, Book 1, lines 415–17, p. 89.

42 Arendt, *The Human Condition*, p. 193.

43 *Ibid.*

44 *Ibid.*, p. 194.

45 Walter Benjamin, 'The Storyteller' from *Illuminations*, trans. Harry Zohn (New York: Harcourt Brace, 1968), p. 97.

46 Arendt, *The Human Condition*, p. 9.

47 Arendt, *Philosophy and Politics: What is Political Philosophy?* from the Library of Congress, Washington DC (Box 40, p. 024446), cited by Simona Forti in *'Vita Della Mente' e Tempo Della Polis*, p. 127.

48 Roland Barthes, *Introduction to the Structural Analysis of the Narrative* (Birmingham: Birmingham University Press, 1966), p. 32.

3

THE DESIRE FOR ONE'S STORY

To portray autobiography as such a solipsistic act is to resign the self to a silent and lifeless 'world' – a 'world,' finally, devoid of self as well as others, since the differentiating circumstances of time and space would be collapsed into a single, all-inclusive consciousness which would have nothing to be conscious of except itself. Was it not in such a non-place that Narcissus drowned?

Janet Varner Gunn, *Autobiography: Towards a Poetics of Experience*[1]

There is a crucial aspect of the *paradox of Ulysses* that Hannah Arendt overlooks. It consists in the fact that, at the court of the Phaecians, the rhapsod's tale encounters unexpectedly the hero's desire for narration. Between identity and narration – and this is our thesis, already announced with Oedipus – there is a tenacious relation of desire.

Such an unexpected encounter is rendered evident above all by the circumstances through which Ulysses is present, incognito, at the telling of his own story. Even if this story already has a fame that reaches 'to infinite heaven' – and thus already has the intrinsic memorability of the hero's actions – it is in fact the first time that Ulysses hears it narrated: that is, he hears *himself* being narrated. His presence in disguise is thus something more than a clever dramatic device. It is rather that which allows the narratable character of identity to come to Ulysses through the unforeseen narration of a story of which he is the protagonist, but not the addressee. The figure of Ulysses is indeed unique because of this very aspect: he seems unaware of his desire *here and now* for the tale of his own story.

This is why, faced with the unexpected realization of his own desire for narration, Ulysses weeps. The story has, all at once, revealed his narratable identity and his desire to hear it narrated. Now he knows *who* he is, he knows *who* he exhibited through his actions; but he also knows that it was his narratable identity that allowed him to perform great actions, because of the desire to hear

32

it *personally* narrated by an other. Now it is clear to him that narratability belongs to the human existent as something unique. It belongs to him as an irrefutable aspect of his life, not as the guarantee of a *post mortem* fame that sees those who follow as the addressees of the story.

We can thus complete the formula, borrowed from Nancy, that defines the existent. Precisely because it is exposable, it is also narratable. Indeed, we are talking about the unrepeatable uniqueness of each human being. We are talking about *who* Ulysses is; this is why, when he hears his story told, he weeps. The *paradox of Ulysses* applies not only to the hero, but to every human being in his or her embodied and unrepeatable uniqueness. Again, the hero simply has the privilege of a spectacular scene of exhibition, which assures him, at the same time, a high probability of narration. The hero, in other words, is the hyperbolic figure of uniqueness, which belongs to two distinct, but resulting, sides of acting and leaves behind a story.

Still, our thesis is that, unlike Achilles, the weeping Ulysses can lend himself to a reading that refuses to focus on the classic link between heroic action and death. Indeed, in his properly heroic aspect, Ulysses is the one who performs great actions because of the desire to 'make of them' an immortal tale. As the emotional listener, he *discovers* that his desire for narration is immediate. The difference between the two hypotheses is remarkable. In the first hypothesis, the desire orients the emphasis on action towards the specter of death; while in the second, the desire orients itself on the *here and now* of the narration. To put it another way, there is a substantial difference between the desire to leave one's own identity for posterity in the form of an immortal tale, and the desire to hear one's own story *in life*.

In fact, after the weeping that accompanies the rhapsod's tale, the recent discovery of the desire to hear his story provokes Ulysses to produce an autobiographical narration of impressive bulk. Biography and autobiography are bound together in a single desire. Although the case of Ulysses at the court of the Phaecians is special, it nonetheless seems that a life-story – while always having its most suited narrator in the *other* – is not totally foreign to the protagonist, as Arendt would have us believe.

Arendt indeed seems to overlook that well-known phenomenon, through which, without effort or intention, every time and in every circumstance, we perceive ourselves and others as unique beings whose identity is narratable in a life-story. Each one of us knows that who we meet always has a unique story [*storia*]. And this is true even if we meet them for the first time without knowing their story at all. Moreover, we are all familiar with the narrative work of memory, which, in a totally involuntary way, continues to tell us our own personal story. Every human being, without even wanting to know it, is aware of being a *narratable self* – immersed in the spontaneous auto-narration of memory.

Indeed, it is not necessary that the personal memory be explicitly solicited in its autobiographical exercise; that is, memory need not make of itself an 'active remembering.' The narratable self finds its home, not simply in a conscious exercise of remembering, but in the spontaneous narrating structure of memory itself. This is why we have defined the self as *narratable* instead of *narrated*. Indeed, the particular contents – the pieces of story that the memory narrates with its typical and unmasterable process of intermittence and forgetting – are inessential. What is essential is the familiar experience of a narratability of the self, which, not by chance, we always perceive in the other, even when we do not know their story at all.

In other words, in personal experience, the narratable self is at once the transcendental subject and the elusive object of all the autobiographical exercises of memory. Subject and object are, moreover, ambiguous terms. It is enough to say that each one of us *lives him or herself* as his/her own story, without being able to distinguish the *I* who narrates it from the *self* who is narrated. We are thus left with a kind of *circular memory*, which simply appears, in perfect and total familiarity.[2] This is why we have defined the narratable self as something *familiar*. The Greek meaning of the word *oiketes* does indeed suggest that the self makes her home, so to speak, in the narrating memory – the inalienable dwelling of her *living her/himself, remembering herself*. In the words of Lyotard: 'the singular knowledge of being here [this *sense*] is ontological [and] derives only from the fact of remembering oneself.'[3]

The narratable self – as the 'house of uniqueness' – is for this reason not the fruit of an intimate and separated experience, or the *product* of our memory. It is neither the fantasmatic outcome of a project, nor the imaginary protagonist of the story that we want to have. It is not a *fiction* that can distinguish itself from *reality*. It is rather the familiar sense [*sapore familiare*] of every self, in the temporal extension of a life-story that is this and not another.[4] This can also be formulated as a general principle: To the experience for which the *I* is immediately, in her unreflecting sense [*sapore*] of existing, the *self* of her own narrating memory – there corresponds a perception of the other as the *self* of her own story. It does not matter whether this story of the other is known in detail, or whether it is totally unknown. The other always has a life-story and is a narratable identity whose uniqueness also consists, above all, in this story. Correcting Arendt, we will therefore say not only that *who* appears to us is shown to be unique in corporal form and sound of voice, but that this *who* also already comes to us perceptibly as a narratable self with a unique story [*storia*].

The person whom we meet is therefore a narratable self, even if we do not know his or her story at all. To put it in a convenient formula: the other is always a narratable self, quite apart from any consideration of the *text*. It does not matter here if the text is written or oral, if it comes from a tale or from gossip, from direct knowledge or from the imagination. The strange possibility of leaving the text out of consideration means simply that it is not necessary for us to know the other's story, in order to know that the other is a unique being whose identity is rooted in this story.

The inessentiality of the text applies also, and chiefly, to personal memory. Everyone – without even wanting to – knows him or herself to be narratable, even when not required to remember the episodes of his/her life, or when he/she is surprised by the uncontrollable work of memory. For every human being, the narratable self has its most familiar sense [*sapore*] in a story without a text; that is, in a narrative attitude of memory which does not cease – even when the memory itself refrains from recounting 'something.' Moreover, even when the memory works on the narration of 'something,' its recounting is mute and *condensed*; or, better, it is the silent condensation of an episode that presupposed the entire life-story, as if this were always internally present, or even unthinkingly sensed [*assaporata*] at any given point in the act of remembering.

Although she is immersed in this tale, the narratable self is not however the *product* of the life-story which the memory recounts. She is not, as the experts of narratology would say, a construction of the text, or the effect of the performative power of narration. She coincides rather with the uncontrollable narrative impulse of memory that produces the text, and is captured in the very text itself. As we know, the contents of this text are necessarily discontinuous – fragmentary, fleeting, and even casual – because the weaving-work of memory is itself discontinuous, fragmentary, fleeting and casual. But the familiar sense of the narratable self is not a result of text itself, and neither does it lie in the construction of the story. It lies rather in a narrating impulse that is never in 'potentiality' but rather in 'actuality,' even when it refrains from 'producing' memories or 'reproducing' past occurrences.

The ontological status of the narratable self becomes distinguished, therefore, from the text of her story; even if it is irremediably mixed up with it. Such a distinction is neither separateness nor self-sufficiency, because the self cannot lie in perfect isolation outside, or beyond, the text of her story. This is not, however, a perfect coincidence, because the text of the story is inessential to the self-sensing [*assaporarsi*] of the self as narratable. Put simply, through the unreflecting knowledge of my 'sense-of-self' [*dell'assaporarmi*], I know that I have a story and that I consist in this story – even when I do not pause to recount it to myself, 're-living' through the memory some episodes through a sort of interior monologue. I could nevertheless not know myself to be narratable unless I were not always already interwoven into the autobiographical text of this story. Such an interweaving is indeed irreparable, and comes irremediably to the self as a reifying experience. The effect of a life-story, whatever the form of its tale, always consists in a reification of the self that crystallizes the unforeseeability of the existent.

In the autobiographical story that the memory episodically – and often unintentionally – recounts, the narratable self is therefore always found to be reified. She becomes, through the story, *that which she already was*. The self is thus also able to recuperate the constitutive worldly and relational identity from which the story itself resulted. In other words, the identity of the self, crystallized in the story, is totally constituted by the relations of her appearance to others in the world, because, even in autobiography, 'the story told through the convention of first-person narrative is always a story which both discovers and creates the relation of self with the world in which it can appear to others, knowing itself only in that appearance or display.'[5]

Someone's life-story always results from an existence, which, from the beginning, has exposed her to the world – revealing her uniqueness. Only in the improbable case of a life spent in perfect solitude could the autobiography of a human being tell the absurd story of an unexposed identity, without relations and without world. The existent is the exposable *and* the narratable: neither exposability nor narratability, which together constitute this peculiarly human uniqueness, can be taken away. The one who is exposed generates and is generated by the life-story – this and not another – which results from such an exposition. Personal memory, intentionally or otherwise, can in fact therefore go on forgetting, re-elaborating, selecting and censuring the episodes of the story that it recounts. Memory nevertheless rarely *invents*, as do the inventors of stories. Personal memory is not a professional author.

Arendt is therefore right in affirming that life-stories never have an author. Biographies or autobiographies result from an existence that belongs to the world, in the relational and contextual form of self-exposure to others. The life-story which the memory recounts to everyone – with its typical, and hardly trustworthy, way of doing things – is thus always the story that every existent left behind and that still continues to persist in its familiar 'sense' [*sapore*] of 'being here'. Even if the precise contents of such a story are inessential to the narratable self, there is no narratable self that is not always already and forever immersed in these contents and in this autobiographical text. In other words, although the text is inessential to the narratability of the self, nevertheless its game of reification is ineluctable and necessary – just as it is necessary and ineluctable that *I* am always the *self* of my narrating memory – enigmatically sensing myself to be familiar.

This necessity is made clear, for example, in the case of traumatic amnesia. The unfortunate one who finds that she has forgotten her story does not know *who* she is, having lost the *text* of her identity. She nonetheless has no doubt about being a narratable self; or rather she has not *forgotten* at all that narratability – the self's unreflective sense [*gusto*] for recalling *itself* – belongs to the existent. Neither has she forgotten that the ones who surround her have an identity because they have a personal story. On the contrary, she knows that she has lost her identity together with her story; because she knows that everyone has a story. In so far as she is a *victim* of amnesia, she finds herself being someone who has suddenly become no one, because she is now merely a sort of empirical life without a story. The identity that materializes in a life-story has no future that is properly *its own*, if it has no past in the present of its memory. We are dealing with a unique existent who has even forgotten her *own*, proper name [*il proprio nome*].

So it is natural that the forgetful one searches in the memory of others for her lost text. By making others recount her own story, she is in fact attempting to stitch her narratable self together with the story into which she was constitutively interwoven. She is attempting to fit her *having been that which she is* into the life-story that has been interlaced with others' stories on the exhibitive and relational scene of the world. For as long as her memory does not *come back* to her, this text, narrated by others, retains the aspect of a total reification that neither comprehends nor consoles. Until the text regains its original union with the narratability of the self, it indeed takes on that performative valence of which post-modern theory is so fond. That is, the text produces an identity that the forgetful one is forced to take upon herself only externally – without that familiar self-sensing recognition [*senza riconoscerne il sapore*]. She is a wretch precisely because she is a narratable self who, by losing her story, has lost her identity. No one can therefore return it to her by retelling to her the text through which this identity is reified. The text is in fact inessential only for those who continue to listen to the tale of memory.

There is therefore a remarkable difference between the forgetful wretch and the Ulysses of our paradox. Just as the first desires desperately that her memory will once again recount her story to her, so too the second is surprised by his desire to hear it told by another. Autobiography and biography, while being different genres of the story, do not seem to be able to manage without one another within the economy of a common desire. But what exactly is desired by this desire?

Obviously, this tale is desired – but, above all, the unity, in the form of a story, which the tale confers to identity. A stork is what is desired. While we have, in many ways, appreciated the Arendtian category of uniqueness [*unicità*], we will not neglect the category of unity [*unità*], as she does. The etymological root that these two terms have in common is a good indication. From the beginning, *uniqueness* announces and promises to identity a *unity* that the self is not likely to renounce.

This is a promise that springs from the elementary reality of an existent being, and not from the untrustworthy promise that the 'subject' has made to her for centuries. As Nancy puts it, the possibility of a thought of the *one*, of the some*one*, of the singular existent, is indeed 'that which the subject announces, promises, and at the same time conceals.'[6] In other words, while claiming to be valid for every*one* that is human – who is rational and thinking, as the experts would say – the subject lets itself be seduced by a universality that makes it into an abstract substance. The fragility of each *one* is thus inevitably sacrificed to the philosophical glories of the One. The *one* who lies in uniqueness, on the other hand, is different because she appears from her birth, she comes and presents herself indefinitely until her death, without her unity ever being a substance.

The baby who is born is always *unique* and *one*. Within the scene of birth, the unity of the newborn is materially visible and incontrovertible through its glaring [*plateale*] appearance. As a result, the newborn absolutely cannot be defined as discontinuous because time is not yet there, even if it begins to pass. This existent which *only just* exists, since she has just shown herself, thus eludes every post-modern perspective because she cannot be thought within a philosophy that is fragmentary or eccentric. The newborn – unique and immediately expressive in the fragile totality of her exposure – has her unity precisely in this totally nude self-exposure. This unity is already a physical identity, visibly sexed, and even more perfect in so far as she is not yet qualifiable.

Despite Arendt's reticence on this point, one must affirm that, being born, there always appears to the world a sexed *who*. The one who is born is always this boy or this girl, even if the absolute nudity that exposes it corresponds with the absolute absence of the *what*. This is because the existent, in the moment of his or her entrance into the world, is naked or bare of this *what* – not because he/she exposes him- or herself at the beginning as a 'bare life.' Indeed, sexual difference does not qualify the existent, it does not specify the *what*, but rather embodies the newborn's uniqueness from the moment of this inaugural appearance. The one who is born does not yet have any qualities; and yet has a sex. How else could he/she be distinguished as 'this and not another,' from the moment of birth and throughout life? 'There exists a sort of gratitude for all that is as it is; for all that has been *given* and has not been *done*,' writes Arendt in a letter to Scholem, including her being a woman among the indisputable facts of her life.[7] The *one* who shows him- or herself, the existent as exposable, therefore has a sex from birth, because this is the way he/she *is*.

Nevertheless, here within the scene of birth, the coinciding of unity and identity, in the as-yet-unqualifiable-nude-*who*, is only a miracle of the beginning. Because *straight away* time begins to flow and the existence of the newborn, which carries on her exposure in time, becomes a story. In the course of this becoming, or rather in the course of her exposure to the becoming-time of existence, the unity of the *who* that unmistakably appears at birth comes to pass – as a legacy of that first announcement – on to the narrating structure of memory as a 'sense' [*sapore*] of her own narratability. And yet, this is not *straight away* for memory, even if the time of the story starts right away.

Indeed, the first and fundamental chapter of the life-story that our memory tells us is already incomplete. The unity of the self – which lies in the miracle of birth, like a promise of its naked uniqueness – is already irremediably lost in the very moment in which that same self begins to commemorate herself. This loss of unity gets turned into the lack that feeds desire.

If everyone is *who* is born, from the start – and with a promise of unity that the story inherits from that start – then no recounting of a life-story can in fact leave out this beginning with which the story itself began. The tale of her beginning, the story of her birth, nevertheless can only come to the existent in the form of a narration told by others. The beginning of the narratable self and the beginning of her story are always a tale told by others. Poor Oedipus knows it well, he who would not give up that story for anything in the world. Oedipus is therefore special only for his misfortune, because there is perhaps no one alive who does not understand what an inalienable right this narration is.

In fact, within the space of this inalienable right, a kind of analogical proof can be found. By making herself a spectator of another's birth, the self can surprise herself by imagining, analogically, the event of her own birth.

This analogical proof does more than skim the surface of the problem. The unity that is familiar to the narratable self indeed continues to show itself as the legacy of a promise whose fulfillment is entrusted to the tale told by another. Even early childhood re-enters into this tale. It is thus understandable that childhood is often described culturally as a loss. It is not only that which 'adult life has lost, a state recognized too late,' but it is also that which personal memory must inevitably register as a loss.[8] Autobiographical memory always recounts a story that is incomplete from the beginning. It is necessary to go back to the narration told by others, in order for the story to begin from where it really began; and it is this first chapter of the story that the narratable self stubbornly seeks with all of her desire.

'I am Odysseus, son of Laertes,' responds Ulysses to the king of the Phae-cians. Without perhaps even knowing it – as often happens – he has recycled the beginning of a story (which others have told him) in an autobiographical tone; he is reproducing a text composed by others. If it wants to begin from birth, autobiography is in fact always a *refabulation* of a story told by others. But it wants to begin with birth, because that which sustains it is the desire for unity that only the narration can offer in a tangible form. This unity is nothing other than the story narrated by someone from beginning to end, or at least, from the beginning *until now*. In other words, the identity of a unique being has its only tangible unity – the *unity* that he/she seeks because it is *unique* – in the tale of his/her story.

One could therefore hypothesize a possible compromise between biography and autobiography: first, my birth, early childhood and my death entrusted to a tale told by others; then, in the middle, self-narration in the first person. But this is not the point. The point is that⌐in any case, the life-story that memory recounts is not enough for the narratable self. Not so much because the memory proceeds like a voluble and discontinuous narration, or because the demon of self-interpretation produces mythical–biographical texts, but rather because memory claims to have seen that which was instead revealed only through the gaze of another.⌐

The memory of every human being is indeed characterized by this structural mistake, which makes it untrustworthy. It doubles itself in the eye of the other and claims to have seen the *daimon*, or the identity of the one who is shown, without that same agent being able either to see, or know, or master *who* is being exposed to the others' eyes. In this way, as happened with Oedipus, personal memory continues to tell us a false story; that is, a story that, although it has the merit of offering worldly contents to the narratable self, also offers a false perspective. In its silent autobiographical exercise, personal memory turns the narratable self into a Narcissus. Its promises of truthfulness are utterly vain, as is the truth of the famous 'autobiographical pact,' theorized by Lejeune, whereby the one who writes her own story does not tell the truth about herself, but rather *claims* to be telling it.[9] Like an impossible game of mirrors, the self is indeed here both the actor and the spectator, the narrator and the listener, in a single person. The self is the protagonist of a game that celebrates the *self as other*, precisely because the self here presupposes the absence of another who truly is *an* other. In this sense, by bringing together the *auto*, the *bios*, and the *graphein*, the self conquers for itself an absolute unity and self-sufficiency. And yet she is not content, because she has the sense [*ne assapora*] that she is being deluded.

At once exposable and narratable, the existent always constitutes herself in relation to an other. With all the inimitable wisdom of a familiar feeling [*sapore*], she knows that she is an unrepeatable uniqueness, but does not know *who* she is, or *who* is exposed. She knows she is a narratable identity, but also knows that only another can correct the fallacy of the autobiographical impulse. The unity of the desire – namely, the unity entrusted to the tale that everyone desires – is not, in fact, an aspect of unconsciousness or a problem of introspection. It is rather the irreflexive object of the desire *for* the unity of the self in the form of a story.

Within a certain contemporary philosophical context (MacIntyre and Ricoeur, to give a couple of names) the sense of identity gets taken back to the 'unity of an embodied narration in a single life;'[10] or to the 'narrative component of the comprehension of the self.'[11] Reflecting on the *narratable self*, we are trying to have a dialogue with these positions concerning the thematic of identity as *unity*. Our philosophy of narration is, however, especially attracted by the intersection of this thematic with the inessentiality of the text. On this score, Arendt becomes once again a decisive point of reference.

Arendt's surprising neglect of the text is indeed consistent with her thematization of the importance of the biographical narration. In other words, in Arendt's view, the problem of narration is never configured as a narratological question; it in no way implies a focalized study of the narrative text that analyzes its style or structural semiotics. It concerns rather – *exclusively* and in total indifference towards the text – the complex *relation* between every human being, their life-story and the narrator of this story. Whether this life-story is a written text or an oral tale, or whether it has or does not have literary dignity – which is more or less classifiable within the disciplinary canons of the biographical genre – all of this becomes superfluous.

Arendt helps us moreover to overturn that crucial movement, from the *outside* to the *inside*, which characterizes the modern conception of the self.[12] Prejudiciously disposed, like Descartes, to the loss of the world, modernity turns its focus from the world itself to the individual, from the public to the private, from the appearing object to the interiority of the subject.[13] Arendt does the reverse. The result of Arendt's move, nonetheless, does not consist in a sort of return to the pre-modern or to a nostalgic recovery of ancient Greece. It consists rather in the anomalous notion of a self that is expressive and relational, and whose reality is symptomatically external in so far as it is entrusted to the gaze, or the tale, of another. Even the utterly modern role of personal memory – namely, the autobiography as an intimate construction of a self that narrates himself to himself – vanishes as a result. It vanishes rather too quickly, perhaps, since it leaves uninterrogated the reciprocity of the narrative scene and its dynamic of desire.

Our thesis indeed adds to the Arendtian horizon the centrality of this desire. To put it simply, everyone looks for that unity of their own identity in the story (narrated by others or by herself), which, far from having a substantial reality, belongs only to desire. The desire orients both the expectations of the one who is narrated and the work of the one who narrates. If Arendt is right in saying that 'the unchangeable identity of the person, though disclosing itself intangibly in act and speech, becomes tangible only in the story of the [...] life', and if 'the essence of who somebody is can come into being only when the life departs, leaving behind nothing but a story,' it is indeed also true that the narration, more than simply translating into words the 'objective' and manifest unity of the protagonist, presupposes it and glimpses it in this story that the protagonist left behind.[14]

41

On the other hand, it is not our purpose here to raise the problem of 'objectivity' in storytelling. Whatever the degree of fidelity invoked by the intentions and the documentary archive in its possessions, the tale indeed, as we know, selects, cuts, and discards. The biographer always has a perspective that excludes other perspectives, and often designs the unity of the protagonist along with the construction of a novel, which, as Roland Barthes would say, dares not call itself 'a novel.'

The very centrality of the text, theorized by Barthes, lies indeed at the foundation of that contemporary thought, which sees, above all – in biography and autobiography – strategies for the rhetorical constructions of the self. The literary narration or the novel, according to more or less obligatory styles, become the implicit models for every *writing* of a life-story. In Barthes' view, writing does not put into words the essence of *who* someone effectively is or was, but rather produces that identity textually and artificially. As a result, taking writing as a paradigm – making every language into a text – also turns every 'real' existent into something definable as 'extra-textual' or 'extra-discursive.' In this way the text, or the traditional form of the biographical and autobiographical genre, wins out over life. Thus, as Carolyn Heilbrun says, 'lives are not what furnish the models, but rather the stories. And it is difficult to construct stories to which lives can be adjusted. We can only renarrate and live according to the stories that we have read or heard. We live our lives through the texts.'[15]

The first consequence of this perspective is that, by swallowing life, the text also risks swallowing the unrepeatable uniqueness of the existent. Omnivorous texts, hungry for life and ready to offer themselves as the more dignified replacements of an all-too-human corporeality – this is how the texts adored by much of the more refined post-modern theory seem to be. I will not dare declare here, as Donna Haraway does, that 'if they are only texts, give them back to the boys,' but we are rather prudently keeping our distance through the theme of desire. We are dealing with a desire for unity which asks the narration of another above all to *be recognized as desire*. This is what the biography responds to – whatever the artistic qualities and the contents of its tale, whatever the intentions and the rhetorical strategies of its narration, and whatever the text its narration inevitably produces.

From this point of view, even the text that puts into words a biography of discontinuous and fragmentary characters (even in the most radical 'postmodern' sense) still ends up unable to flee from the unity, which, *listening to* the tale with the ear of its desire, is conferred upon it by narratable self. Our Ulysses is an example of this, although the blind rhapsod might be defined as anticipating post-modernity within the multi-perspective narrative style that is typical of Homer. Ulysses still does not discover *who* he is in the instantaneous refiguration of his single actions, but rather in the tale of his life-story. To cite Arendt again, what the tale of the rhapsod *signifies* and 'translates into words is the story to narrate, *not* the action itself *nor* the agent.'[16]

The narratable self that listens to her story, and is *one* because of the familiar, narrative structure of memory, transfers this irreflexive unity, even in the most manifest fragmentarity of the text. Moreover, it is above all the autobiographical impulse of memory that produces discontinuous and fragmentary texts, which, although untrustworthy and elusive, can nonetheless never be exchanged for someone else's story – as happens in the magnificent textual games of Jorge Luis Borges. This everyday certainty of the self, which comes from sensing oneself to be 'this and not another,' indeed continues to resist both the inimitable pleasure of Borges' inventions, and the more refined enticements of contemporary theory – which continue to impose upon the self the pleasure, if not the necessity, of the infinite dissolution of her *internal* and multiple alterity.

Significantly, with this spontaneous resistance – which seems, at first sight, to be based upon the banality of good sense – the narratable self ends up doing a good service for philosophy. Indeed, philosophy ought to be more cautious in playing around with the endless game of the *other*. By continuing to transport the category of alterity into the intimacy of the self, contemporary philosophy in fact produces the inevitable consequence of impeding every serious naming of the other in so far as he/she is *an* other.

As Arendt teaches us, a unique being is such only in the relation, and the context, of a plurality of others, which, likewise unique themselves, are distinguished reciprocally – the *one from the other*. The story of a unique being is obviously never the monotonous and monolithic story of an *idem*, but is always the unpredictable and multi-vocal story of an *ipse*. Although it changes in the course of its life and in the course of its story – even to the point of no longer seeming or feeling the same – this *ipse*, like Oedipus, is 'this and not another' from the beginning to the end of this life and this story.

We have pointed out the way in which Ulysses differentiates himself from Achilles because the latter chooses to entrust the essence of his identity to death, an identity that is condensed in the definitive greatness of his heroic actions. Even the *eudaimonia*, through which Achilles reassures himself, is thus an extraordinary manifestation of his desire for unity, which is given over directly to the tale. The example of Achilles is therefore quite important in order to clarify another aspect of the question. His capacity to summarize all of his life 'in a single act, such that the story of the act ends with the life itself,' indeed exemplifies how the unity of the self can also be entrusted to a single act. Put another way, the desire for unity that the narratable self manifests does occasionally translate itself as the conviction that there is a moment in which one's entire destiny, or rather one's entire story, can be summarized.

In *The Life of Tadeo Isidoro Cruz*, Borges writes that 'any life, no matter how long or complex it may be, is made up essentially *of a single moment* – the moment in which a man finds out, once and for all, who he is.'[17] True to this principle, Borges does not then recount all the nights of Isidoro, but rather only 'the night in which he glimpsed his own face, the night in which at last he heard his name. Fully understood, that night exhausts his story; or rather, one moment in that night, one deed.'[18]

This is an instance in which Isidoro comprehends *who* he is from the other, and suddenly sides with the enemy in battle – the other who is confronting him, weapons in hand – because he understands 'that the other man was himself.'[19] Through a curious twist on the Arendtian rule that entrusts the identity of the *who* to the gaze of the other, Borges does not abandon the perspectival dislocation of the self within the specular game of the double (which is so dear to him). Beyond this symptomatic narrative invention, the tale of Isidoro still has something in common with that of Achilles. It illustrates how a single act can summarize an entire life-story. Tellingly, a desire for unity-of-self, which prefers synthesis, becomes evident. No identity can in fact gain a better unity than that which condenses itself in the narration of a single act of the hero.

Next to this condensation in a single act, which has fascinated narrators for centuries, we might add (on the equally ancient side of the collective imagination) the age-old conviction that the dying man reviews in a single instant his own, entire story. We could put it more elegantly, with Benjamin, according to whom 'a sequence of images is set in motion inside a man as his life comes to an end – unfolding the views of himself under which he has encountered himself without being aware of it.'[20] With the very last act of his narcissistic impulse, the memory of the dying turns him into the spectator of the film of his life-story. Even in this popular belief, there is an important clue. It confirms the desire for unity, which gets doubly satisfied by death – whether as the final chapter of the tale, or as the summarizing gaze that watches the story.

The unity that the narratable self asks of the tale is never a question of the text. It is rather the question of her innate desire, which can turn in many directions – to the narration for the thread of the story, or to a single act, or to a summary of the dying one. Indeed, if Ulysses weeps, it is not because the story of the rhapsod faithfully *reproduces* that identity which the hero himself does not know and does not control. Rather, it is because the text that he is unexpectedly given clearly recognizes – or, better, reveals – his desire to him. In fact, since it arises so unexpectedly, the desire itself leads the hero to engage in a lengthy self-narration, more than is generally respectable for an autobiographical narration.

It is occasionally said that autobiography responds to a rather precise question: who am I? The autobiographical project 'would thus obey the order given by the Delphic oracle, the commandment *gnothi se auton*.'[21] It seems rather that one could maintain the exact opposite. Autobiography does not properly respond to the question 'who am I?' Rather, it is the biographical tale of my story, told by another, which responds to this question. 'Know thyself,' in the case of a self for whom self-knowledge is constitutively precluded, cannot help but become the total self-predisposition to listening to his own biography. In different ways, Ulysses and Oedipus are also figures of this theorem.

NOTES

1 Janet Varner Gunn, *Autobiography: Towards a Poetics of Experience* (Philadelphia: University of Pennsylvania Press, 1982), p. 137.
2 This phrase is liberally taken from Roland Barthes' *The Pleasure of the Text*.
3 Jean-François Lyotard, *Lectures d'enfance* (Paris: Galilee, 1991), p. 58.
4 [TN: See footnote no. 39 in the Translator's Introduction.]
5 Janet Varner Gunn, *Autobiography: Towards a Poetics of Experience*, p. 141.
6 Jean-Luc Nancy, Introduction to *Who Comes After the Subject?*, ed. Eduardo Cadava, P. Conner and J. L. Nancy (New York: Routledge, 1991), pp. 4 and 7.
7 Arendt, *The Jew as Pariah*, p. 270; see also Françoise Collin, 'Plurailità, differenza, identità' in *DWF [Donna Woman Femme]*, 2–3 (1995), p. 88.
8 Cf. Carolyn Steedman, *Past Tenses* (London: Rivers Oram, 1992), p. 140.
9 Cf. Philippe Lejeune, *On Autobiography* (Minneapolis: University of Minnesota Press, 1989).
10 Alasdair MacIntyre, *After Virtue: a Study in Moral Theory* (Notre Dame: University of Notre Dame Press, 1981), p. 243.
11 Paul Ricoeur, *Oneself as Another* (Chicago: University of Chicago Press, 1992), p. 201.
12 Cf. Charles Taylor, *Sources of the Self: the Making of Modern Identity* (Cambridge: Cambridge University Press, 1989).
13 Arendt, *The Human Condition*, p. 254.
14 *Ibid.*, p. 193.
15 Carolyn Heilbrun, *Writing a Woman's Life* (New York: Norton Press, 1988), p. 36.
16 Hannah Arendt, *The Life of Mind*, p. 133.
17 Jorge Luis Borges, *The Aleph and Other Stories: 1933–69*, translated by Norman Thomas di Giovanni (New York: E. P. Dutton, 1968), p. 83.
18 *Ibid.*
19 *Ibid.*, p. 85.
20 Walter Benjamin, *Illuminations* (edited and with an introduction by Hannah Arendt; trans. by Harry Zohn (New York: Schocken Books, 1986)), p. 94.
21 Christophe Miething, 'Le grammaire de l'ego: phénomenologie de la subjectivité et théorie autobiographique,' in *Autobiographie et biographie*, ed. M. Calle-Gruber and Arnold Rothe (Paris: Nizet, 1989), p. 150.

Part II

WOMEN

4

OEDIPUS ERRS TWICE

Long after, Oedipus, old and blinded, walked the roads. He smelled a
familiar smell. It was the Sphinx.

Oedipus said, 'I want to ask one question. Why didn't I recognize my
mother?'

'You gave the wrong answer,' said the Sphinx.

'But that was what made everything possible,' said Oedipus.

'No,' she said. 'When I asked, What walks on four legs in the morning, two at noon, and three in the evening, you answered, Man. You
didn't say anything about woman.'

'When you say Man,' said Oedipus, 'you include women too. Everyone knows that.'

She said, 'That's what you think.'

Muriel Rukeyser, 'Myth'

Oedipus, reread in the brief poetic version of Muriel Rukeyser, is twice
mistaken.[1] Or, better, in keeping with his response, he is destined to meet a
double monstrosity. This is, we know, a correspondence totally internal to
philosophy, of which Oedipus is here the involuntary champion. The logic of this
is well known: Man is not only monstrous in so far as he is the abstract, universal
name that engulfs the uniqueness of each human being, but is also monstrous on
account of his claim to include women, while at the same time naming them in
the masculine. In other words, Man is at once the entire human species, and one
of its two genders. Man is neuter and masculine. Man is both, neither of the two,
and one of the two. Whether written with the first letter capitalized or not,
whether invoked by philosophical texts or everyday language, the effect of Man's
arrogance does not change. The whole of the Western tradition, with philosophy
at its base, becomes Man's field of self-representation. Notoriously, despite the
variety of its styles, the Western tradition is a patriarchal, androcentric, and
phallocentric culture; it is a culture that seems destined to survive into the

second millennium, and which has sung the glory of its protagonist, Man, from the beginning. Every feminist scholar has on her shelves hundreds of volumes that testify to the misdeeds of Man, and denounce his arrogance.

In the version of Muriel Rukeyser's myth, the Sphinx nonetheless seems to lead Oedipus into another, later trap. There is the risk that his error, rather than making amends, doubles itself. One might expect from a philosopher (as Oedipus shows himself to be – capable as he is of making himself immediately at home in the universal), a final response that adds Woman to Man. 'Man and Woman' would in this case be the response to the riddle about the legs. Oedipus does not give this response; but – after reading Rukeyser's poem, or perhaps even before – we feel it vibrate in the air as a reticence of the myth, as an uninterrogated side of the mistake. In truth, the trap is seductive, even for us. It would be enough to add Woman to Man and everything would turn out fine.

Adding Woman to Man, however, means duplicating the representation of the universal without freeing oneself whatsoever from its abstract valence, without abandoning whatsoever the ancient error of metaphysics. Of course, the incontrovertible given that there are two sexes of the human species makes of this duplication a homage to the minimal sense of appearing. However, as happened with Man, Woman can still be nothing but *all* women, precisely because it is none of them. Its presumed reality, substantiated in the universal sign of the capital letter, belongs to the mystic register of collective representation. Like Man, Woman leaves behind no life-story. One cannot ask about Woman *who* she is, but only *what it is*.

The monstrous Sphinx is nonetheless a feminine creature. 'A woman in the shape of a monster/a monster in the shape of a woman/the skies are full of them' writes Adrienne Rich.[2] Therefore the trap that she seems to set for old Oedipus in the poetry of Rukeyser might turn out to contain something of use for the fate of her sex. Making himself a philosopher in the name of Man, Oedipus shows that he embraces the tradition of the masculine subject, which places the woman as an object (denying her, so to speak, the capital letter). In other words, in the long philosophical succession that Oedipus inaugurates, the woman is notoriously in the position of the object; or rather, she is thought, represented, defined from the point of view of the Man. In so far as she is the woman *of* Man and *for* Man, different *from* him since he is the paradigm of the human species, the woman – though a noun [*nome*] – is never universal. She consists rather in a series of images, which represent, from time to time and according to the context, *what* a woman must be in the economy of masculine desire: for the most part a mother or a wife, and, on occasion (as seems to be the case!), a combination of the two. From the point of view of the Sphinx, by pushing Oedipus to the edge of an answer which joins Man and Woman, the enigma is a sort of challenge or, perhaps, a practical joke, not without humor.

50

Indeed, what is the Sphinx herself if not one of the most explicit figures of these androcentric representations of woman? What is she if not the feminine monster – the frightening side of the animality which Man sees in the feminine – confronting him, the King?

Therefore, by pushing him to the edge of an error which he does not even imagine, the Sphinx challenges Oedipus on a level of epistemic coherence. She invites him to place Woman next to Man – in the position, always denied her, of the subject. What is more, with this response she, who with her ferine body walks on four legs, could permit herself a certain variety of deambulating styles. While philosophical discourse on the universal – the definitory art that loves the abstract – is a rather large mistake, it does not diminish the weight of the androcentric arrogance that reserves for Man the role of the subject. In its classic profile, philosophy is the child of Oedipus alone, not of the Sphinx.

In another poem by Muriel Rukeyser, 'Private Life of the Sphinx,' the voice of the monstrous singer is developed in a long monologue.[3] She says at the beginning:

> On the rock I asked the shaky king
> one foolish question to make him look at himself –
> He looked. Beheld himself and kingdoms. Took
> My claws and smile transferred into his myth.

Obviously the question is ridiculous because she speaks of the number of legs. But it is especially ridiculous in and of itself, stupid, *foolish*.[4] However, its aim does not consist in the completion that Oedipus' response, equally foolish, could confer upon it. Rather, it consists in pushing Oedipus to look at himself, to ask himself who he is. Indeed, he looks: but he looks in the wrong direction and thus does not see himself. He sees the kingdom instead, and sees himself as the King of Thebes, husband of Iocasta, a powerful man. He takes everything right away – even the Sphinx, who is by now reduced to a figure in his myth, to a signifier of his story. Oedipus, we might say again, heads decidedly towards the possessive destiny of the phallocentric subject, totally ignoring *who* he himself is.

Of course Oedipus (who bears the foot [*pous*] in his very name) – the Oedipus who was stolen as a child, but is now great and powerful, with his feet on the ground, mid-way through life; the Oedipus who will soon be blind and forced to walk with a cane – could have sensed a warning when confronted with the riddle of the legs.[5] He could have found there, in the foolish question, some good reasons for looking at himself, or at his story. But the rewriting of the myth, in Muriel Rukeyser's brief version, offers us another solution. The key does not lie in the allusive words of the riddle, but rather in the link between the wrong answer and the incest – that is, in the crucial consequence of the error.

Indeed, what is truly strange is the question that old Oedipus dares pose to the Sphinx: 'Why didn't I recognize my mother?'

As the frightening face of the first enigma, the Sphinx evidently remains, in Oedipus' opinion, the supreme lady of all enigmas – especially this one, which he does not know how to solve. However, the solution, which the Sphinx reveals, lies precisely in his response, which – by saying 'Man' without mentioning women – commits the first error. Believing that he has given the correct response, Oedipus won in this way both the kingdom and the queen. But, since the response was wrong, he married his mother without being able to recognize her. His response 'made everything possible,' even the incest.

Old Oedipus still does not understand – not yet. On the contrary, he repeats the old error. Indeed, in order to justify himself, not only does he assume that the term Man includes women as well, but he emphasizes that this is something which everyone knows, that it is common and indisputable knowledge. 'That's what you think,' retorts the Sphinx to the poor blind man. Oedipus' last response, the extreme defense, the obvious justification for a chain of errors, is in truth the worst of all. From Man – in which there still lived the uncertainty and the trembling of the challenger, in the risk of the old response – Oedipus now intends the universality of Man as the *obviousness* of a general knowledge.

Therefore the enigma of the incest, which follows as a consequence of the mistaken answer to the first enigma, becomes clear. Indeed, how could he have recognized his mother, who was *obviously* a woman too, under the name Man? How could he ever have recognized her who, in all logical rigor – and as Aristotle argued – should then also say that man is born of Man?

Only later, we know, does Oedipus learn at his expense that his mother is *this one*, she and not another – the one from whom he was born, he and not another. Only too late is Oedipus forced to learn that the abstract language of Man prevents one from recognizing the face, which is always unique and unrepeatable, of the existent. Old Oedipus, whom the Sphinx encounters in Rukeyser's poetry, is therefore an absent-minded man with a short memory. Futilely warned by his life-story, as though no one had ever told it to him, he returns, by a kind of tragic distraction, to the old vice of philosophy.

There is a way in which the story of Oedipus is a tragedy that could only happen to a man. In other words, the tragedy of the originary scission between the universal Man and the uniqueness of the self, between the abstraction of the subject and the concreteness of the uniqueness – in a word, between the discursive order of philosophy and that of narration – is an entirely masculine tragedy. Even in the recent 'fulfillment' of the emancipatory model (which ends up legitimizing that which Oedipus, in the late justification of his formidable error, considers to be obvious), rather few women in fact seem disposed to recognize themselves in the universality of the term Man. The clear refusal by women – which has exploded in the contemporary era – to recognize themselves in the images of women thought for millennia by Man, has some significant precedents in a long history of mute feminine resistance.

Having been estranged from the form of the subject, and deported into the place of the object, women now find themselves, unpredictably, in a rather fortunate position. Namely, they are able to extract themselves [*sottrarsi*] from the emphasis of the old game in which self-representation is entrenched. For millennia, the question 'what is woman?' has concerned a definition – a hundred definitions, a thousand contradictions – for which no one of course expected a woman to answer. The discourse on the universal, with its love of the abstract and its definitory logic, is always a matter for men only. The scission between universality and uniqueness, between philosophy and narration, signals from the beginning a masculine tragedy.

There is therefore a shade of truth in the usual stereotype by which women would be allowed a kind of aptitude for the *particular*. Just as the proverbial care for the fragile, the little, the vulnerable, the delightfully feminine has indeed for centuries been the care for a particular that – far from wanting to supersede itself in a higher universality – enjoys being such, and does not aspire to transcend itself. We are dealing with the particular, resplendent with finitude and content with existing; whose glory takes the form of uniqueness.

Taken as a concept, uniqueness corresponds with the extreme form of the particular – or better, to the absolute 'one;' or, rather, to a form of the particular that is *free* [*sciolta*] of any universality that tries to redeem it, or erase the miracle of finitude. Because this, from Plato onwards, has been precisely the mission that philosophy, seduced by the universal, originally decided to take upon itself: to redeem, to save, to rescue the particular from its finitude, and uniqueness from its scandal. This task of redemption, however, logically transformed itself into an act of erasure. As Hegel admits – and as Arendt does not fail to point out – 'philosophical contemplation has no other intention than to abolish the accidental.'[6] *To save by suppressing* is of course an ancient law that philosophers call dialectic.

It is therefore wise not to turn to philosophy at all if one truly wants to save the accidental that is in every life, or rather the accidentality [*accidentalità*] of being 'this and not another,' which happens to everyone as the *given* of their very being-here. Rather than salvation, the accidental needs care. To tell the story that every existence leaves behind itself is perhaps the oldest act of such care. The story is not necessarily one that aspires to immortalize itself in the literary empire – as Arendt herself would want, when she thinks of Homer – but rather the type of story whose tale finds itself at home in the kitchen, during a coffee-break, or perhaps on the train, when even those who do not want to hear it are forced to listen. In the kitchen, on the train, in the corridors of schools and hospitals, sitting with a pizza or a drink – women are usually the ones who tell life-stories. As Françoise Collin puts it, 'communication between women unfolds as the comparison of life-stories, rather than as the reciprocal exchange of ideas.'[7] Throughout the ages, the aptitude for the particular makes them into excellent narrators. Cornered in weaving rooms, like Penelope, they have, since ancient times, woven plots with the thread of storytelling. They have *woven* [*intessuto*] stories, letting them casually tear the metaphor of the *textum* of professional men of letters. Whether ancient or modern, their art aspires to a wise repudiation of the abstract universal, and follows an everyday practice where the tale is existence, relation and attention.

Entrusted to such a feminine art, it thus seems that a philosophy of narration is by now the only cure that could save the very name of philosophy from its tragic fate.

NOTES

1   Muriel Rukeyser, 'Myth,' from *The Collected Poems* (New York: McGraw Hill, 1984), p. 498.
2   Adrienne Rich, 'Planetarium,' from *Lies, Secrets and Silence* (New York: W.W. Norton, 1979), p. 47.
3   Muriel Rukeyser, 'The Private Life of the Sphinx,' from *Collected Poems*, p. 278.
4   [TN: *'foolish'* is italicized in English in the original.]
5   Cf. Jean-Pierre Vernant and Pierre Vidal-Naquet, *Odipe et ses mythes* (Bruxelles: Editions Complexe, 1988), p. 101.
6   Georg Wilhelm Friedrich Hegel, *Lectures on the Philosophy of History*, Vol. 1 (Oxford: Clarendon Press, 1984), p. 8.
7   Françoise Collin, 'Pensare/raccontare' in *DWF [Donna Woman Femme]*, **3** (1986), p. 37.

5

ON THE OUTSKIRTS OF MILAN

> The gift of the written story which connects thoughts and saves one from letting herself go is an exquisite image of what we have tried to explain, that is, that in women's struggle, the symbolic revolution – the representation of oneself and of one's fellow women in relation to the world – is fundamental and must come first.
>
> The Milan Women's Bookstore Collective

In one of the most famous books of Italian feminism, *Non credere di avere dei diritti* [*Don't Think You Have Any Rights*], a true story gets reported.[1] We are in the 1970s, and the protagonists are two friends with assonant names: Emilia and Amalia. They attend, in Milan, *'la scuola delle 150 ore'*.[2] The story which concerns them appears in the book as a report of Amalia, after the premature death of her friend, who died at fifty-three years of age.

Emilia, in the early days, 'was pretty boring: she went on telling her story umpteen times a day,' says Amalia.[3] The latter has the gift of being able to express things well, whether out loud or on paper, which the other lacks. In their exchange of writing exercises, the gap became evident. 'When I let her read what I had written,' continues Amalia, 'especially when I was talking about my hometown, about the farmers and particularly about my life, she cried.'[4] She too 'needed to tell about her life,' notes Amalia in order to explain this weeping, 'but she wasn't able to connect any of it up, and so she let herself go.' Amalia then decides to take an interesting initiative: 'once I wrote the story of her life, because by then I knew it by heart, and she always carried it in her handbag and read it again and again, overcome by emotion.'[5]

The episode almost seems like a transposition of the Homeric Ulysses on to the outskirts of contemporary Milan. There is the weeping in the listening/reading of a story, and there is the same emotion in the recognition of one's own life-story narrated by another. There is, however, also, beyond the oral or written form of the story, a substantial difference. In the Homeric scene, the rhapsod and Ulysses are strangers: the first does not know that he is singing the story of the second in his presence, and neither had Ulysses ever told the rhapsod anything about himself. Amalia and Emilia, on the other hand, are two friends. The first writes the story of the second because Emilia had continually recounted her story, in the most disorganized way, showing her friend her stubborn desire for narration. The gift of the written story is precisely Amalia's response to this desire. Now Emilia can carry the text of her story with her and reread it continuously – moved every time by her own identity, made tangible by the tale.

Of course, Emilia could have written an autobiography with her own hand – in fact she tried. Like Arendt, we nonetheless begin to suspect that what prevented her from successfully completing the undertaking was not so much a lack of literary talent, but rather the impossibility of personally objectifying the material of her own desire without falling into the perspectival mistake of memory. In other words, the *who* of Emilia shows itself here with clarity in the perception of a narratable self that desires the tale of her own life-story. However, it is the other – the friend who recognizes the ontological roots of this desire – who is the only one who can realize such a narration. This means that Emilia obstinately manifests the desire that the course of her life trace a stork, that her uniqueness leave behind a story. By writing the story for her (not in her place, but for her), Amalia gives it a tangible form, sketches a figure, suggests a unity. Amalia herself, moreover, finds success in autobiographical narration as well. She even makes her friend weep. Her friend weeps because she recognizes in that narration the object of her own desire. Autobiography and biography come thus to confront each other in the thread of this common desire, and the desire itself reveals the relation between the two friends in the act of the gift.

As a young maidservant in contemporary Milan would note at this point, women everywhere, and quite often, set themselves to telling their stories to one another, as though through each story there passed their own existence and personal identity.[6] The fact is that this passage does indeed occur. Not only for the reasons that psychoanalytic theory could ably indicate, but also for those reasons that the political thought of Arendt, reinterpreted in the light of feminist experience, helps us to better understand.

As we read in *Non credere di avere diritti*, the aim of women who have returned to school in order to attend the 150-hour adult classes is indeed to 'think that my "I" exists.' Emilia does not seem to have any doubts about the importance of this ontological affirmation. For her, such existence coincides with the very narratability that desires to make itself materialize in a tale. Emilia knows that a life about which a story cannot be told risks remaining a mere empirical existence, or rather an intolerable sequence of events. What is intolerable, therefore, is not so much a life that 'has always been a "no" ' and which seems poor at fifty-three years of age, married and without children; but rather the fact that the life-story that results from it remains without narration.[7] She thus passes, from the failed autobiographical attempts, to the biography that her friend gives to her as a gift. This biography is highly tangible, all the more so in so far as it is written. By always carrying it in her purse and rereading it continuously, Emilia can touch with her hand and devour with her eyes her personal identity in a tangible form. She can, like Ulysses, be moved by it.

The paradox of Ulysses functions therefore also in this case, but the comparison between Ulysses and Emilia works only up to a certain point. Indeed, Ulysses is a hero; that is, he has had the Trojan scene as an interactive space for exhibiting his own uniqueness. To use Arendt's language, Ulysses is the archetypal actor who, performing actions in a shared political space, reveals *who* he is to his peers. The life-story that results from these actions corresponds with a specifically human existence in so far as it is political. Emilia, however, has had no such public scene of reciprocal and interactive exhibition. Emilia, as happens with many women in Italy (and elsewhere), has probably had the domestic scene as the setting for her existence. If the principle – according to which the unexposable is the non-existent – is valid, then Emilia has lived a life in which her uniqueness has remained partially unexposed due to the lack of a shared scene of co-appearance [*comparizione*], the lack of a true political space.

It is helpful to recall once more that we are using the term 'political' in Arendt's anomalous sense. We are not pointing out the well-known historical phenomenon of women's exclusion from political institutions; but rather the phenomenon through which many women, like Emilia, have no experience of a plural and interactive space of exhibition that is the only space that deserves the name of politics. Actually, the best comparison here is not a Milanese worker [*operaio*] – the most likely masculine equivalent of Emilia's condition – but rather it is that ancient hero who, despite his suspect virility, keeps us company here. The fact is, as Arendt herself emphasizes, it also happens that men too are excluded from participating in a political space of interaction. As many scholars maintain, but as Arendt more than others is able to argue, Western history is a history of depoliticization. Replaced by the rule of the few over the many; or rather replaced by various models of domination, throughout this two-thousand year history – the political as a shared space of action disappears, or rather reappears only intermittently in revolutionary experiences.

Nonetheless, the dominant social codes, which ascribe different roles to men and women, make this lack-of-politics [*impoliticità*] different for each. For women, the absence of an interactive scene, where uniqueness can be exhibited, is historically accompanied by their constitutive estrangement from representations of the subject, which rule in the patriarchal symbolic order. As was noted earlier, the tradition which, by ignoring uniqueness, celebrates the glorious accomplishments of Man, is the same tradition that consents only to human beings of the male sex the ability to recognize themselves in this abstract universal. Whether on the level of expression or on the level of representation, women find themselves trapped between a double powerlessness that concerns both *uniqueness* and *quality*. In other words, for women – in addition to the general absence of political spaces where each human being can show to others *who* she or he is – there is the pervasiveness of a symbolic order where the androgynous subject is what defines *what* they are: mothers, wives, care-givers, bodies to be enjoyed … the list goes on.

Again, from our point of view, there nonetheless is an appreciable advantage in all of this. Women have somewhat less of a chance of committing that formidable error that consists in exchanging the 'unrepeatable uniqueness' for the abstract 'Man.' In other words, the exhibitive impulse of uniqueness, in the case of a woman, finds obvious obstacles in being erroneously supplied with the representation of a universal subject that is clearly masculine.

Our friend Emilia can testify to this. Her double powerlessness makes it so that she wisely orients her desire where existence finds its only and genuine expressive outlet; namely, towards the scene where uniqueness constitutes itself 'in relation.' This relation does not yet have the luminous characteristics of the public scene, in so far as it arises from the obscurity of the private sphere; but it is first of all in the private sphere that the relations of the feminine experience become a friendship. Contrary to the widely held opinion that maintains that feminine friendship is founded above all on the solidarity of misery and oppression, we are here offered a friendship that has conspicuous narrative characteristics. What is more, we women know how the habitual side of feminine friendship consists in this reciprocal narrative exchange – continuous though interrupted, intense though diverting [*svagato*] – of our own life-stories. For female friends, the questions 'who are you?' and 'who am I?', in the absence of a plural scene of interaction where the *who* can exhibit itself in broad daylight, *immediately* find their answer in the classic rule of storytelling.

This immediacy has its first cause [*causa prima*] in the symptomatic fear that a life led in the absence of a public space of exhibition leaves behind no life-story. *What* Emilia is we could, in fact, try to define with a good approximation: she is a Milanese housewife; she is poor, married, without children … in short, she is a woman like many others who have a difficult lot in contemporary cities. In this sense, she is the champion of a certain sociological 'type.' *Who* Emilia is, on the other hand, eludes this classification. This *who* is precisely an unrepeatable uniqueness which, in order to appear to others, needs first of all a plural – and therefore political – space of interaction.

With respect to Arendt's theory, Emilia and Amalia – or feminine friendship in general – pull off a curious transgression. Arendt would like the narration of the story to follow the actions of the hero from which the story itself results. In other words, Arendt would like the question 'who are you?' to respond to the revealing action of identity; only *after* and *because of* this action does a life-story result, which then needs a narrator. Emilia and Amalia, however, seem to go *immediately* to narration, as do many women in the course of a narrative friendship. The uniqueness, partially unexpressed due to the absence of political scenes of interaction, therefore gets concretized in a narratable self, who entrusts the inalienable sense of her existence to the narration. Emilia, not having had political spaces of exhibition, fears that she may not leave any story behind which is worthy of narration. She wants this narration in the tangible form of a written tale at any cost. It is as if, contrary to Arendt's theory, the narrated story that produces the reality of the self then regards, first of all, the revealing quality of political action, or regards the process of narrating this life-story as if it were already a political action.

Surprisingly, it is.

The typical feminine impulse to self-narration can indeed be recognized even in the phenomenon of 'consciousness-raising groups,' which characterized Italian feminism in the 1970s.[8] This phenomenon is, at its root, the passage of a rather diffuse habit in the everydayness of female relations to the relatively stable and organized form of the group. The desire is still that of expressing *oneself*, in the double sense of actively expressing one's own self and of finding the words that translate that exposition into narrative form. In the practice of 'consciousness-raising,' the feminine custom of self-narration thus finds a political scene – that is, in the Arendtian sense, a shared and interactive one. The thesis 'of an intrinsic authenticity of the personally lived,' which has always sustained the female friendship-relation, can finally make itself explicit and come to an interactive significance that assumes the exhibitive characteristics of action. Nothing, in fact, is lacking, because this experience can, in Arendt's sense, define itself as political: a shared, contextual, and relational space is created by some women who exhibit *who* they are to one another. There is nonetheless an utterly peculiar aspect with respect to Arendt's criteria: the exhibitive action coincides here with a self-narration. Arendt's criteria are thus transgressed – if not the principle according to which the action can consist in a discourse, at least the principle that declares autobiography to be ineffective.

In the practice of consciousness-raising, the narratable self, pushed by the justifiable fear that the partially unexposed is partially non-existent, comes by herself to satisfy her own desire for a narrated story. The life-story, having come into its own tale, puts into words an identity – at the same time and in the same context in which the women present generate a political space that finally exposes them. Put another way, there is a privileging of the word as the vehicle of a desire for identity that only the narrated form seems able to render tangible.

And there is, at the same time, the creation of a relational space of reciprocal exhibition, which is clearly perceived and affirmed as political. The insistence on the *relationship between women*, on the *contextuality of the practice* and on '*starting from oneself [partire da sé]*' – that has characterized the feminist political lexicon in Italy since the 1980s – therefore finds a fundamental source in the consciousness-raising groups. Its uniqueness consists in a horizon that sees politics and narration intersect.

Moreover, the exclusively feminine setting of such a horizon in the consciousness-raising group becomes important. The stories of women, which intertwine on the *separatist* scene, allow them 'to deconstruct a point of view on the world, which claims to be neutral, but in reality conforms largely to masculine desires and needs ... to learn to narrate themselves as women means in fact to legitimate for themselves a definition which is outside the gaze of the other.'[9] Or rather, outside the standards of the gaze of Man. In other words, the relational context, in which the uniqueness of each one can finally expose itself, renders simultaneously visible not only the concrete sensation that pertains to the uniqueness of each one; but also the sexual difference which is shared, and which shows itself capable of working as a point of view that is independent of the masculine one. Since the expression of personal identity comes also to express a gender identity, the fact that each is a woman and not a man risks therefore betraying itself in the super-personal paradigm of Woman. It risks betraying itself in a *representation* of Woman and being satisfied with that. It risks falling into the trap of the Sphinx which old Oedipus avoided (not because he was smart, but because of a defect of memory).

However, the gender identity cannot avoid producing, in this context, a contradictory effect, in so far as it invites the uniqueness of each woman to identify herself with all other women. In the reflection of the one in the other, the very personal identity that is consigned to the tale of an unrepeatable life-story runs the risk of losing its expressive reality and founding itself in the common 'being women' that is represented here. 'I am you, you are me, the words which one says are women's words, hers and mine.'[10] The empathy risks producing a substance. Put simply, *who* I am and *who* you are seem to surrender to the urgency of the question of *what* Woman is.

Even if universalism of the masculine type is amended, the old error of Oedipus returns all the same. The uniqueness of the self sacrifices itself to the hypostatization of the female gender and, while it gains a critical perspective on the patriarchal tradition, it nonetheless deviates from its original desire. Yet beyond this assimilating effect (which goes on relatively quickly to close the experience of consciousness-raising groups), the phenomenon is still of extreme interest. As Ida Domanijanni writes, 'Here the original figures of the thought of sexual difference come to light, and here one finds that particular form of interaction of the feminine "I" with the order of discourse and representation which constitutes the nucleus of the debate over politics of the symbolic.'[11] Already at the inaugural point of feminist practices, it becomes evident how the usual feminist impulse to self-narration, at the moment in which it generates a political space, roots itself – implicitly or explicitly, spontaneously or reflexively, genuinely or hypothetically – in a self that is constitutively sexed.[12]

Reread in the light of this phenomenon, the Arendtian category of the *who*, precisely in so far as it is expressive and relational, thus is materialized in the specificity of the feminine sex, showing how the uniqueness of human existence deals constitutively with sexual difference [*la sessuazione*].[13] Not only because, if it is correct to follow Arendt and say that 'men, and not Man, live on Earth and inhabit the world,' it seems even more fitting to say that not Man, but rather men and women live there and inhabit it; but especially because the phenomena in question stage [*inscenano*] the exhibitive impulse of a *who*, which, by distinguishing itself, exhibits at the same time the distinction of its sex.[14] To use Arendt's terms, it must be decided if the fact that I am a woman and not a man belongs to the order of my qualities (*what* I am), rather than to my uniqueness (*who* I am). At the heart of the first alternative there is a subject, unique and unrepeatable, which nonetheless is born 'neutral' as far as sex goes and thus can make of its feminine *quality* a hypostasis that can be entrusted to the realm of representation. At the heart of the second alternative there is a uniqueness, equally unique and unrepeatable; birth shows who the newborn is – namely, sexed [*sessuata*], and given over to the contextual and relational realm of expression.

The maidservant in Milan, could therefore once again suggest for us a rather simple summary. From birth, the uniqueness which appears, and which provokes the fundamental question 'who are you?,' is an embodied uniqueness and therefore sexed. Neither the political scene nor the narrative scene, nor their extraordinary coinciding in the consciousness-raising groups, can ignore this sexedness [*sessuazione*][15] if, on this scene, it is truly the *who* that shows itself.

Beyond the naïve gaze of the housewife, it is above all the advent of feminism that permits us to twist the Arendtian categories towards the concretion of the self. The self-expression of identity reveals itself here to be rooted in a desire which could call itself ontological, since some of the existence of *who* is revealed 'goes' ['*ne va*'] into this desire. Although women live in the world, this is an existence that the patriarchal tradition tends to synthesize within the catalog of feminine qualities that reduce the *who* to the *what*: a mother, a wife, a nurse. Outside of these qualities, or rather outside of the phallocentric representative order, women would end up existing only in the empirical sense, in such a way that their life would be a *zoe* rather than a *bios*. It does not amaze us, therefore, that the in-born [*in-nata*] self-exhibitive impulse of uniqueness comes together for many women in the desire of the *bios* as the desire for biography.

The fact that masculine friendship is rarely of a narrative type – or that many men would rather speak of *things* (football, cars), or of *what* they are (lawyers, tennis-players), instead of *who* they are – is a rather interesting symptom. Of course, this could be taken as a sign of androcentric guilt. In this guilt (which throughout the ages has satisfied in Man the 'metaphysical vampirism' of men), the *biographical* impulse of masculine-friendly relations overshadows the uniqueness of the *bios*.[16] As dear Oedipus had to pay a high price to learn.

Now, Emilia encountered the gift of her story written by another in a precise context. The two friends attended the 150-hour adult school, which, with good reason, went hand in hand with the consciousness-raising groups in the events which, in Italy, opened up some political spaces for women in the 1970s.[17] The episode of Amalia and the same phenomenon of consciousness-raising call us therefore not to underestimate the crucial intersection of politics and narration. Even if their perfect coincidence is probably unrepeatable and, anyway, hardly obligatory, it is indeed interesting not to lose sight of this narrow bond, seeking perhaps to comprehend it in all of its latent potential.

In this regard, Arendt's suggestion concerning the inessentiality of the text gains a splendid proof. Indeed, we do not come to know the adored pages that Emilia preserves in her handbag. What this singular episode of narrative friendships teaches is precisely the relation of desire between Emilia and the biographical pages – which are unknown to us, and which were written for her by Amalia. The relationship between Emilia and her narrated story is indeed a stubborn relation of desire. This desire appears to place itself, not between the empirical reality of a self without a story and its narratability, but rather between a self that always already senses herself to be narratable and the act of narration. From this perspective, both the text that results from the awkward autobiographical attempts of Emilia and the written work of Amalia can easily remain outside of our analysis without affecting its 'completion' or 'rigor.' Our concern leads back to a human being's desire for narration, in which uniqueness and unity coincide once again, after birth. From the point of view of this desire, Barthes' theory, according to which narrator and characters are 'beings of paper,' is not valid at all.[18] Consider, as a refutation, the fact that Emilia weeps over the pages that she preserves in her handbag.

It is moreover significant that the relational familiarity of a narratable self has its most explicit figure in the narrative character of feminine friendships. In this case, the narratable selves of the friends are undeniably what drive the scene. The scene consists in the intersection of autobiographical narrations, which make sure of the result of the reciprocal biographical activity. Put simply, I tell you my story in order to make you tell it to me. At work, therefore, is a mechanism of reciprocity through which the narratable self of each woman passes on to the self-narration, up to the point at which the other woman is familiar enough with the story to be able to tell it herself. They are able to tell stories to one another, of course, but above all to tell the story *again* to the one who is its protagonist. The suspected psychoanalytic dynamic that supports narrative friendships is therefore rather the scene of a narratable self that offers autobiographical materials to a biographer, who, in turn, is an accomplice in the whole operation.

In this way, the criterion that differentiates friendships from acquaintances can be identified. The difference between acquaintances and friends consists indeed in the circumstances through which only the latter are *capable* of telling that story, although the former do not doubt that we have a story and might even know its broad outline. Whether they then go on to tell it or not, in whatever form or circumstance, does not affect the significance of our proposition. Within the general horizon of human relations that causes us to perceive one another as narratable selves, friendship is a specific horizon where this narratability can be meaningfully translated in the act of a reciprocal narration. Although, as Gertrude Stein would say, there is 'the need to have always met whomever we know,' with our acquaintances we only have rapports [*rapporti*]; with friends we have a relationship [*relazione*].[19] Even lovers too, as one can say with a certain moralistic irony, have a *relationship*. Indeed, in love too the reciprocal narrative exercise often occupies the scene.

The self – to the extent to which a *who* is not reducible to a *what* – has a totally external and relational reality. Both the exhibitive, acting self and the narratable self are utterly given over [*consegnati*] to others. In this total giving-over, there is therefore no identity that reserves for itself protected spaces or a private room of impenetrable refuge for self-contemplation. There is no *interiority* that can imagine itself [*autoaffabularsi*] to be an inexpressible value.

What is more, since the scene of action is contextual and mutable, the reality of the self is necessarily intermittent and fragmentary. The story that results therefore does not have at its center a compact and coherent identity. Rather, it has at its center an unstable and insubstantial unity, longed for by a desire that evokes the figure – or rather, the unmasterable design – of a life whose story only others can recount.

In the same years in which Amalia writes for her friend her story, but in another far-away place, the South African writer Elsa Joubert writes the biography of a black woman, giving her the fictitious name of Poppie Nongena. They are not friends; Elsa Joubert is a 'white lady,' the other is a maid: 'the only rung of contact, frequentation and acquaintance which [a black woman in times of apartheid] can establish with whites.'[20] It happens that they have the occasion to meet each other, and the first asks the second to let her memory flow in a long autobiographical tale in order to then put it into words.

To collect oral testimonies and re-elaborate them in writing is, notoriously, a part of the specialized work that characterizes anthropology and oral history. Much of modern knowledge is provided by the *story-taker* – the one who solicits and listens to life-stories told by others, in order to then transcribe them into the scientific canons of his discipline. As Carolyn Steedman rightly emphasizes, this figure finds its most famous and influential variants in psychoanalysis. The psychoanalyst might indeed be interpreted as a *story-taker* [English in the original] whose purpose is 'to give back to the patient the story of his or her life, welded into a chronological sequence and narrative coherence, so that at the end of it all, the coming to psychic health might be seen as the re-appropriation of one's own life story.'[21] No one therefore seems to better embody the desire that wants the other to tell her own story than the patient herself. Put another way, even if this only works one way, and without reciprocation, the intersection between autobiography and biography concerns quite evidently the narratable self of the psychoanalytical scene. In this sense, the *story-taker* who works in the field of anthropology or oral history is somewhat less involved in the work of *restituting* the story *to* his or her interviewees. Moreover, when the interviewees – the autobiographical narrators at the source – belong to another culture and speak another language, there emerges the problem of writing a text that they themselves cannot understand. In this case, this is a text that they can understand neither at the level of simply reading it, nor at the level that implies 'a conflation of the production and consumption of texts.'[22]

The Long Journey of Poppie Nongena is a written text in the form of a novel, the autobiographical tale of Poppie. Symptomatically, the most original choice of the author concerns the writing itself. Elsa Joubert in fact decides to write the book not in her language, English, but rather in Poppie's language; that is, 'the Afrikaans language of the blacks, colored with frequent expressions from *xhosa* – an idiom which has not been used as a literary language; indeed, which has never been used in writing.'[23] The English edition, which came out two years later, thus acquires the curious status of 'translation' from Afrikaans.

A text has many addressees, even more so when it gets elaborated by one whose profession is the art of narration and who thus also keeps editorial needs in mind. The choice of the Afrikaans language allows us nonetheless to hypothesize that the South African writer wanted to put the life-story of Poppie into words first of all *for* Poppie. Having met each other regularly for two years, it is indeed likely that the white lady's project of *story-taking* – of translating the oral autobiography of the black woman into a biographical novel – had found a space in the context of a narrative relationship that went beyond the rapport of an intellectual 'landlady' [*'padrona'*] and an illiterate 'maid.'

The risk of cultural colonialization and of instrumental appropriation, which manifests itself in all relations of this kind, is rather strong. Again, as a story of an

African woman, of her family and of the feminine genealogy that sustains its memory, *The Long Journey of Poppie Nongena* runs the further risk of appealing to those who speak the Afrikaans language but do not know how to read it.

Joubert herself seems still to have wanted to solve this problem. On her initiative, for the family and friends of Poppie, a theatrical performance of the novel was arranged.[24]

NOTES

1 It has been published in English under the title *Sexual Difference: the Milan Women's Bookstore Collective* (Bloomington: Indiana University Press, 1990).

2 [TN: 'Le scuole delle 150 ore,' 'the 150-hour schools,' were schools founded by the Italian Left in the 1970s, whose purpose was to provide supplementary education in the arts and sciences for workers or housewives who lacked higher education – workers were allowed to take 150 hours, paid, out of their work year in order to attend these schools.] Cf. *Sexual Difference: the Milan Women's Bookstore Collective*, pp. 102–7.

3 *Ibid.*, p. 105.

4 *Ibid.*, p. 106.

5 *Ibid.*

6 I allude here to the Platonic figure, which according to Plato embodies feminine knowledge. I discuss this figure of the young maidservant in *In Spite of Plato*, trans. Serena Anderlini-D'Onofrio and Aine O'Healy (New York: Routledge, 1995), pp. 31–57.

7 *Sexual Difference: the Milan Women's Bookstore Collective*, pp. 105–6.

8 *Ibid.*, pp. 40–59.

9 Manuela Fraire, 'Arte del fare, arte del disfare,' in *Lapis*, **28** (1995), pp. 12–13.

10 *Sexual Difference: the Milan Women's Bookstore Collective*, p. 44.

11 Ida Domanijanni, 'Il desiderio della politica,' from the Introduction to Liz Cigarini, *La Politica Del Desiderio* (Parma: Pratiche, 1995), p. 11.

12 [TN: There is an error in the printed Italian text, which has 'sensed' ['*sensato*'] for sexed [*sessuata*].]

13 [TN: I here translate *la sessuazione* as 'sexual difference', whereas Serena Anderlini-D'Onofrio and Aine O'Healy, who translated Cavarero's *In Spite of Plato*, coin the term 'sexedness'. They give a lengthy explanation for their decision to employ the word 'sexedness' in the 'Translator's Note' to that book.] Cf. *In Spite of Plato*, pp. xx–xxi.

14 Arendt, *The Human Condition*, p. 9.

15 [TN: There is another error in the Italian text here, which I have amended in the English. In addition, here I thought it best to follow Anderlini-D'Onofrio and O'Healy's translation of *sessuazione* as 'sexedness,' for syntactical reasons.]

16 Cf. Luce Irigaray, *Sexes and Genealogies*, p. 128.

17 *Sexual Difference: the Milan Women's Bookstore Collective*, pp. 40–3.

18 Barthes, *Introduction to the Structural Analysis of Narrative*, p. 40.

19 Gertrude Stein, *Everybody's Autobiography* (New York: Cooper Square, 1971), p. 46.

20 Itala Vivan, 'Nota Critica' to Elsa Joubert, *Il Lungo Viaggio di Poppie Nongena* (Florence: Giunti, 1991), p. xi.

21 Steedman, *Past Tenses*, p. 172.
22 *Ibid.*
23 Itala Vivan, 'Nota Critica,' p. vi.
24 I owe this information to a conversation with Itala Vivan.

6

IN A NEW YORK BOOKSTORE

A woman enters a bookstore and browses the bookshelves. She stops, and takes up a volume of essays on Hegel and feminism, but quickly puts it back in its place. She changes places and picks up the new 'mystery' by a feminist author and reads the end of it. She looks at the new biography of 'X,' and carefully observes the cover, reads the information on the in-set, looks at a page or two, and then goes to the eight pages of photographs which accompany the text and she looks them over very carefully, with care and concentration.

Liz Stanley, *The Auto/biographical I*

In the passage reported above, the English feminist sociologist Liz Stanley describes for us a scene that she probably saw in Manchester, where she teaches – but which we, following our provincial imaginations, freely place in a New York bookstore. In any case, the message is clear: women show a great interest in biographies and happily read them. That a biographical story is, in general, more palatable than a volume of philosophical essays is certainly understandable. That it is more palatable than a mystery is even more telling. Life-stories seem to earn the highest popularity-ratings among readers.

The reader browsing through this New York bookstore is probably a feminist, just as it is likely that the 'X' of the title and the author of the book are female. We can therefore define a rule: women – feminists included – are happy to read biographies of women, written by women. Put conversely, there are many women who write life-stories of other women, in order to appeal to the reading public of women. They are bound together by a kind of pact. On the seal of this pact, suggests Liz Stanley, lie *lives-with-meaning*.[1] We are therefore not too far from the principle of a narrated identity as the tangible expression of existence. We are also not very far removed from the design of the stork. Some difference remains, however. Besides being a different approach to the question – e.g. Liz

Stanley's perspective as a sociologist – all of this depends upon the post-modern or post-structuralist horizon that characterizes the feminist debate in the English language, especially in America. This is why we have chosen New York instead of Manchester.

Given the vivacity and the internal conflicts of this debate, it is obviously risky to speak about it in synthesis, or through a generalization. Already, since the 1980s, we have witnessed a significant migration of French post-structuralism into America, which, according to some, has produced a rapid colonialization of feminist theory.[2] More attentive than most to the complexities of things, an authoritative philosopher like Rosi Braidotti prefers instead to link the origin of contemporary feminist thought to post-structuralism through the riverbed of the same epochal crisis, underlining their progress by *dissonances*.[3] Of course, there is no lack of mediating positions, or of forceful critical revisitations – Liz Stanley herself is commendable for this. This phenomenon is nonetheless largely hegemonic in all theoretical environments, including those that concern themselves with life-stories. In this field, critical feminist literature that is inspired by post-structuralism is particularly abundant.

Put simply, and generalizing under the 'American' etiquette a reality that has major resonances beyond the boundaries of the United States and the English language, the theme of the debate can be summarized in the following way.

In accordance with post-modern standards, American feminists denounce the metaphysical foundations of classical autobiography (which the traditional literary criticism of autobiography obviously tends to reflect). The classical forms of autobiography are commonly registered in some famous masculine prototypes; especially Saint Augustine, Rousseau and Goethe. What they have in common is the unitary and substantial model of a self that finds a coherent affirmation in his self-narration. In the classical form, as both author and protagonist of the story, the self proposes himself as a compact subject, whose uniqueness means exceptionality; or, rather, the presupposed greatness of a *real* self that the autobiographical narration – the confession – claims to faithfully reflect. The implied theory is that there exists in the first place a self-conscious subject who, setting to write his life-story, translates in words the substantial reality of the 'I' – which precedes and is independent of the text.

The anti-metaphysical horizon of post-structuralist theory – 'which den[ies] the self any status whatsoever outside language,' and, therefore, outside the text as well – cannot but refuse this theory and, of course, overturn it.[4] Post-modern theory indeed maintains that it is rather the narrative text itself that *constructs* the self, providing him with coherence and unity. The claimed substantiality – attributed by metaphysical thought to the *real* and materially living self, who then makes himself the author of his own story – besides being presupposed, is thus only the fantasmatic product of the textual self; or, rather, the result of the performative power of the text and its rhetorical strategies.

Neither does this critical mechanism change much when one is dealing with a biographical exercise instead of an autobiography. Within the post-modern perspective, the demiurgic centrality of the text indeed continues to produce the heroes of the narrated story, even when the hero himself does not narrate it. Invented stories and life-stories, novels and biographies or autobiographies, reveal themselves as adhering to the same model: the rhetorical construction of a substantial and self-referential self, intent on valorizing his own interiority; in other words, 'the classical subject.'

For the majority of American feminists – in both biography and autobiography, there is, frighteningly, afoot a self about which substantiality is most feared by post-modernity: namely, the metaphysical profile of the subject. Because of its stubborn affection for the fragmentation of the classical subject, the post-modern view, moreover, finds suspicious – in principle – the *uniqueness* of the self, in so far as it is too perilously close to the idea of a unitary, substantial and self-referential subject. As has already been indicated, we live with a tradition of critical reflection that privileges the text, inaugurated by Barthes, and that remains in continual tension with the formula for which the self is only an effect of language. The problem of autobiography is therefore prejudiciously focalized on the *graphein* to the detriment of both the *bios* and the *self* [*auto*].

Even from the perspective that privileges the text, feminists still sound a call to arms. Indeed, the so-called gender difference intervenes. The fundamental accusation is that both traditional criticism and text-centered criticism have never 'fully accounted for the peculiar characteristics of autobiography (and biography) written by women, having limited themselves to looking at those written by men – or, worse still, to excluding them from analysis, or treating them as a sort of subgenre.'[5]

Taking the classical model back through the long 'ideological history of the self,' Anglo-American feminism, as articulate and complex as it is, lands upon a common principle:[6] the uniqueness of the self (even more strikingly alleged to be a real and material existent), is nothing more than an ideological construction of traditional and patriarchal autobiographical standards, which, as such, is refuted. Different theoretical strategies are opened here: for example, discovering whether women have always signified a difference in this narrative genre; or, indicating the correct way of writing and reading life-stories within the horizon of post-modern feminism.

Now, since this horizon is post-modern – while there are a variety of approaches – an agreement on general principles nonetheless emerges. One of these affirms the peculiar non-univocity of the self – that is, its constitutive fragmentation – in auto/biographical feminist writing.[7] Another emphasizes the

69

way in which 'the individual course intersects continually with the collective, in the conviction that something of their own life is shared with the lives of many other women.'[8] And another one denounces the risk of an auto/biographical model of 'white women' that would come, guiltily, to hegemonize the field of feminist criticism itself.

When analyzed from a historical–semantic, or formal linguistic, perspective, or read from the point of view of a literary scholar or sociologist, the central role of the text, to be sure, remains untouched. The specificity of the feminine is a specificity of the text. The feminist approach to auto/biography, more than deferring to the sexed unity of the existent, denies its materiality and, even before that, its unity. Actually, given the familiar metaphysical unfolding of the One in philosophical phallocentrism, it is above all *unity* that becomes demonized within the post-modern or post-structuralist horizon that these feminists embrace; with the odd result, as Christine Battersby would say, of confirming the traditional patriarchal meaning that wants 'women to be a fragmented self, incoherent and resistant to every synthesis.'[9]

It is equally odd that this theoretical perspective faces obstacles within the very scene in the New York bookstore cited above. It is more than likely that our reader shows an interest not so much in a deconstruction of the text, but rather for a life-story that is capable of narrating the *uniqueness* of its protagonist. Indeed, what else is she looking for in the photographs if not this uniqueness in the form of body and facial expressions? What else attracts her attention if not this material 'proof' of a woman who really lived, in flesh and bone, in a time and a place?

A photograph, too, is a text; and it clearly has an author, or rather an image that is constructed by a particular point of view. A photograph, too, therefore constructs a subject, as Liz Stanley herself argues convincingly. We can nonetheless suppose that the New York reader seeks the living material of this subject *beyond and in spite of* its photographic construction. After all, who among us who passionately devour auto/biographies would not have wanted to meet Virginia Woolf in order to be a direct spectator of her actions and her appearance before us? Who of us does not look at her photographs – placed here and there on the walls of rooms 'of our own' – as a surrogate of that missed encounter?

Virginia Woolf is a fitting example. If it is true that all human beings are unique, it is equally true that some are also remarkable, exceptional. The fact remains that not only the exceptional leave behind a story. The narratable self is a figure of uniqueness, not of exceptionality. Women who write biographies and autobiographies have understood this for a long time. Alongside auto/biographies of famous women, it is in fact not uncommon to find in the bookstore some that are dedicated to *any old* woman [*donne* qualunque]. Indeed, here lies the magic of the biographical text: any woman, who is the biography's protagonist, shows herself to be unique and unrepeatable. Her life-story, before bearing witness to the historical typology of a class or a condition of women, puts into words, above all, the uniqueness of her personal identity.

We are in a bookstore. The editorial horizon that envelops us means that the narration does not appeal to the protagonist of the story, as though it were a personal gift, but rather to the reading public. At work here, therefore, is neither the gesture of Amalia nor the paradox of Ulysses. Nevertheless it is still uniqueness that subtends the question of *who* – and which sustains the classic rule by which the story gets recounted and read. Other intentions of writing or reading are obviously possible. Indeed, they are inevitable or obligatory – but they neither deny nor affect the motive or the result of the classic rule.

The approaches to an auto/biographical text are numerous. Narratology, at least the peculiar post-modern version, is, indeed, interested in the text as a construction of identity – which is more or less fragmentary and insubstantial, multiple and eccentric. Sociologists, on the other hand, are more interested in the typological complexity, or the social–historical context, which shines through the story. It is too much trouble to enumerate the broad number of interests that literary critics have. What the New York reader of our *fable* seeks, and finds, is nonetheless something that precedes these ways of reading, and renders them possible.

Biographies and autobiographies, before being textual sites of a refined and professional hermeneutics, are life-stories narrated as a written text. For as much as they are necessarily constructed according to diverse standards, or according to the epoch or the tastes of the time, they nonetheless tell the story of a narratable self whose identity – unique and unrepeatable – is what we seek in the pages of the text. It is this identity, which may be *rendered* as a fragmentary or multiple segmentation of the self, which would deny its *unity*. Our thesis, once more, is that the etymological root that the terms *uniqueness* [unicità] and *unity* [unità] share does not flatten them out into a homogeneous substance, but rather renders them signs of an existence whose life-story is different from all others precisely because it is constitutively interwoven with many others.

There is undoubtedly a flattening effect regarding the narrated identity in the form of a story. As two phrases of Arendt (which we never tire of repeating) state – in biography 'the unchangeable identity of the person' becomes tangible, 'the essence of *who* he is.'[10] For Arendt, who is interested neither in the text nor in the infinite hermeneutics of the reader, this identity is unchangeable precisely because the tale comes after the flow of action from which the life-story results. In the same way, the *who* appears in the tale as an essence because the narration is always retrospective – it *halts* that which is, in the expressive flux of the existent, not stable or fixed.

It nonetheless seems to us that, more than immutability, it is the unity of the self, made tangible by the tale, which moves the desire of the narratable self to seek the narration of a life-story. In other words, the narrative familiarity of memory, which constitutes the self as a narratable identity, has, in the unity of this identity, *the ideal* of her desire. The unity is therefore the figure of an in-born and inexhaustible tension: it is the design promised, from birth, to a unique existent, in so far as she exposes herself to the world, leaving behind herself a story. The one who is unique is also one in the very act of self-exhibition. She is this way first of all in her birth, when she is already a *who* without yet being a *what*; when, in her very new beginning, she is a *unique unity*, about whom multiplicity, or fragmentation or discontinuity, cannot yet be predicted.

Moreover, the pleasure principle is always a good criterion for identifying desire. The New York reader, like many others, likes auto/biographical texts. That is, she likes life-stories in which the reifying effects of narration, whatever the style or intention, render tangible the unrepeatable unity of a self in the unity of its story. This unity does not have to be understood as a homogeneity. On the contrary, it is likely that it is precisely the inhomogeneous personality of the protagonist that attracts the contemporary reader's interest.

Thus, a possible ambiguity is clarified. From a relational and expositive identity, which is immersed in the flux of existence and which is unpredictable by definition, the life-story of a self whose identity gives itself as a *simple* unity, as the coherent development of an immutable substance, certainly cannot result. This unity is rather the temporal succession of *an* unrepeatable existence, which, continuing to appear, made a story for herself – or, rather, the temporal configuration of an *ipse*. In other words, the text narrates the story of the insubstitutable *who*, not the *what*, of the protagonist. The unity lies precisely in this *insubstitutability* that *persists* [*permane*] in time because it continues to present itself in time.

In accordance with the various rhetorical strategies enacted by auto/biography, it indeed seems that the insubstitutability of a self that persists throughout the whole time of her existence, from birth to death, arouses few doubts in the common sense of the New York reader and in our proverbial housewife. Indeed, we should seriously take into account this common sense, which wisely states that every human being is born and lives until he/she dies. No one can fully walk in another's shoes; neither can anyone become another in order to get out of his/her own shoes. We might respond in the following way to the classical question of the experts: the young Emilia, the adult Emilia, the Emilia who is moved after receiving the gift of her story ... is she always the *same*? Can one say about her that she is *ipse* or *idem*, or, better, *ipsa* or *eadem*?

Yes, she is always the same – comes our response. Emilia, like Oedipus, like every human being, is *who* is born and lives until she dies. The ambiguity of these questions regarding the persistence of identity lies in fact in the confusion of the status of the *who* with the *what*. The *what* – that is, the qualities, the character, the roles, the outlooks of the self – changes and is inevitably multiple and may be judged or reinterpreted in many ways. The *who*, on the other hand – as the uniqueness of the self in her concrete and *insubstitutable* existence – persists in continual self-exhibition, consisting in nothing else but this exposure, which cannot be transcended.

Arendt, in this regard, notes that – in so far as personal identity cannot be exchanged with another – identity maintains a sort of curious intangibility which eludes all efforts at unequivocal verbal definition: 'the moment we want to say *who* somebody is, our vocabulary leads us astray into saying *what* he is; we get entangled in a description of the qualities he necessarily shares with others like him; we begin to describe a type or a 'character' in the old meaning of the word, with the result that his specific uniqueness escapes us.'[11]

Arendt therefore leads us to an important theme. Not only does the *who* – that is, identity – elude verbal definition; but the definitory exercise (which works in relation to it) produces an ambiguous nomination of its *what*. The discursive order that says *who* someone is, in fact, does not belong to the (genuinely philosophical) art of definition, but rather to the art of biography. Personal identity, which – in the gaze of the other or in a momentary encounter – cannot be exchanged for another, thus finds in his or her life-story a temporal extension; or, the continual dynamism of his or her persistence. In other words, the verbal response to *who* someone is always consists in the narration of his or her life-story; that is, in the tale where this someone has used up already her time (at least her time up until now) – the unrepeatable existence of *a single* insubstitutable being.

Obviously, in a life-story, qualities of the protagonist get narrated as well. Since there is no *who* that is not always already intertwined with its *what*, or that is inseparable from it, the tale also tells *what* someone was and is – and thus offers interesting material to historical or sociological, if not literary, analyses. In this sense, the tale sometimes makes the protagonist into a 'character' or 'type' – even a 'type' of existential fragmentation – making him or her exemplary under this profile, and thus exchangeable with many others. If we did not fear the ambiguity of the term, we might therefore say that the biographical tale tends to evidence the various identities through which the same protagonist passes. (For example, in the case of Emilia, her identity as an urbanized proletariat or as re-educated housewife.) But it is not *this* type of identity that we are talking about. Following Arendt, the term identity must indeed be understood not as that which results from a process of identification, or from a social construction of that identity, but rather as that which a singular existent designs in her uncategorizable [*incatalogabile*] uniqueness. Although it is inextricably intertwined with various plural, typological identities – just as the *who* is always intertwined with the *what* – it is above all a unique, unrepeatable, personal identity whose story a biographical text narrates. This identity, which is rendered tangible by the story, is what moves Emilia and arouses the interest of our New York reader.

From the point of view of the narratable self – or, rather, in the economy of her desire – the stylistic intentions of the text do not count; indeed, the text itself does not even count. The New York reader bears ample witness to this. We do not know what she has found, but we know fairly well what she was seeking. She was looking for a life-story, and devoured with her eyes the photographs of the protagonist. Before reading the text, and thus before encountering its styles or intentions, her desire turned toward a biographical tale without any perceptible critical orientation.

It is indeed quite probable that the desire to read auto/biographies of others is a sort of spontaneous reflex of the narratable self's desire for narration. And it is symptomatic that, in the perspective of reading others' stories, the distinction between biography and autobiography no longer counts. Unlike what happens in narrative friendships, there is here neither relation nor exchange. In this case, the narratable self decontextualizes her desire and transfers it to the ready-made work below. Amalia and Emilia knew each other and narrated to each other in turn: the one was a narratable self *for* the other, who manifested *to* the friend her desire for narration. The New York reader, on the other hand, neither tells stories, nor, in the anonymous context of the bookstore, asks to be told a story. She limits herself to looking, in the text, for the story of another woman. Once again, what orients this search is simply the conviction that each narratable self has a life about which a story can be narrated.

The predilection for auto/biographical texts obviously does not concern only women, and neither does it confine the pleasure of readers to a circle of writers or heroes of their own sex. The phenomenon of a wholly feminine – if not feminist – circle of auto/biographical publishing is nonetheless salient. There are many reasons for this. In the first place, there is the pleasure of reading stories of women as commendable reactions to the immense auto/biographical literature dedicated for centuries to men, a literature that seems to make men themselves the only protagonists of a life that deserves to leave behind a story. In the second place, there is the effect of a 'revindication' of female existences, which, even within the decidedly traditional confines of social standards, live *lives-with-meaning* (though obviously a specific and different meaning). Third, and more simply, there is the sympathy or empathy that like finds in like. And yet, these are not the fundamental points.

Indeed, it seems reasonable to hypothesize about an effect of *literary orientation* due to the narrative character of feminine friendships. In other words, the auto/biographical text replaces the storytelling friend, in the absence of a reciprocal relation. As was already indicated in reference to the episode of Emilia, the traditional exclusion of women by the two-thousand-year-old exploits of the subject – or, better, of its representations – indeed functions as an advantage in the feminine practice of narrative exercise. The double scene in which Oedipus moves sketches a tragedy that could only happen to a man. This does not take away the fact that many men have always been – and, for some centuries, exclusively – some of the great narrators: of epic, of the novel, of auto/biography and so forth. Nonetheless, they were great narrators only inside this enormous tragedy.

There is thus some truth in the feminist critique of the fantasmatic centrality of the classical subject in the masculine auto/biographical and narrative tradition. However, the conclusions that feminists draw from this critique seem less true – namely, the temptation to welcome a fragmentary and multiple narration of the self as a particularly feminist practice. What appears more productive, instead, is the valorization of the experience that seems to have destined women to be saved from the claws of this tragedy. Put positively, the habit of not universalizing the undeserved, contradictory, and impossible self in Man, has made women into great narrators, through reciprocal, friendly relations, even when there were very few *texts* to *attest to this*.

It is indeed equally unlikely that the classic subject casts its shadow in the pages written by Amalia for Emilia. Neither does it seem that Emilia requested immortal fame from these pages – a fame capable of overcoming death, which the hero, beyond Arendt's analyses, seems to take on as the measure of his existence. In so far as it refigures the feminine paradigm of the narratable self, the Milanese episode has above all the merit of making evident the essentiality of the context and the inessentiality of the text. The text is obviously there; indeed, Emilia weeps because it is there. But the text is invisible to us: we cannot 'study it' or 'judge it' in order to proceed *from* the text to Emilia's identity. We cannot make her 'self' into a textual self, identifying, for instance, the performative effects of the writing. This text only exists in relation to Emilia's desire and in the context of her relationship with Amalia.

We could therefore even say that, in this text, Emilia assumes the modern status of 'character,' or, rather, risks embodying 'a psychological essence,' encountering, moreover, the figure of her identity in the form of an irrefutable reification.[12] On the other hand, the reverse becomes oddly true for Emilia as well. Her finding herself as a 'character' functions in fact as a confirmation of her having been 'an actor;' that is, of having been the one *who* exhibited herself in action and left behind a story. In the economy of desire, the effect of the text is therefore polyvalent.

This desire, however, does not move towards a narration that has the power to go beyond the death of the protagonist. Rather, it moves here and now – in the actuality of its tension, so to speak – towards the promise of the unity of the self which the other, beyond simply satisfying, can actually recognize. Self-immortalizing is something that heroes do; or perhaps poets, artists, navigators; or, more recently, industrial leaders or university professors. It therefore comes as no surprise that, from their ivory towers, they see the text with a posthumous gaze, continuing to perpetuate the virile habit of measuring themselves against death.

There is even the old dispute between the narrator and his heroes. The immortal fame of the latter depends upon the former. As Horace – whose verses erect a 'monument more lasting than bronze,' making his 'undying I' grow in the praise of his descendants – knew well, 'many heroes lived before Agamemnon; but all are overwhelmed in unending night, unwept, unknown, because they lack a sacred rhapsod.'[13] The narrator is therefore the one who, in the last analysis, gains the greater fame. The theory of the inessentiality of the text has thus the additional merit of rendering superfluous this malicious dispute over immortal fame.

Sometimes, however, a bit of malice is not such a bad thing. One could indeed maliciously suspect that the whole affair about the centrality of the text, which reduces the existence of the living to a *status* of extra-textuality, depends on the well-known tendency of intellectuals to represent the world in their likeness and image. This is, of course, an ancient vice. It originates, perhaps, with Parmenides – the first professional *thinker* – who declares that 'being and thinking are the same.' The 'I think, therefore I am' of Descartes, and the 'all that is real is rational' of Hegelian memory, echo him through the millennia. After which, in more recent times, the subject fades away – but not the sacredness of intellectual work, which, for centuries, has claimed to put it into the world. On the contrary, such intellectual work, tirelessly speculating upon itself, decides that the very same speculators are a fictitious product of the speculating game. With a rather democratic gesture, the text thus consumes everyone's existence – philosophers and housewives, heroes and poets, characters and authors – in a single mouthful.

It is therefore not the case that our New York reader reveals a strong interest for life-stories, furnished with nice photographs, and not for literary or philosophical criticism. Evidently, however, she has already become bored with books written by someone who, though appearing by name on the cover, endeavors with delight to argue for the unreality of his own existence, and additionally for the unreality of our reader's existence as well.

NOTES

1 *Ibid.*, p. 20.
2 Cf. Kathleen Barry, 'Biography and the search for a women's subjectivity,' *Women's Studies International Forum*, **12** (1989), p. 571.
3 Rosi Braidotti, *Dissonanze* (Milan: La Tartaruga, 1994).
4 Janet Varner Gunn, *Autobiography: Towards a Poetics of Experience*, p. 30.
5 Laura Mattesini, 'Scrivere di sé: una rassegna critica sull'autobiografia femminile', *DWF [Donna Woman Femme]*, **2–3** (1993), pp. 28–47. [TN: my translation.] As the title indicates, the article is a very useful review of feminist literature, especially American, which is dedicated to autobiography; and has the merit of reporting in a long, documented bibliographic note, to which I refer the reader. Especially in the English-speaking world, this type of study has seen a marked, and interesting, increase in recent years, with an end nowhere in sight.
6 Cf. Felicity A. Nussbaum, *The Autobiographical Subject* (Baltimore: Johns Hopkins University Press, 1989), p. 12.
7 The neologism of the term 'auto/biography' appears in the text and title of the book by Liz Stanley, according to theoretical criteria explained by the author. The use that I make of it here must be understood as a choice of mere typographical convenience. By auto/biography I mean simply both autobiography and biography.
8 Laura Mattesini, 'Scrivere di sé: una rassegna critica sull'autobiografia femminile', p. 39.
9 Christine Battersby, *Gender and Genius* (London: The Women's Press, 1989), p. 151.
10 Arendt, *The Human Condition*, p. 193.
11 *Ibid.*, p. 181.
12 Roland Barthes, *Introduction to the Structural Analysis of the Narrative* (Birmingham, UK: Centre for Contemporary Culture Studies, 1966), p. 32.
13 Horace, *Odes* 3, 30, and 4, 9; from *Odes and Epodes* (Cambridge, Massachusetts: Harvard University Press, 1988).

Part III

LOVERS

7

THE NECESSARY OTHER

About six weeks ago Gertrude Stein said, it does not look to me as if you
were ever going to write that autobiography. You know what I am going
to do. I am going to write it for you.

Gertrude Stein, *The Autobiography of Alice Toklas*

Gertrude Stein succeeds notoriously in disturbing the fundamental tenets of the
autobiographical genre. Writing *The Autobiography of Alice Toklas*, she runs up
against the elementary rule by which the protagonist of an autobiography is also
its author. In the book in question, this rule explodes. As the title announces,
Gertrude Stein writes and signs the autobiography of another woman; namely,
The Autobiography of Alice Toklas, where Alice speaks in the first person. Alice lives
with her: she is her friend and lover. Their relationship is by now quite strong. In
this strange autobiographical enterprise, there is a strict collaboration, which sees
them as accomplices. Gertrude writes by hand and Alice types. Alice therefore
rewrites, copying word for word *her* autobiography, written by another, where
she herself ends up as the narrator.

One could thus regard this as an ingenious trick, which consists in disguising
as autobiography – writing in the first person instead of the third person – that
which is instead a biography of Alice written by Gertrude. There is a trick, but
this is not it. The book, in fact, does not speak of Alice, but rather of Gertrude
and of her relations with the Parisian intellectual scene. In other words, in the
text, Alice Toklas recounts an autobiography that is centered above all on
Gertrude Stein and on the extraordinary people whom she encounters.
Obviously Alice too participates in this extraordinary scene, but in a secondary
role; she participates as the companion, the 'wife,' of the brilliant Gertrude
Stein.

In the last analysis, *The Autobiography of Alice Toklas* is therefore an autobiography of Gertrude Stein, written by Gertrude, where Gertrude herself appears in

the text, however, as a character narrated by Alice. The play of this fiction could also be formulated differently. One could indeed say that, in *The Autobiography of Alice Toklas*, Alice herself – while figuring in the autobiographical role of the first person – nevertheless ends up playing the role of Gertrude Stein's biographer. In short, the fiction is complex and entertaining precisely because it is explicit. The autobiographical and biographical genres are superimposed upon one another. The roles of the narrating self and the narrated self confuse Alice's name with Gertrude's, perplexing the reader. There are numerous possible interpretations of this transgressive gesture that sustains the text, not the least of which is the one adored by the post-modern paradigm. From an elementary point of view, one thing nevertheless remains true. Gertrude writes her life-story, *making it* told by another; by Alice, her friend and partner, her lover.

As many interpreters have noted, this is a life-story that does not at all resemble the classic profile of the tale, and resembles even less what is inspired by the 'confession' or the 'novel.' On the contrary, the privileged viewpoint is given to a vision rooted in the actuality of the happening.[1] Alice – in the famous experimental writing of Gertrude – watches, and writes what she sees. She sees some quite extraordinary characters enter into Gertrude's Parisian house, albeit from her angle of vision – which is, of course, secondary. And, as she sees them, so she tells of them. In the same way, she sees and describes Gertrude's visits to the shows or the studios of the most famous painters of the period. Even in the digressions that abound in the text, forward and backward in time, the visual technique remains a fundamental choice.

The privileging of the gaze indicates therefore another crucial trick. Gertrude constructs a text where she watches herself with the eyes of the other; or, rather, in Arendtian terms, she constructs a scene where she paradoxically appears *to herself* in the only way in which she can appear – to the gaze of others.

Many remarkable artists of the period appear before the gaze of Alice and are described, or recounted, by her. But Gertrude remains at the center of the vision, and orients it. Indeed, the presence of others – observed and narrated by Alice – allows Gertrude's story to make clear the interwoven character of others' stories, which constitutes the expositive and relational reality of the self. The gigantic egotism of Gertrude Stein thus succeeds in producing a literary fiction of stories that intersect where she herself stands out, and where Alice – the lover, the friend – still appears as the other who watches her and as the other who tells her story. Put another way, the text functions as a sort of theater of the self in which Gertrude stages her exhibitive impulse and her desire for narration. Alice, who watches and recounts, more than simply being a literary artifice, is here *the necessary other*.

The dynamic of the text indeed bears witness to the fact that Alice does not play a merely instrumental role. This dynamic is, moreover, developed by the position of the one who watches and recounts. In other words, Gertrude Stein does not simply create an ingenious narcissistic mechanism, but rather adapts the writing as much as possible to the perspective, narrative position of the other. For example, she lets Alice – who is not involved in a conversation between Gertrude and Picasso – have the time to observe alone, from her point of view, the paintings that hang on the wall. The privileging of the visual orientation – totally immersed in the actuality of a present which makes the narrative coincide with the description – thus produces the curious absence of any sentimental accent. Lacking in introspective satisfactions and psychological enquiries, the text is a feast of exhibition and appearance. The reality of the self, far from possessing an interior, is totally *external*. Alice narrates that which she sees in the moment in which she sees it. Like Picasso's paintings, Gertrude appears to the gaze or the senses of the other. 'I met Gertrude Stein. I was impressed by her coral brooch and by her voice,' recounts Alice in the text written by Gertrude.[2] That meeting signals the beginning of a love-affair that the tale still refuses to infuse with any retrospective sentimentalism.

As the fruit of a curious fiction that clearly refutes itself, the text is therefore interesting not only as the transgression of the autobiographical genre, but also for the desire that sustains its ingenious mechanism. That this desire is tightly bound to a lesbian relationship has been made clear by feminist literary criticism.[3] What is remarkable, however, is the capacity of the book to stage a relationship between Alice and Gertrude that refigures itself in terms of both a visual and narrative reciprocity. Indeed, the game is found out. The two are accomplices. Alice types – or, rather, first reads, and then rewrites, the pages that Gertrude has written by hand. Alice was not a typist by trade. She had to learn how to use the typewriter in order to support Gertrude's work. Their life together is in large part modeled on the traditional couple, where one – the writer, the genius – plays the role of the 'husband,' while the other – the cook, the secretary – plays the role of 'wife.' Gertrude writes. Alice recopies.

The text that results from this is obviously important; indeed, it is exemplary as literary experimentation – but this is first of all a part of the game. The text, in fact, succeeds in producing curious rhetorical strategies precisely because it refigures the real relationship and itself functions as the reciprocal desire, both lived and narrated, that characterizes it. Put simply, *The Autobiography of Alice Toklas* transgresses the classical tenets of autobiography because it puts into writing the relational character of a self that the autobiographical genre – as such – is prevented from putting in words.

From a rigorous perspective, even Gertrude Stein's text does not escape this rule. Indeed, it is written by Gertrude and it narrates chiefly *about* Gertrude. The Alice who recounts in the first person is only a pretext. Due to the particular nature of this pretext, the text nevertheless, in a certain sense, eludes this rule –

at least as far as it is possible to elude it. Indeed, in the pretext, it is the other who watches Gertrude and tells her story. The complicity of Alice in the undertaking adds to the trick, and renders it perfect. One of the most shameless examples of egotism in contemporary literature thus gives us a lesson in altruism.

Prior to being a generous life-style in the service of others, altruism is indeed the foundational principle of a self that knows itself to be constituted by another: *the necessary other*.

If not only Emilia, but also Gertrude Stein (who proclaimed herself, without mincing words, to be a genius), can interpret the figure of a 'narratable' self and her desire, an obvious question arises. Is all of this a narcissistic orgy centered on the pleasure of hearing one's story told? Is this perhaps an auto/biographical twist on typical modern individualism, in feminist clothing?

The Arendtian hero, who has accompanied us from the start, has in effect often been accused of exhibitionist narcissism; indeed, the Arendtian sense of politics has been judged to be constitutively narcissistic. Reserving some doubt with regard to Gertrude Stein, we realize, nonetheless, right away, how difficult it is to make the same judgment regarding Emilia. Not only because narcissism is a question between self and self, where the other (if there is one) functions only as a spectator to be dazzled – but also since the uniqueness that exposes itself, in Arendt's sense, brings to the scene a fragile and unmasterable self. Both the exhibitionist self of action and the narratable self are completely given over to others. In this total giving-over there is therefore no identity that reserves for itself protected spaces or private rooms of impenetrable refuge for self-contemplation.

This is why autobiography is a mistake of desire, the vicious circle of a mistaken course. This is why Gertrude Stein challenges the autobiographical genre by writing a text where it is the other who tells her story. The narrative character of memory is indeed everything in which the narratable self consists, without yet being able to keep any distance from itself. To tell one's own story is to distance oneself from oneself, to double oneself, to make of oneself an other. It is not by chance that narratology must deal with 'the anomalous coincidence of author, narrator and character,' which is typical of the autobiographical work.[4] There is, in autobiography, the strange pretense of a self that makes himself an other in order to be able to tell his own story; or, rather, of a self which, using his memory as a separated mirror in which he inseparably consists, appears to himself as an other – he externalizes his intimate self-reflection. The *other*, therefore, is here the fantasmatic product of a doubling, the supplement of an absence, the parody of a relation. Gertrude Stein knows this well, and she challenges the very mechanism by introducing into the autobiographical scene an other who really is *an* other.

Moreover, in the autobiographical exercise, the real existence of the other, even just as an addressee, is always taken into account, whether he or she is a listener of an oral narration, or an ideal reader to which the text appeals. The oral tale is, however, always an act, which happens here and now, in relation to the listening of an other, who in turn is necessarily 'here and now.' The written, on the other hand, does not have these characteristics of material relation in the context. On the contrary, as Derrida says in reference to Nietzsche, a written text can call itself *auto*-biographical not 'because the one who signs [it] tells his life-story [...] but because he tells *himself* this life-story, because he is the first, if not the only, *addressee* of the narration.'[5] 'I will tell myself my life-story,' writes Nietzsche in the famous autobiographical pages of *Ecce Homo*.

It is nevertheless odd that Derrida does not emphasize how, even in Nietzsche, the solipsistic intention is clamorously betrayed. For as much as he refuses with disdain to recount himself to his contemporaries who could never understand him, he in fact does not keep an intimate diary, but rather writes for his descendants, for future readers to whom he commands: '*Hear me! For I am such and such a person. Above all, do not mistake me for someone else.*'[6] 'I do not want to be mistaken for another – therefore I must not mistake myself for another,' he repeats a moment later with emphasis. The Nietzschean autobiography thus ends up citing Oedipus, almost to the letter, inside a text that begins importantly with the programmatic task of '*saying who I am.*'[7]

In the autobiographical exercise, writing and orality indicate, in effect, a difference. For millennia, human beings have written their life-stories in solitude, but only madmen tell themselves their own stories out-loud, making of themselves their only listeners. Emilia knows this difference perfectly well. She distinguishes her solitary writing exercises from the continual oral narration with which she tires her friend. And yet it is precisely by virtue of the relationship implied by this orality that Emilia obtains, in the end, her written biography from Amalia.

What the narratable self of Emilia desires, even without knowing it, is thus, from the start, a narration of her story from the hand or the mouth of another. From the perspective of the story, which responds to the desire of the narratable self, the written or oral form is indeed of secondary importance. The written text has the advantage of a greater tangibility; or the advantage of the pages jealously held in the purse, continually reread. The oral tale, on the other hand, as Arendt would say, has no lasting material consistency. Nonetheless, in both cases, what matters from the beginning is the narrative relation that rendered them possible and that renews itself in them.

In other words, in the biography given by the other, both the written and the oral put into words above all the uniqueness of an identity which, *only in relation*, is *bios* instead of *zoe*.

In the case of Gertrude Stein, characterized by a precise literary vocation and by an extraordinary intellectual circle, the relation is obviously more complex and, so to speak, already oriented towards writing. Narcissism is, moreover, a vice to which Gertrude is certainly not immune. *The Autobiography of Alice Toklas* finds an ingenuous way of giving it an outlet, intertwining it with the altruism that belongs to the relational character of the self. Of course, some doubt remains regarding the motive for this inventive negotiation of the narcissistic pitfall.

Aside from the experiment of Gertrude Stein, it seems, however, unjustified to accuse the exhibitive *who*, which we have borrowed from Arendt's theory of politics and narration, of narcissism. Its reality is in fact totally relational. And then, as Maria Zambrano would say, there is no narcissism in the one who 'does not look at himself but gives himself to be seen, which is the gift of the one who does not pause to look at himself in the water or any other mirror.'[8] Fragile and contingent – and already marked at birth by a unity that makes of herself first a promise, and then a desire – the narratable self is an exposed uniqueness that awaits her narration. The text of this narration, far from producing *all* the reality of the self, is nothing but the marginal consequence, or symptom, that follows that desire.

What moves the desire of the narratable self, indeed, is not fame, just as the manner in which its desire is measured is not death. On the contrary, within the narrative scene, where each desire engenders the reciprocity of storytelling, death is constitutively excluded from the tale. The tale of death can indeed only be a posthumous tale. It never belongs to a scene where the other is present.

In the formula 'tell me my story,' there speaks a narratable self that always already sees the beginning and the end of her life-story entrusted to another's tale; that is, the story of her own birth, which goes back to early childhood, and the story of her death. Beginning and end, although belonging to her story, are not however on the same level. Rather than being an unavoidable end, from the perspective of the desire for narration, the end that coincides with death is in fact the *inaudible* conclusion of the tale. The beginning, on the other hand, is the essential chapter in which the self becomes narrated before even knowing herself to be narratable. The unity of the self, which the desire for narration makes manifest, finds in the others' tale her indispensable *incipit*, but never her *final* pleasure.

The finale that coincides with death has, moreover, its greatest appeal only from the perspective of absolute fulfillment, which continues to flirt with the ethic of the hero. That sort of partial completion, which the biographical exchange stages, reveals itself to be somewhat less solemn, but much more significant. Within this scene, a 'momentary completion' is indeed often perceptible, one which is capable of contenting itself in the present of the here

86

and now, and which coincides simply with the *actual* end of the story.[9] In other words, the biographical tale can always enjoy the momentary completion of its unity in the story 'up until now,' even if this unity finds its formal perfection – which is necessarily inaudible to the ear of desire – in the *final* word written by death.

Whether absolute or momentary, the completion of the tale of a life-story is still peculiar. Even when the last word is written, it never gives in to the illusion of a complete totality. That which 'in the end' comes to completion in the tale is in fact never the *total sense* of the self, but rather the lifetime that death cuts off. In other words, death does not coincide with the final stroke that *brings to an end* the design of the stork. Never closed in a perfect line that rejoins the first point with the last, the stork can be retraced at many points of the tale. The existent, which is insubstitutable for the duration of his/her life-span, is never an *all* – although it is born into the promise of the *one*. Still less does he/she find in death 'an adequate base for establishing in what sense the totality of Being-there can be talked about.'[10] Only a perspective that is obsessively focused on death can in fact read existence in terms of totality. Even the posthumous horizon that characterizes the motive of many autobiographical writings supports this obsession.[11]

Precisely because of this irremediable exposure to others, uniqueness – although it speaks the desiring language of the *one* – rejects, at the root, the synthesis of the *all*. The *en kai pan*, the One and All, belong to the doctrine of Parmenides, not to the design of a life traced by human footsteps on the terrain of unforeseeability and contingency. Fragile and exposed, the existent belongs to a world-scene where interaction with other existents is unforeseeable and potentially infinite. As in *The Arabian Nights*, the stories intersect with each other. Never isolated in the chimerical, total completion of its sense, one cannot be there without the other.

The narratable self thus re-enters into what we could call a relational ethic of contingency; or, rather, an ethic founded on the *altruistic* ontology of the human existent as finite. Already exposed within the interactive scene that Arendt calls 'political,' there lies at the center of the narrative scene a *who* which – far from enclosing herself within the pride of a self-referential ego meant to last forever – gathers the in-born matrix of an expositive and relational existence. She wants and gives, receives and offers, *here and now*, an unrepeatable story in the form of a tale.

This ethic finds therefore a fundamental principle in the recognition that every human being, whatever her qualities, has her unjudgable splendor in a personal identity that *is* irrefutably her story.

This is not a recognition that belongs to the classical realm of moral theory, and neither is it a principle whose ethic can be *deduced*. This is rather an irreflexive recognition, already at work in the exhibitive nature of the self, which is rendered even more explicit in the active and desiring practice of reciprocal storytelling. The relational character of the ethic that responds to this is not therefore the fruit of a choice; or, rather, the object of a possible appraisal or the result of a grandiose strategy. It is rather the necessary aspect of an identity which, from beginning to end, is intertwined with other lives – with reciprocal exposures and innumerable gazes – and needs the other's tale.

Thus, all universalizing ethics (or politics) that are founded on Man, and those that champion the modern individual, end up being refuted. Although in different ways, both of these doctrines ignore the *who* and focus instead on the *what*. It is enough to cite the rational and political animal of Aristotle, or the *homo homini lupus* of Hobbes. These respond, in different ways, to the same question: what is Man? This insistence on the *what* to the detriment of the *who* is symptomatically even truer when the 'individualistic theory' refuses to emphasize the competitive nature of the single, or 'dissolves' it into the political principle of equality. The fact is that human beings live together. Whether natural or artificial, their community is involved with a problem of acting and of living together that cannot refrain from taking the other into consideration. This is precisely why – coinciding in some cases, as happens in the Greece of Plato and Aristotle – ethics and politics often go hand in hand.

Within the individualist horizon, the other – different or equal, according to criteria of categorization – is, however, someone who is before us and with whom we must establish rules for living together. He or she never embodies the constitutive relationship of our insubstitutible identity. The other is rather someone who *is also there* and occupies, more or less peacefully, the same territory. In fact, according to the doctrine of natural law, in the classical formulation of individualism, *residing together [stare insieme]* – rendered possible and disciplined by politics – is the 'artificial' result of an agreement, not the founding condition of humans, in so far as they are constituted by a *being together [essere insieme]*, which, within the plural space of appearance, shows their uniqueness and guarantees their reality. It is hardly necessary to refer to Hobbes, and to his famous theory of the war of all against all, in order to take note of the way in which the foundations of the individualist doctrine ignore precisely the constitutive relation of the self *with* the other. *Ut singuli*, in Hobbes' radical formulation, but, nonetheless, separable – indeed, originally separated from one another – the individuals of the modern doctrine are sources of values and rights for themselves. Their greatest burden is that they must take account of others – they must negotiate rules, accept limits, make compromises.

Neither is it any longer worth the trouble of illustrating by extension, the neuter–masculine model that substantiates individuals, and towards which feminist thought has for a long time now directed its criticism.[12] Indeed, our actual approach to the problem consists in a more malicious criticism. It consists in indicating an odd aspect of the modern doctrine – one which both shows itself ready to enthusiastically adopt the category of individuality, and, on the other hand, reveals itself to be predisposed to restrict with disdain the category of uniqueness. As the elementary lexicon of democracy demonstrates, individuality is indeed a repeatable, atomized, serial paradigm. Each individual, in and of himself, is as valid for *one* as he is for any other; he is equal because he is equivalent. Uniqueness, on the other hand, ends up rendering useless both the concept of repetition and the principle of generalization that nourishes the individualist theory. Uniqueness is an absolute difference, which, as Arendt never tires of arguing, changes the very notion of politics.

Thus, difference is absolute because each human being is different from all those who have lived, who live, and who will live.[13] Not because she is free from any other; on the contrary, the relation with the other is necessary for her very self-designation as unique. We come to suspect therefore that the bad reputation from which the term uniqueness suffers, both in the moderns and the post-moderns, depends upon the erroneous way in which it is mistaken for an idea of romantic origin. On the contrary, in the uniqueness of the *who* there is no homage to the self-centered and titanic subject of romanticism. The *who* does not project or pity herself, and neither does she envelop herself within her interiority. The *who* is simply exposed; or, better, finds herself always already exposed to another, and consists in this reciprocal exposition.

To summarize: the ontological status of the *who* – as exposed, relational, altruistic – is totally *external*. Therefore, one of the centuries-old problems of philosophy becomes superfluous; namely, the unsayability of the individual, already decreed by Aristotle, and which in modern times regards autobiography as an expressive modality 'which gives voice, as much as possible, to an ineffable individual, in contrast to the discovery of regularity by the natural sciences.'[14] On the contrary, within the expositive horizon of the *who*, the individual is not ineffable at all. What ends up being ineffable in all of this is, if anything, a supposed *internal,* profound, hidden nucleus; namely, a mysterious interiority, which the *who*, in its total exposition, does not possess. As Arendt puts it, 'An interior "I," if it exists, never appears to the internal sense, or to the external senses, from the moment when nothing of its interiority possesses those stable, relatively permanent, traits which – being recognizable and identifiable – characterize the individual's appearance.' Or, even more radical: 'inside, we are all alike.'[15]

In the light of a unique and unrepeatable identity – irremediably exposed and contingent – the other is therefore a necessary presence. He or she is the one who consents to the very event of an appearance [*apparire*] of the existent, which – as Nancy would say – is always a co-appearance. *Appearing to each other* [*Comparendo*], they reciprocally appear as *an* other.[16] They thus do not lend substance to the anonymous face of an indistinct and universal alterity – namely, that face of the abstract altruism which is too easily identified as a generic benevolence or pious intention. The altruism of uniqueness is neither sacrifice nor dedication, nor mortification, nor renunciation. It is rather the ontological status of a *who*, which is always relational and contextual, for whom the other is necessary.

The altruism of uniqueness has thus the additional merit of avoiding that 'rhetoric of alterity,' which the philosophical discourse of the twentieth century seems to adore. 'The Other' or 'the other,' capital or lower-case, often gets invoked by contemporary philosophers as a proof of their good intentions with respect to the individualistic spirit of the times. Whether it is the alterity that invades the self, rendering him nomadic and fragmented, or the alterity that lures the self more subtly with his embrace, these others never have the distinct and unrepeatable face of each human in so far as he is simply *an*other. Intolerant, as usual, of many elementary givens of existence – a large part of contemporary philosophy disdains the ontological status that binds the reality of the self to the (well, yes, empirical) material presence of some*one* other.

As we never tire of repeating, the ontological status of reciprocal appearance [*comparizione*] belongs to the existents – distinct and plural, each one *for* and *with* another – of a living context like life. Continuing to live as a unique existent, *here and now*, in flesh and bone, this and not another, the *who* therefore avoids both the usual language of ethics and of politics. *Constitutively* altruistic, rather than by choice, the ethics and politics of uniqueness indeed speak a language that does not know general names. They tend, moreover, to coincide in the relational character of the very same scene – where the other who interacts, watches and recounts is the inassimilable, the insubstitutable, the unrepeatable. She is a unique existent that no categorization or collective identity can fully contain. She is the *you* [*tu*] that comes before the *we* [*noi*], before the plural *you* [*voi*] and before the *they* [*loro*].

Symptomatically, the *you* [*tu*] is a term that is not at home in modern and contemporary developments of ethics and politics,. The 'you' is ignored by the individualistic doctrines, which are too preoccupied with praising the rights of the *I*, and the 'you' is masked by a Kantian form of ethics that is only capable of staging an *I* that addresses itself as a familiar 'you' [*un 'io' che si dà solamente del 'tu'*]. Neither does the 'you' find a home in the schools of thought to which individualism is opposed – these schools reveal themselves for the most part to be affected by a moralistic vice, which, in order to avoid falling into the decadence of the *I*, avoids the contiguity of the *you*, and privileges collective, plural pronouns. Indeed, many 'revolutionary' movements (which range from traditional communism to the feminism of sisterhood) seem to share a curious linguistic code based on the intrinsic morality of pronouns. The *we* is always positive, the *plural you* [*voi*] is a possible ally, the *they* has the face of an antagonist, the *I* is unseemly, and the *you* [*tu*] is, of course, superfluous.

It is therefore interesting to note the way in which – by allowing the *we* of the context to be modeled on the relationship between the *you* and the *I* – the narrative practice of the consciousness-raising groups already ends up subverting this curious morality of pronouns. This shift towards an altruistic ethics of relationality is the right direction, and facilitates the course that the feminism of sexual difference follows in its most recent developments. As evidence, consider the way in which the Italian Left regards as incomprehensible the feminist lexicon that is *bizarrely* centered on the link between 'starting from oneself' and 'the relation between women.'[17] Within this horizon (which we now take to heart), the crucial problem still does not consist in this congenital incomprehensibility, but rather in the empathetic trap into which each scene of narrative reciprocity risks falling.

The empathetic theory is quite familiar to literary criticism, which occupies itself with the cultural and social construction of the self in modern narrative. It illustrates how, beginning with the eighteenth century, the sense of the 'self' is articulated above all through the use of a history of suffering and tribulation told by another – most of all by someone who belongs to the ranks of the oppressed.[18] This is therefore a type of empathy that functions typically within the constitution of a self that metabolizes the story of the other. In other words, this is a recognition in which uniqueness, as such, disappears.

Although the feminist practice of consciousness-raising does not deal with literature, it can be analyzed from the perspective of this empathetic theory. In the exchange of auto/biographical tales, the recognition of the uniqueness of the other and her desire for narration is, within the narrative scene, often mixed with the tendency to recognize the meaning [*senso*] of one's own self within the other's story, especially if that story speaks of suffering and misery. The comfort of similarity wins out over the relational status of distinction. The effect – or, perhaps, the empathetic motive for reciprocal narration – thus risks frustrating that reciprocal appearance [*comparire*] of *uniqueness* that qualifies the dynamic of recognition as an ethic. To recognize oneself *in* the other is indeed quite different from recognizing the irremediable uniqueness of the other.

This phenomenon must be carefully considered. In the last analysis, the risk of constructing the common 'being woman' ['*essere donne*'] as a substance, as the Woman that responds to their common experience, can be traced to the generalization of this empathy within the groups of consciousness-raising. In the words of *Non credere di avere dei diritti*, 'the practice of self-consciousness presupposed and favored a perfect reciprocal identification. I am you, you are me, the words which we say are women's words, hers and mine.'[19] Who I am and who you are are thus passed over in favor of the question 'who are we,' which is simply an ontological error of the language.

What we have called an altruistic ethics of relation does not support empathy, identification, or confusions. Rather this ethic desires a *you* that is truly an other, in her uniqueness and distinction. No matter how much you are similar and consonant, says this ethic, your story is never my story. No matter how much the larger traits of our life-stories are similar, I still do not recognize myself *in* you and, even less, in the collective *we*. I do not dissolve both into a common identity, nor do I digest your tale in order to construct the meaning of mine. I recognize, on the contrary, that your uniqueness is exposed to my gaze and consists in an unrepeatable story whose tale you desire. This recognition, therefore, has no form that could be defined dialectically; that is, it does not *overcome* or *save* finitude through the circular movement of a higher synthesis. The necessary other is indeed here a finitude that remains irremediably an other in all the fragile and unjudgeable insubstitutability of her existing. Put simply, the necessary other corresponds first of all with the *you* whose language is spoken by the shared narrative scene.

Within the horizon of the narratable self, the pronoun of biography is in fact not *he* [*egli*] but *you* [*tu*]. The one who tells *us* our story speaks the language of the *you*. Within the shared narrative scene, the addressee of the tale and its presence wins out over the classic role, in the text, of the absent protagonist.

NOTES

1 Cf. Simona Cappelli, 'Le autonarrazioni di Gertrude Stein,' *DWF [Donna Woman Femme]*, 2–3 (1993), p. 52.

2 Gertrude Stein, *The Autobiography of Alice Toklas* (New York: Modern Library, 1993), p. 6.

3 Cf. Catharine R. Stimpson, 'The mind, the body, and Gertrude Stein,' *Critical Inquiry*, 3 (1977), pp. 459–506; Leigh Gilmore, 'A signature of lesbian autobiography: Gertrude/Altrude,' *Prose Studies*, 14 (1991), pp. 50–68; Sidonie Smith, *Subjectivity, Identity and the Body* (Bloomington: Indiana University Press, 1993), pp. 65–82.

4 Andrea Battistini, *Lo Specchio di Dedalo: Autobiografia e Biografia* (Bologna: Il Mulino, 1990), p. 129.

5 Jacques Derrida, *The Ear of the Other* (New York: Schocken Books, 1985).

6 Friedrich Nietzsche, *Ecce Homo*, translated by Walter Kaufman (New York: Random House, 1967), p. 217.

7 *Ibid.*

8 Maria Zambrano, *I Beati* (Milan: Feltrinelli, 1992), p. 77.

9 Carolyn Steedman, *Past Tenses*, p. 48.

10 Martin Heidegger, *Being and Time*, trans. John Macquarrie and Edward Robinson (New York: Harper, 1962), p. 372.

11 Cf. Maurizio Ferraris, *Mimica* (Milan: Bompiani, 1992).

12 I have dealt with this question in 'Equality and sexual difference: amnesia in political thought,' in *Beyond Equality and Difference: Citizenship, Feminist Politics and Female Subjectivity*, edited by G. Bock and S. James (London: Routledge, 1992), pp. 32–47.

13 Hannah Arendt, *The Human Condition*, pp. 8, 127.

14 Maurizo Ferraris, *Mimica*, p. 9.

15 Hannah Arendt, *The Life of Mind*, pp. 32, 34.

16 Cf. Adriana Cavarero, 'Birth, Love, Politics' in *Radical Philosophy* **86** (1997), pp. 22–3.

17 See the analysis of Ida Domanijanni, 'Politica del simbolico e mutamento' in *Cultura e politica delle donne e la sinistra in Italia* (Trimestrale della Fondazione Istituto Gramsci di Roma), **3** (1992), pp. 131–57.

18 Cf. Carolyn Steedman, *Other People's Stories: Modernity's Suffering Self*, presented also at the conference on *Autobiography: Strategy for Survival* (University of Warwick, October, 1996).

19 *Sexual Difference: the Milan Women's Bookstore Collective*, p. 44.

8

ORPHEUS THE POET

Hic, ne deficeret metuens avidusque videndi
flexit amans oculos, et protinus illa relapsa est.

Ovid, *Metamorphosis*

Eurydice dies; Orpheus seeks consolation in his art. 'But he, solacing love's anguish with his hollow shell, sang of thee, sweet wife – of thee, to himself on the lonely shore,' Virgil tells us.[1] The poet sings for himself, narrating about her on the solitary bank, but his song is heard by others – listeners who grow in number and let themselves be seduced by the poetic verse: men and beasts, infernal gods and dead souls. In this way, the memory of Eurydice is circulated and the song can be repeated, from generation to generation, becoming immortal – even beyond the lifetime allowed to Orpheus.

Orpheus has essentially two faces, which cross a long literary tradition dedicated to the myth. On the one hand, he is the very symbol of poetry, of the language that enchants the hearer, of the magic verse that has 'the capacity to break down the barrier between life and death, and even to bring the dead back to life.'[2] On the other hand, he is the ultimate lover, the one who challenges the gods of Hell in order to have his beloved back and, because of his tremendous passion, undoes his own undertaking. Virgil's Orpheus, who sings precisely of her, of the loved one, serves to bring together these two faces, linking the narrating verse to the amorous relationship. This is a tragic link, however. As his name says, Orpheus is an *orphan*: his song comes from an inexorable loss, from the death of the loved one. As the symbol of the poetry of love, Orpheus inaugurates the stubborn tradition, which wants the loved woman to be a dead woman.

As the poet *par excellence* – not only the poet of love, but the very symbol of poetry – he is, however, also able to impersonate the direct adversary of the poet *par excellence*, Plato.

Ever since philosophy decided to call itself such, and to define its disciplinary status with the work of Plato, it has declared war against the art of poetry, and proudly differentiates itself from it. After Havelock's famous studies there are no longer any doubts about the original cause of this series of events.[3] The extraordinary stance of hostility which Plato reserves for the poetic art – or, for the various types of *narration* (epic, tragedy, poetry) that dominate Greek culture at the time – is a consequence of the gesture with which he comes to found philosophy as an alternative genre of discourse. Briefly, the epochal passage from orality to writing, from Homer to Plato, is, above all, a passage from narrative verse, which enchants the hearer by evoking images in the seductive and irreflexive flux of the tale, to philosophical discourse, which proceeds rather with method to define and to fix its terms. 'The crucial movement of philosophy is born with the repudiation of poetry,' the work of abstraction is born of the repudiation of the pleasure of narration.[4] From the *stories* of Homer we pass to the 'immobility without history' of *ideas*. What Oedipus learned at his expense is, for Plato, a principle – indeed, it is the very principle of philosophy.

With the typical seriousness of his irony, Plato has no scruples when it comes to making fun of Orpheus. In the dialogue on love, *The Symposium*, he takes delight in interpreting the myth from a perspective that tries precisely to discredit Orpheus as the figure of the poet. Plato makes Phaedrus say how the gods showed to Orpheus, at Hades, 'only the shadow of the woman he came for, without giving him the woman herself, because they judged him to be weak, just like a cithara-player.'[5] To the illusionist effect that, according the philosopher, characterizes the poetic art, the gods have correctly responded with the illusion of a shadow [*phasma*], or rather with the phantom of Eurydice, her deceptive image, her *copy*. Orpheus, the cithara-player, is weak for Plato. He is a purveyor of shadows and deceptions, who receives in exchange the mocking deceit of a shadow. In fact, for the philosopher, there is nothing more harmful, more anti-pedagogical, more Platonically anti-political, than an art that appeals to the weakness of the passions – which is, not by chance, totally feminine. Nothing is more perilous than a tale that stages human fragility, inducing the spectators to participate in it and to share in its emotions. With the pride of the founder, Plato opposes this art – which narrates of singular existents, and their fragility, as a goodness – the disciplining exercise of philosophy; namely, the work of thought, which can, by right, be defined as 'reasonable and detached, in relation with external forms; masculine and mature, and capable of attracting students, the province of an elite;' in short, a school for the best boys.[6]

For Orpheus, poet and lover, the consequences are not small. Indeed, from Plato's perspective, philosophy is not only a discipline, which, as Foucault would say, stylizes Man on the model of his abstract, discursive order. Philosophy – which is obviously polemic in relation to the 'vulgar' love, which attaches itself to the bodies and the passions – also turns 'celestial' love, between two souls filled with *logos*, into an ascendant course that draws on the truth of the ideas.[7] In this way, love doubles itself into its vulgar figure and its ascetic figure. The first is left to the weakness of the little people, the women and the cithara players. The second conducts philosophy in a realm of pure thought, which is entirely like the realm of death.

'Throughout the whole history of philosophy,' writes Arendt, 'persists the truly singular idea of an affinity between philosophy and death.'[8] Philosophers from Plato to Heidegger (and beyond) proclaim this emphatically. The common people, for their part, figure this out rather quickly – and have fun ridiculing them. However, what distinguishes the philosopher from the common people is the very tone of this emphasis. The activity of thought consists in fact always and everywhere in a solitary experience, which temporarily abandons the world of appearances – or, rather, the world of life and plurality that we inhabit together with our peers. Since, for human beings, 'the most radical experience of disappearance is death, and the retreat from appearances which is equal to death,' the analogy between death and thinking has an obvious foundation.[9] Making thought into his favorite activity – indeed, into his very profession – and qualifying this activity as 'a living for death,' the philosopher simply registers the way that things are. His ingenuity consists in the emphatic tone with which he announces this rather common experience to the profane. He pretends to smuggle as a discovery and a privilege something that is, instead, actually obvious.

From this emphasis there nonetheless follow, for the philosopher, even more serious crimes than the sin of naïve vanity. The greatest of all, according to Arendt, is that of making himself at home in the realm of pure thought and of judging the world of human plurality to be superfluous. Universal Man thus comes to eclipse the uniqueness of each human being. The *theory* expels the politics of plural interaction and replaces it with the rule of the few over the many. In other words, the metaphysical tradition is centered on the category of death – to which Arendt opposes her political conception of action and birth.

It thus becomes clear why Arendt refutes the very name of philosopher, preferring that of political thinker. For the love of human plurality, she indeed embraces a speculative horizon, which – against the philosophical custom of separating itself from the world – opens a worldly scene, plural and shared, where each one exhibits *who* he or she is, and leaves behind a story. The role of the poet and the narrator, in Arendt's anomalous theory, finally gets recuperated after centuries of neglect. We might expect therefore that Arendt finds some excellent arguments for *defending* Orpheus from the malice of Plato. Amazingly, this is not the case.

The brief reference that Arendt reserves for the myth of Orpheus is in fact inserted by her into a broad reflection dedicated precisely to the activity of thought. The argument regards the fact that thinking always takes as its object something *invisible*; that is, some 'de-sensitized sensible objects,' rendered this way by the imaginative work of memory. The myth of Orpheus has the merit of illustrating efficaciously 'that which happens in the instant in which the thought-process interrupts itself in the ordinary world of life,' or rather that which happens when we stop thinking and return to the reality of the world: 'every invisibility vanishes again.'[10] Put another way, in its constitutive separation from the world of visible appearances, the one who thinks has in his mind some invisible objects – that is, some desensitized images. When, detaching himself from the activity of thinking, he *turns* once again to the world, these images disappear along with the thought.

The myth of the crucial *turning around* [*voltarsi*] therefore functions rather well. In the context of Arendt's argument, Eurydice impersonates the role of the *invisible*, while Orpheus – in, for him, a somewhat anomalous role – represents *thinking*.

Within the perspective of this surprising reading, Orpheus's decision to turn around when he gets close to the light finds an easy explanation. The physical visibility of the objects – which is obvious in the world of the living, illuminated by the sun – is indeed hypothetically possible only when, rising from Hell and 'on the very verge of light,' Orpheus turns around in order to 'look back at Eurydice.'[11] This is mad, of course, because in a flash the loved one dissolves. He has fatally disobeyed the condition of never turning around, imposed by Proserpina. 'Something worthy of being forgiven, if Hell knew how to forgive!' notes Virgil with a quite human lyricism.[12] But the point is, Arendt would say, that not even the gods of Hell *are able* to pardon the one who violates the law that separates thought from the world of the visible. The condition, imposed by the gods, is that Orpheus should not turn around to look at the loved one who walks behind him. Apparently, this is not a prohibition that absolutely denies to the living the vision of dead souls, because the poet does see the specters of the deceased, which gather in throngs around his song. The prohibition only goes for Eurydice; that is, for the one who, being the object of thought, the image of the mind, is necessarily incompatible with the physical visibility that concerns the gaze.

Since the Arendtian discourse on the activity of thought here concerns the invisible, even the narration enters inevitably into the argument. 'Therefore the simple *telling* of what happened ... is *preceded* by the de-sensing operation,' notes Arendt in order to corroborate her thesis.[13] Like thought, narration has to do with invisible objects. The imagination is common to both.

Now, the reading which Arendt reserves for the myth of Orpheus turns out to be rather surprising. Not so much because, identifying the poet *par excellence* with the activity of thinking, she upsets the Platonic revindication of the opposition of the roles; but above all because she loses a good chance to lead Orpheus back to that model of the *storyteller* which would suit him better. As the narrator, who always has a retrospective gaze because he turns to the past, to what has been and is no longer, Orpheus indeed sings of the loved one because she is not there, because she is dead. As is the task of the poet, he offers a narration *post mortem* to the one who has completed her sojourn in the world of *sensible appearances*. Rather than turning him into a philosopher who is irritated by the world interrupting his thoughts, the error of turning around makes Orpheus into a poet who transgresses the rule of his art, because of an overflowing passion for love.

If it is indeed true that both thinking and narrating share the rule that requires that their objects be invisible, is it equally true that these 'objects' are not the same? The beloved Eurydice, the Eurydice of poetic memory, is absolutely different from the ideas contemplated by Plato. To say it somewhat romantically, the memory of *who* one loves is never deferred to the cold splendor of the universal.

It is, moreover, curious that, to have read the myth of Orpheus in reference to thinking rather than narrating, Arendt ends up neglecting the possibility of reinterpreting the myth as a dramatic version of the blind poet. Like Homer, Teiresias, and Ulysses' rhapsod, Orpheus *cannot* in fact see the one whose story he narrates. As the ancient image of the poet has it, he – at least symbolically and, certainly, in a sudden and unexpected manner – experiences the blindness that is typical of the narrator. Although temporary, it renders even more significant the drama of the gaze, which Orpheus plays out with his 'turning around.' The myth plays on the effects of an inexorable sequence. Turning his back on the light, Orpheus looks backwards. Eurydice returns into the darkness from which she came. In that moment – aligning himself with the classical figures of the rhapsod and the soothsayer – the poet, by antonomasia, becomes blind.

This cannot be said about the classical figure of the thinker – let us say the 'philosopher' – even if he shares with the poet the invisibility of the object. Again, for Arendt, the philosopher – more than being blind – is 'dead to the world' and, what is more, is happy that way. His professional characteristic consists in abandoning the world in order to set himself apart in the splendid activity of pure thought – the luminous region from which he never returns voluntarily to the darkness of the cave.

The very splendor of the objects of thought in fact nourishes the well-known Platonic metaphor, according to which what is invisible to the physical eye becomes maximally visible to the gaze of the mind. Accustomed to a contemplative life that is similar to death, the philosopher is never blind; on the contrary, he sees more than others – with an acute eye undisturbed by the worldly appearances – the intrinsic luminosity of the ideas. Those 'who have no clear visual models in their souls' are more similar to the blind.[14] The philosopher therefore applies the metaphor of blindness to others. Those who have eyes that are obscured by the *mere* appearances of the world do not know how to look at ideas. Given his familiarity with appearances, the poet is obviously one of their number.

For as much as invisibility ends up being the object that thought and narration have in common, in the ancient image, only the narrator has a special link with blindness. This is a classical link that Homer embodies in an exemplary way. Unlike Arendt, we begin to suspect that there is, in this, something more than the allusion to the posthumous gaze of the narrator.

If his blindness indicates the fact that the things which he narrates are not seen by him directly because they are already *past*, then nothing would forbid the poet from not being blind *within the scene*. Or, rather, nothing would forbid the rhapsod from being able to physically see the Ulysses whose story he is unknowingly narrating. In fact, in the physical sense, Orpheus the poet is not blind at all. And yet, even for him, there arises inexorably the law of blindness in the sudden dissolving of Eurydice. The blindness therefore seems to indicate not so much – or not only – the physical invisibility of narrated things, but rather the exigency that the narrator *not see* he or she whose story he tells. Put another way, in the examples cited above, the blindness of the poet comes to underline the necessity of the *lack of relation* [*l'irrelazione*] on the narrative scene. It does not amaze us, therefore, that – as definitive as the disappearance *of the narrated person from the scene* of the world is – death becomes a perfect image of this lack of relation. The one who narrates the story of a deceased person certainly does not narrate it to its protagonist.

The Arendtian thesis, according to which 'the essence of *who* one is comes into being only when life departs, leaving behind nothing but a story,' has been cited repeatedly.[15] We suspect that in death – in which Arendt too finds inspiration – there is something more than the realization of the *eudaimonia* as the lasting condition of a personal identity that is no longer subject to change. There is also a critical allusion to the separation, which *ideally* keeps the one who becomes narrated, at a distance from her narrator. Therefore, the scene of the Phaecians (which, in theory, would resist this thesis) provides a significant instance of it. Ulysses is in fact alive and is there, but the rhapsod does not know him, and does not see him because he is blind. Between them, there is only a story that results from the actions of the hero and that the rhapsod casually narrates to him. Neither can the narrator see Ulysses' tears. The posthumous gaze of the blind poet symbolizes at the same time a logic of 'unrelation' [*irrelazione*].

Arendt's preference for the heroic epic poem and for the blind poet thus risks confirming this same logic. Consumed by the theme of death, the possible contextual relations that the narrative scene contemplates disappear. All the attention is concentrated on the classical figure of a scene where the ideal death of the one who gets narrated, and the blindness of the one who narrates, sustain each other by symbolizing the absence, *between* the two, of any relation.

In the Milanese episode of Emilia and Amalia – while it is not as canonical as Homer, although it is certainly just as important – the contextual relation itself between the one who narrates and the one who gets narrated comes to undermine both the metaphor of blindness and the metaphor of death within the narrative scene. In the relationship between the two friends, there comes to the fore a narratable self who frustrates the two central elements of the ancient figure.

Immune to heroism, here the self once again finds her familiar sense [*sapore*] in the active relation [*relazione in atto*] with the one who grants her wish to hear herself narrated. Moreover, the self often makes of this relation her fundamental theater of reciprocal narrativity. The *invisibility* of memory thus comes to encounter a happy correspondence in the *visibility* of the one who asks for and receives the narration of her story. Just as blindness was a metaphor for the absence of relation, *seeing* is here a symbol for all five senses. It indicates simply that the relation is perceived, empirical, present. In the end, whether this text is oral or written ends up being, in the last analysis, inessential.

The horizon in which the narratable self inscribes her meaning [*senso*] is in fact a horizon of desire that manifests itself and nourishes itself in the relation of two *living* uniquenesses. This desire flows in the life-blood and has in death its natural, physical limit – not its object *in view* of an immortal fame. Emilia certainly does not want an identity, which, in the tangible form of the written text, can outlive her. Emilia wants her friend to tell her story to her, while she is still alive. Put another way, storytelling is the living's desire for narration, not the desire for the immortal fame of the dead.

Obviously the dead too have a story. Or, better, the dead are by now *nothing but* the tale of this story [*il racconto di questa storia*]. It is, however, a story *for us*, not for them. This is already true when the pronoun *we* indicates a general public; we read biographical texts. But it is, above all, true when the dead are *our* dead. The one who dies, always dies *to* someone (or at least it should be so). He or she is missed. A relationship is broken, and in the memory of the one who lives there remains a life-story whose tale can no longer be heard by the protagonist. In this way, the story gets told to others. Especially to those who already know it. The story, far from being valuable for its *newness*, is indeed in this case a co-memorative [*con-memorante*] repetition. The elaboration of the mourning lies in the narrative work of a memory, which requires the complicity of others in the evocation of a story of someone who is no longer with us. As if the link with the absent consisted in the thread of the tale, the story gets repeated until it is broken by forgetfulness [*l'oblio*].

While, for the one who dies, life ends perfectly in the moment of death, for the one who remains, only the overcoming of forgetfulness renders that death definitive. It happens that forgetfulness – the proverbial, merciful gift of time – is experienced by some just as guilt is felt by a murderer – especially by those who have their only consolation in looking after the narrative thread of a now lost relationship. We know well how this comes about. There are white-haired mothers who recount the story of their dead child, as though fifty years had not passed. Less dramatically, family meals and the reunions of old friends are full of stories of the dead, which intertwine with those of the living.

As for lovers, the phenomenon is not so clear. They in fact risk remaining entrapped in the tragic emphasis of a literary imagination that has for centuries celebrated the *authenticity* of love precisely in death. The death of the other, as the highest figure of un-relation [*irrelazione*], becomes the horizon in which love sustains itself. The preceding scene, that of the amorous relationship between two living creatures, becomes oriented in advance towards its mournful outcome. The love story seems not to contemplate reciprocal narrations worthy of interest. It lives rather in the *post mortem* tale, which legitimates itself through the loss of the other.

In the myth of Orpheus, if one looks closely at this legend, which by now has undergone two thousand years of interpretation, one point becomes clear. Founded as it is on the triad – love, poetry, death – the myth makes evident and instills in the Western imagination the great pathos of the lack of relation [*l'irrelazione*]. In other words, its fascination lies above all in the *mise en scène* of the separation between the two lovers; and in the absolute impossibility of bridging that separation – whether through the resurrection of Eurydice, which is interrupted by Orpheus's turning around, or through the poetry which sings of her, and enchants – because she is dead, she is not there, she is unreachable, lost forever. Drawing his inspiration from the now-dead Eurydice, Orpheus sings *of* her but not *to* her.

Perhaps this is why he mischievously turns around.

If he had turned around *afterwards* – outside the mouth of Hell, where seeing Eurydice, by then safe, was allowed – he would have had to tell her the story *about* her that had opened the doors of Hell for him. If he had turned around afterwards, along with an improbable happy ending, we would have been able to enjoy a love brought back to the narrative scene of the relationship – a banally happy love, a love accessible to all.

Instead, as we know, he turned around *before*: pushing her back in order that he enter into the myth.

NOTES

1 Virgil, *Georgics*, Book IV, vv. 464–6 (Cambridge, Massachusetts: Harvard University Press, 1916).

2 Charles Segal, *Orpheus: the Myth of the Poet* (Baltimore: Johns Hopkins University Press, 1989), p. 207.

3 Cf. Eric Havelock, *The Muse Learns to Write: Reflections on Orality and Literature from Antiquity to the Present* (New Haven: Yale University Press, 1986).

4 Mark Edmundson, *Literature Against Philosophy: Plato to Derrida* (Cambridge: Cambridge University Press, 1995), p. 13.

5 Plato, *The Symposium* 179d–e. See *Plato's Complete Works*, edited by John Cooper (Indianapolis: Hackett Publishing, 1997).

6 Mark Edmundson, *Literature Against Philosophy: Plato to Derrida*, p. 7. See also my *Figures of the Body: Philosophy and Politics* [translation forthcoming from the University of Michigan Press].

7 This is, of course, the central argument of Plato's *Symposium*. I refer the reader, for brevity, to my *In Spite of Plato*, p. 96.

8 Arendt, *The Life of Mind*, p. 79.

9 *Ibid.*

10 *Ibid.*, p. 85.

11 Virgil, *Georgics*, Book IV, v. 490–1.

12 *Ibid.*, v. 489.

13 Arendt, *The Life of Mind*, p. 87.

14 Plato, *The Republic*, 484c–d.

15 Cavarero, *The Human Condition*, p. 193.

9

THE VOICE OF EURYDICE

Why did you turn back,
That hell should be reinhabitated
Of myself thus
Swept into nothingness?

H. D., 'Eurydice'

The most famous modern transposing of the myth that gives voice to Eurydice is that of the poet Rainer Maria Rilke, who 'transfers its interpretive key from Orpheus himself to Eurydice.'[1] Actually, in 'Orpheus, Eurydice, Hermes,' she pronounces a single word; or rather, a question: 'who?' The fatal monosyllable is nonetheless crucial in the context.

The Rilkean poem describes a spectral scene, suspended in dark colors between the world of the living and the world of the dead, where only Orpheus and Hermes participate – with attention and intention – in what is happening. Eurydice knows nothing of Orpheus's undertaking, she knows nothing of the one who goes on ahead of her during the return among the living. She knows nothing of his desire and his impatience. This heightens the tension of the tale. She is no longer the blonde woman

who'd sometimes echoed in the poet's poems,
no longer the broad couch's scent and island,
nor yonder man's possession any longer.

[die in des Dichters Liedern manchmal anklang,
nicht mehr des breiten Bettes Duft und Eiland
und jenes Mannes Eigentum night mehr.]

Full of her own death, once again a virgin: 'her sex had closed like a young flower at the approach of evening,' she is by now a creature of the subterranean

103

world, perfect and indifferent. She is the sublime figure of absolute un-relation. The god Hermes, who walks alongside her, guiding her return, cannot help but show his disappointment when Orpheus turns around. 'He turned,' exclaims Hermes in pain, sharpening the tension of the tale. And it is precisely in response to this exclamation that Eurydice asks – 'who?' The monosyllable, in its inimitable dramatic brevity, thus indicates the total estrangement of Eurydice to what is happening around her. Eurydice is the central figure of the myth rewritten by Rilke, but the plot of the myth does not concern her.

While the title of the myth bears three names – *Orpheus, Eurydice, Hermes* – the text of Rilke's poetry omits them, preferring to impersonally name 'the man,' the 'god' and she, 'the so-beloved,' *die So-geliebte*. The *who* of Eurydice's questions thus resounds with a double importance. On the one hand, the response can in fact only consist in a name: Orpheus. On the other hand, it is precisely of Orpheus that Eurydice – 'full of her great death, so new that everything was incomprehensible to her' – conserves no memory, not even the memory of a name. The god therefore, in his divine wisdom, does not respond. The drama, the *pathos* of the scene indeed belongs only to the man and the god. Eurydice, futilely led along the path that leads upwards, does not know *who* walks ahead of her; 'wrapt in herself like one whose time is near, she thought not of the man who went before them.' She does not even know that she is following someone. 'Her paces circumscribed by lengthy shroudings, uncertain, gentle, and without impatience,' she is equally indifferent to her return down the road after Orpheus turns around. She, so-loved, is indeed now in her absolute solitude without any relation to the other, without any memory, and without any story. This is why the god did not respond to her question: 'who?' because, for the response to make any sense, he would have had to follow the name of Orpheus with the tale of his story.

An etymological approach to the names of the myth seems to curiously fit within the Rilkean perspective. We have already noted that the *orphanos*, which resounds in Orpheus, alludes to an abandonment, to a deprivation of the loved one. The name, moreover, is also significantly connected to the peculiar blindness of Orpheus, who – even more so as a poet – is *blind* [*orbus*], that is deprived [*orbatus*] of the sight of she who slips further away into the distance. The etymology of Eurydice seems rather to indicate, in the term *eurus*, a vastness of space or power, which, joining to *dike* [and thus *deiknumi*, to show], designates her as 'the one who judges with breadth' or, perhaps, 'she who shows herself amply.' Even the etymological guess, therefore, allows us to bind the figure of Eurydice to the vastness that resounds with her name – whether this is a boundless territory that she inhabits, or something that concerns her power to judge and to show; or, better, to judge by *showing* simply herself instead of referring to intentional words or gestures.

In Rilke, as Maurice Blanchot suggests, Orpheus is in fact constitutively rooted in her lack – 'twice lost' – because 'only in the song does Oedipus have power over Eurydice. But in the song too, Eurydice is already lost.'[2] The Rilkean Eurydice, on the other hand, has no roots *in the other*, but rather only in her intimate fullness that inhabits the vast quietude of Hell – 'her patient footsteps' showing her to be without intention and without aim. The Eurydice who is closed within her autonomy and undisturbed fullness is thus also the Eurydice of absolute un-relation. That is, she is a Eurydice who inhabits the narrative context, without, however, belonging to it. She is totally indifferent to a story that is no longer her story, totally dead in the irreversible death of her narratable self. The *who* of her question therefore appears as a word that, while inserting her voice into the plot of the Rilkean tale, nonetheless keeps her external to it.

Put another way, for as much as the god watches over her and the man holds her in the eyes of his impatient desire; for as much as the tension of the myth lies in a logic of the gaze – in the eyes which look ahead but project themselves (while hearing, 'like scent, remains behind') through the vision of what is happening behind – the point of view of Eurydice is nevertheless an empty gaze. Serenely immersed in the unintentional time of the pure present, she no longer has a past or a future, and thus she cannot have any story. Since, in the eternal present of death, the narratable self has vanished, Eurydice no longer has a story to tell or to listen to. The god, who does not respond to the *who*, knows full well how the circumstances render moot the classic rule of storytelling.

Rilke's poem, 'Song of the Woman to the Poet,' thus comes back to mind, like an inevitable echo. Already, the 'Woman' of the title excludes uniqueness, and thus the singularity of a story. Moreover – just as 'all's now unfolding; we are too, for we are nothing but such blissfulness' – 'Woman' is here a choral and de-individualized presence that has no personal story. Unlike Eurydice, however, it asks the poet to say the 'Infinite [which] keeps going' in it. 'You, the mouth, that we may apprehend it, you, you us-expresser, must remain,' it demands of the poet – the 'us-expresser' [*Uns-Sagender*].[3] If Eurydice is the figure of un-relation [*irrelazione*], then these women within the collective presence entertain with the poet a relation that makes of them the impersonal figure of an infinite cosmos that transcends them.

The one who expresses *them* does not tell their story, neither do they manifest the desire to hear the poet narrate a uniqueness that they do not, fatally, embody. As a feminine instrument of inspiration, they are only there *for* the poet.

If Rilke's Eurydice is the perfect figure of un-relation, the Eurydice of the American poet, Hilda Doolittle (1886–1961), more commonly known by her initials H.D., is instead the tormented figure of a relationship with Orpheus who renders herself autonomous only at the end, through a proud detachment.[4]

In the poem that bears her name, she recites a monologue that is staged immediately following the tragic turn of Orpheus. The initial verses, inaugurated by the exclamation 'So you have swept me back,' have the tone of a deep rancor. Perhaps citing the Rilkean version of the quiet fullness of death, and turning directly to Orpheus, Eurydice tells him that:

> If you had let me wait
> I had grown from listlessness
> Into peace,
> If you had let me rest with the dead,
> I had forgot you
> And the past.

Instead, Orpheus came in order to bring her back to the world of the living, and then he turned around, pushing her back down again. In the words of Eurydice, who, by now close to the light, is forced to return 'Where dead lichens drip/Dead cinders upon moss of ash,' he is not at all the courageous lover who has challenged the gods of Hell and, turning around, has erred due to his overflowing passion. Rather, he is arrogant and cruel. He is, in other words, the one on whose desire and error the whole story, the whole plot of the story, turns. He is the classical Orpheus, rewritten over and over, capable of charming new generations of poets and readers, who are moved first of all by the spell of his singing and by the tragedy of his story. In the verses of H.D., Eurydice, who is dragged up and down without being able to intervene, discovers the extraordinary possibility of commenting upon this story from her point of view. The story reveals itself to be one of cruelty and arrogance, always decided by he who has acted and erred in order to possess her again, without asking himself, or asking her, what the other's desire is.

If we think about it, the Orpheus of the classical myth is rather strange. He is a magician of words, and master of verse. He knows that the loved-one walks behind him, and yet he says nothing to her; he does not call her, does not communicate, does not ask anything. This poetic enchanter is suddenly mute, and is entrapped in the logic of the gaze – strange indeed.

Ovid himself had already emphasized this visual entrapment. The song of Orpheus has the power to paralyze [*stupuere*] and petrify those who listen to it. When Orpheus turns around and is 'struck' by the vanishing Eurydice, Ovid can thus make fun of him by comparing him with someone turned to stone by the gaze of Cerberus. The enchanting effect of Orphic poetry is therefore character-ized by a stupefying valence, which has its mythic model in the petrifying gaze: Cerberus, at the gates of Hell and, obviously, Medusa. Besides, in the Ovidian version, it is Eurydice herself who figures 'as an inhabitant of Hell, who transforms into stone any who looks upon her and who must go back inside (like Cerberus) to her infernal abode.'[5] Supported by the logic of the gaze, the song of Orpheus is a vocalization that immobilizes the listener. Orpheus is silent during his ascent out of Hell, and never speaks to Eurydice, who follows him mutely; this is why he pays the price for turning around – in a stupefied paralysis without words.

The way in which H.D., parodying this same logic, allows Eurydice to revisit the myth by focusing on the arrogance of the gaze of Orpheus, thus becomes rather significant.

She indeed asks him what he saw on her face when he turned around. The whole scene plays on the effect of the earthly light that filters into the margins of the exit and reflects upon her face, rendering her 'hyacinth colour caught from the raw fissure in the rock.' He possesses his own light. Turning his back towards the exit, his head is back-lit and is 'caught with the flame of the upper earth.' He therefore sees on the face of Eurydice the very reflection of that earthly light that his own turning-around renders, for her, unattainable.

The stenographic direction is truly subtle because – by reversing the perspectival focus that traditionally centers on the gaze of Orpheus (who, by turning around, looks at the loved-one, and we who look at him looking) – it transfers the attention on to her. Indeed, Eurydice is here, contrary to the poem by Rilke, an active center, and, at the same time, passive to vision. Or, rather, she is the one who sees the scene and describes it from her point of view, discerning in front of her the light that filters and the flames surrounding the head of Orpheus that create the back-lighting effect. But she is also the one who, seeing herself gazed upon by Orpheus, asks him what he is seeing and suggests the answer; or, rather, she usurps the usual privilege of the other's perspective.

The poem of H.D., in which everything plays out around this gesture, thus becomes legible in terms of the 'centrality of the system of the gaze in cinematic representation,' which Teresa De Laurentis rethinks from the perspective of feminist theory. In effect, the text of H.D., which almost follows De Laurentis's advice, seems both to take account of, and reverse, the classical modality of identification, which implies for the female spectator 'both positionings of desire, both the active and passive objectives; the desire for the other and the desire to be desired by the other.' The result is an inversion of the meaning of the story. In this poem, as in Plato and perhaps Ovid, there is neither pity nor emotion for the unhappy undertaking of Orpheus. Nor is he here the poet; rather, he is the ancient protagonist of the story, who is dethroned from his mythical function, and, thus, from his role as poet and narrator. The protagonist and narrator, the heroine and the poetic voice, turn out now to be Eurydice.

After having been illuminated by the reflected light that comes from the earth and from Orpheus, and after having glimpsed the azure sapphires and the gold crocuses 'on bright surface' of the earth – all flowers which are by now lost – Eurydice makes her home in perfect autonomy, in the colorless dark of her abode. 'At least I have the flowers of myself,' she says, 'I have the fervour of myself for a presence and my own spirit for light.'

Unlike the Eurydice of Rilke, whose fullness springs from the death of consciousness and intention, the Eurydice of H.D. acquires her full autonomy through the knowing and intentional course with which, although she cannot change it, she is able to rewrite the plot of her story. There is obviously a transition, filled with rancor and pride, from the love of the other to self-love. The latter is symbolized by the Hell that opens 'like a red rose,' according to the most famous metaphor of the feminine sex. What is a closed sex for Rilke, through a new virginity of impenetrable fullness, becomes an opened sex for H.D., albeit through the pleasure of a self-love that rejects the other – Eurydice embodies in both cases a figure of un-relation [irrelazione].

While she is self-conscious and combative in H.D.'s version, Eurydice sings her story only to herself, in the form of a monologue. The narration – which returns to the tone of an autobiography, while repeating the *pathos* of the ancient play – renounces the amorous scene and keeps the lovers separate.

NOTES

1 Charles Segal, *Orpheus: The Myth of the Poet*, p. 165.
2 Maurice Blanchot, *The Space of Literature*, trans. Ann Smock (Lincoln: University of Nebraska Press, 1982), p. 173.
3 English translation of Rilke's poetry taken from *New Poems*, trans. by J. B. Leishman (London: New Directions, 1964).
4 Hilda Doolittle, 'Eurydice,' in *Selected Poems* (New York: New Directions Books, 1988), pp. 36–40.
5 John Heath, 'The stupor of Orpheus,' *The Classical Journal*, **9(4)** (1996), pp. 363–4.

10

EROS AND NARRATION

Slowly I bend over you, slowly your breath
Runs rhythms through my blood
As if I said
I love you
And you should raise your head
Listening, speaking into the covert night:
Did someone say something?
Love, am I in your light?
Am I?

Muriel Rukeyser, 'Three Sides of a Coin'

We would like to tear Eurydice and Orpheus away from the funereal *pathos* of the ancient myth. We would like to imagine a different outcome for the story and picture the lovers, together once again, enraptured in the delight of a reciprocal tale. Similar to feminine friendships, love is indeed often characterized by a spontaneous narrative reciprocity. The reciprocal desire of a narratable self — which throws itself into autobiographical exercises in order to make the other into a suitable narrator of her story — is of course part of the narrative. In love, the expositive and relational character of uniqueness plays out one of its most obvious scenes. On the stage of love, the questions 'who am I?' and 'who are you?' form the beat of body language and the language of storytelling, which maintain a secret rhythm.

We are all — at least those of us who have had the fortune — perfectly familiar with this secret rhythm which, through the alternation of caresses and narration, lets the loved-one play out this desire. In the community of love, however, the other [*l'altro/a*] to whom the existent reciprocally appears is simply the beloved [*l'amato/a*].[1] And these bars that gender language could go on forever, because love is the clearest proof that the uniqueness of the *who* always has a face, a voice, a gaze, a body, and a sex; we could even say a soul, if we did not fear its traditional meaning of invisibility and substantiality. In love, the *who* is clearly an unrepeatable, embodied, uniqueness: this and not another, through the indissolubility of flesh and spirit. The *who* is not a *person*, but rather is always a *you* [*tu*]. If we choose to exemplify the whole discourse through the grammar of heterosexual love, it is not simply to pay homage to Orpheus and Eurydice, but rather to free the writing from the 'alienating' effect of this barred gendering [*sessuazione*] of language, which alerts us to its illegitimate one-sidedness.[2]

One never loves the *what* of the loved-one, rather one loves *who* he/she is. Indeed, one often loves the other in spite of what he/she is. 'You are unique,' 'you are the only one' ['*sei unico*,' '*sei unica*'] say lovers to one another. And in this way they simply say what is *obvious* about the existent. The relationship of lovers is indeed a privileged relationship where two uniquenesses appear *to each other* together, drawing on a corporal and verbal language of meaningful transparency. To say, as one does on occasion, 'I love your defects,' is simply part of the amorous game. What is assumed in this game is that 'I love you, despite your defects,' or, better, 'I love your defects, because they are yours,' or, rather, 'I love *who* you are, although I disapprove of *what* you are.' Even maternal love speaks this same language. It is the language of the 'in spite of' [*del 'nonostante'*], the language – which is, in a certain sense, immoral – of 'beyond good and evil;' where the judgment on the *what* of the loved-one becomes powerless before the appearance of *who the beloved is*. And this apparition is the unexpected, which we were nevertheless always waiting for. The paradox gets expressed in the words – 'you were made/born for me' ['*tu sei nato per me*']. And yet, this is not exactly what we mean; rather we mean that 'you appear as unique to me now as you did when you were born.'

As many have noted, the language of lovers is anti-social. And it is obvious that this should be the case, because *society* – all the more so in the modern understanding of the term – is perhaps the greatest impediment to the in-born [*in-nata*] self-revealing of uniqueness. Within the social scene there appears in fact only the *what* of the protagonists, never their *who*. In society, needs and forces expose themselves – as infinitely negotiable, replicable, and substitutable *whats* [*cose*]. The unique, rather, in its absolute difference, is constitutively insubstitutable. All loved-ones are unique for the lover, just like all children are unique for the mother. It is therefore not difficult to understand why, for millennia, lovers have challenged social rules and conventions, transgressing divisions of caste and subverting hierarchies. Such structures limit themselves to defining what someone is, and indeed, increasingly, what someone has. Social qualifications, even more than the qualities of the loved-one, thus become the inauthentic surface or appearance [*scorza*] of the *who*, which must be torn down by lovers.

The joy of love lies indeed in the nakedness of a shared appearance [*comparizione*] that does not tolerate qualifications but simply exposes two uniquenesses to each other. It is then possible that the lovers will *remember* the twofold movement of the relation with the mother, at once passive and active: the originary impulse toward self-exposure. All the fragility of finitude is here again, in the entirety of the human existence, which refuses, or mocks, every internal distinction between its flesh and spirit; since the only active distinction [*distinzione in atto*] is now rather that of two unrepeatable uniquenesses, who distinguish themselves by mutually appearing together [*comparando insieme*]. There is therefore no fusion into unity, despite the myth that we have heard told to us for millennia. The myth is false – because it is false to celebrate existence in rites of dissolution, turning the impulse to love into a desire for death.

The myth indeed tells us how love and death, *eros* and *thanatos*, willingly merge – despite some circumstantial shudders – in the seductive myth of dissolution. The two uniquenesses, fusing into the one-all, disappear into a whirlpool of nowhere [*gorgo del nessun luogo*] – the very same place, says a well-known variant of the myth, from which they emerged, namely, the mother. Birth and death, the eternal seduction of the inorganic, would therefore amount to the same thing – provided that the finite, if it is allowed some fleeting shimmer of glory, burns out in the act of its annihilation; provided that the infinite conserves its supremacy, and death its voracity.

But, despite the ancient myth, lovers do not want to die, merging *into* each other. Rather, they want the full splendor of the finite according to the reciprocal uniqueness that exposes them and distinguishes them. Loving each other, they are simply reborn into the inaugural fragility of their existence. Love indeed offers no protection against the fragility of the *who*. Its exposition is total and irremediable: it asks to be accepted, not to be nullified. The sexual rite, therefore, is not one of a fusion, which would nullify uniqueness, frustrating the act itself. It is, if anything, the rite of repeating the beginning: exposing once again the naked exposure, not yet covered by any 'what,' that inaugurates the appearance of every human being as unique, because only in the moment of birth is every human being a pure *who*, to which is in no way added any *what*. Put another way, the one who has just been born is *exemporarily* without qualities – although it is already, as Oedipus well understood, this existent and not another. The newborn's body, her face, her sex are indeed not *qualities* of the existent – rather, they are the spiritual matter of its uniqueness. Appearing to each other with indifference regarding qualities – an indifference which finds its height in the orgasm – lovers therefore come to repeat the beginning of their existence. They do not return into the womb of the mother; on the contrary, they are ousted again into the inaugural nudity of an appearance – one which now has the perfect relational character of a co-appearance [*comparizione*].

While not condoning its falsity, we can thus understand the error on which the credibility of the myth hinges. It is, in fact, the very experience of orgasm that is often identified with death – where the pleasure would coincide with self-annihilation within the impersonal and autonomous logic of the flesh. Nonetheless what dies here, or what is already dead, is nothing else than the inflated *subject* of its qualities. The loss of the meaning of *what* one is, and knows oneself to be – the total *oblivion* of one's own personal qualities and social markers – thus get mistaken for the death of the self. However, we are dealing with a repetition of birth, undergone by a self without qualities who, precisely because of this magnificent stripping away of qualities, can suddenly *remember* the originary coinciding of life and existence. The prevalence of the body is indeed here only the inherence of the existence of the body – or, rather, the spirituality of the flesh and fleshiness of the spirit, which makes their indiscernibility the miracle of uniqueness. Lovers undress themselves in order to caress their naked bodies, and yet only in the orgasm is the nakedness of the existence truly such, in so far as it is stripped of every quality.

There is a great deal of common sense in the proverbial 'love at first sight.' The expression signifies that one can fall in love with someone suddenly and at first sight. But at first sight one cannot see anything but a physical appearance, and thus one can only fall in love with the beauty that it embodies, as Plato would say. And yet we know well that this is not so. We fall in love, rather, with *who* shines through that body and that face; these become beautiful because they are his or her body and face. They are beautiful in so far as they are unique and felt to be such with an indisputable intensity. Since the criterion for this beauty does not belong to the realm of judgment and, perhaps, not even to taste; rather it belongs to the realm, indifferent to the 'what,' of the sudden manifestation of uniqueness. Here too, therefore, in this immediacy that *strikes* the gaze, the flesh and spirit of the loved-one are united and reveal an unrepeatable uniqueness, while its qualities rapidly begin to vanish.

Love – always the phenomenon of the unexpected which we were always waiting for – has some uncontrollable and bizarre times, both in its upspringing and in its end. Love, as we often lament, is brief. It easily succumbs to the unhappy prevalence of qualities over the irremediable uniqueness of *who* we loved. And we are then amazed by the fact that we had never seen *what* he or she is. But it is precisely this 'what' of the luminous revelation of the existent that occupies the entire scene of mutual apparition, and which we could not see. We could not see the qualities that render him or her similar to many others, the *judgable* qualities. As the saying goes: love is blind – not because it turns upon the *invisible*, but because it is without judgment with respect to that which others see. It experiences another type of gaze – a gaze that comes from the agonizing experience of a finite being's appearance, in its constitutive fragility.

Lovers, indeed, fully perceive the fragility of their reciprocal appearing. Trusting in the *touch* of each other, once more naked like the day they were born, they then entrust *one another* to the language of the body. It is said, by the way, that women know how to *touch* the loved-one delicately, because of their habit of 'handling' newborns. The truth is that the human being, when totally exposed, is totally fragile – even, perhaps more so, in its adult flesh. The maps of the erogenous zones are thus a ridiculous technical support (a product of the scientific community of sex) for those who ignore the fact that they are touching a unique existent in the wholeness of his/her self-exposure. He/she is touching a *who*, all over the deep surface of his/her irresidual appearance – because this is love: a relationship that constitutes an existence as an intimate exteriority, as a singular unity always already exposed to the other.

The misery of love lies in loving without being loved. Precisely because the exposition of uniqueness wants the relationship, or wants the mutual apparition, the loved-one who does not love back is here in fact the only *apparent*. The other creature, the lover, remains instead an inapparent existence due to the lack of relation [*irrelazione*] – because, no matter how much she exposes herself, her uniqueness appears to no one. The status of existence as co-appearance has precise rules and, in love, rules that are rather cruel. The one who exhibits herself without appearing to the other remains, paradoxically, an unexpressed uniqueness. She remains a *what*, in front of a *who*. This is a well-known infelicity, which, on occasion, leads to suicide; in such a way that, in this case, love and death really do go together. The suicide of the unhappy lover is nonetheless a paradoxical figure, or, rather, the figure of a paradoxically unexpressed uniqueness. 'I kill myself because you do not love me and because I do not exist for you,' thinks the unhappy one; after my death, you will understand *who* loved you and, thus, you will love me. The suicide thus follows the logic of a desperate contradiction. On the one hand, it comes to confirm the death of a *who*, who died because of the inappearance of her exhibition and – on the other hand – tends to fabricate the posthumous presence of a *who*, who would gain, thanks to her disappearance, the right of co-appearance [*comparizione*].

I kill myself because you do not love me, and because for you I do not exist. After my death, you will understand *who* it was that loved you, and therefore you will love me. In the paradox of the suicide, there is thus, in the end, the desire of a narratable self, which dislocates itself, tragically, through its posthumous narration.

This tragic side of love depends in great part upon its exclusive character. Love 'captures' the lovers in the dual scene of their relationship and keeps them *out* of the world. The world, others, are only the background of this scene – a territory in which they can take an excursion, or an agreeable setting for the amorous tourist or, sometimes, a public to be shocked. It is indeed this exclusive character that distinguishes love from friendship. Friendship is a type of love where the other is unique and yet does not appear to the exclusion of others. Friendship does not leave out the world, it lives in the everyday. Friendship knows, furthermore, that, in being human, the flesh is spiritualized even without being touched. Friendship is the co-appearance of the *who* without the emotional confirmation of *eros*. It is a co-appearance that multiplies itself, making 'two' into a network of friends.

Given its affinity with friendship, it is therefore not by chance that love shares with it the narrative impulse. Telling one another one's own story – and, as often happens, preceding body-language with an autobiographical tale – the lovers testify to the way in which the narratable self coincides with the expositive *who*, who finally comes, in love, to her nude co-appearance. In other words, *who* appears to the other always has her uniqueness in a story which, on the level of its insubstitutable physical identity, makes the loved-one this and not others. In so far as he or she loves *who* the other is, every loved-one knows that their own narratable self is a part of this co-apparition. 'It seems like I've always known you,' says the lover on occasion; but, in truth, she wanted to say, 'it is as though, from the beginning, I knew your whole story.'

In the amorous relationship, the frequent reciprocity of the autobiographical exercise is therefore above all a finalized exchange that constitutes the other as one's own biographer. The dynamic is always the same, as we already identified in female friendships: I will tell you my story in order to make you capable of telling it to me. The narratable self's desire for narration manifests itself in autobiographical exercises in order to entrust one's own story to another's storytelling. It is helpful to note that, again, what is at stake is not an assessment of qualities, or the frequency of a biographical response. Rather, the point is that I become for you a narratable identity, someone whose story you can tell, since my identity is by now in the care of this story that you know by heart.

As we know well, thinking of the loved-one is indeed always recounting the loved one to one's self [*raccontarlo fra sé e sé*]. By offering to the loved-one this very tale, the lover makes the amorous game into a scene in which two narratable selves complete each other, through the complicity of their desire.

Texts, which can be soon forgotten, are inessential for the lovers, who reiterate their narrations without getting bored. Perhaps the text could come later, reconstructed through the infidelity of voluntary memory, often with rancor when the love is no longer there. Biographical exercises of love are indeed only valid within the context – in the secret rhythm that alternates back and forth between the language of the body and the language of storytelling.

We can thus consider another well-known myth, which the tradition stubbornly continues to tell us, to be false. This myth wants to make us believe not only that the language of the body does not need to involve the language of storytelling – but that the first is most perfect when the second is totally absent. 'Carnally loving a stranger,' is its basic message, updating the autarchy of the *eros* with a sort of positive spin on the 'vulgar' love despised by Plato. Consider, as an example, the film *Last Tango in Paris* by Bernardo Bertolucci, where the knowledge of the other's story signals, tragically, the end of a love entrusted entirely to the language of the body. Like the myth about love and death, there is a grain of truth to the myth about the isolation of eros. In its modern sense, the autarchy of eros is traditionally attributed only to the male sex; while women would be – through a strange tenacity of the romantic stereotype – 'sentimental' and inclined towards the language of storytelling, if not to fantasizing [*affabulazione*]. The grain of truth in the myth is therefore easily revealed; it alludes to the fact that the narrative character of feminine friendships signals a female specificity, a conception of love that is nauseating to the champions of autarchic eroticism.

As pointed out earlier, through the scission between 'body' and 'soul' that characterizes the subject, women have an easier time approaching the experience of the narratable self. In other words, their so-called sentimentalism is the coherent aspect of a gathering of uniqueness, which, in the amorous scene as well, confirms itself through the familiar indistinguishability of embodied existences and life-stories. As poets of both sexes know well, love is too complex a phenomenon to leave to the advocates of autarchic eros.

The dream of this autarchy, on the other hand, might be diagnosed as one of the most blatant pathologies on the subject. It ought not to amaze us that, after having founded itself on the dichotomy of body and soul, the subject succumbs rather easily to the unstoppable progress of its internal scissions. The clinical description of this pathology is familiar enough: reason, the passions, the emotions, the feelings, impulses and so forth all become *parts* of the subject, which must be located in an apposite site, according to variable maps, but always tending towards a precise regionalization. The region of the 'vulgar' eros, which Plato located in the bowels, is one of the more stable. Eros too has its traditional territory deep in the body, reclaiming an autonomy from both reason and the sentiments.

Only the modern age, however, makes this territory into a paradox. For the moderns, this is both an individual 'vice,' and the thrill of de-individualization; the subjective *libido* and the impersonal law of the flesh, or, the act of loving a stranger in order to become a stranger to oneself. Seduced by the autarchy of eros, modernity thus ends up losing the secret rhythm, which, by interpolating the language of the body and the language of storytelling, makes love into a feast of uniqueness. It ends up losing the identity of *who* we happen to love, and the unjudgable reasons for which it is he or she that we love and not another.

We would like for eros and narration to be inseparable for the inconsolable Orpheus, whom we would like to separate from his myth. Basically, a slight shift of perspective is enough, and the myth changes. By saying that the poet sings of Eurydice, the loved-one, of her story, Virgil himself becomes an accomplice in our game. The fatal 'turning around' can, subtly, take on a different meaning.

Indeed, Orpheus turned around not only to see Eurydice and touch her, but also to sing this story *to her*. In spite of the fact that the myth has made of him the poet of Hell and of death, his inability to resist turning around is the gesture of a lover who cannot refuse love as a scene of reciprocal narration and co-apparition. The *lived* amorous experience has oriented, from the start, the everydayness of a gesture that even the gods of Hell would have had to forgive. The lovers look at each other, they touch each other and they tell each other their stories. There is no god who can ignore this, not even those who promise the impossible.

Orpheus turned around, therefore, not because of weakness or malice, but because it was cruelly foreseen that he give in to the call of a secret rhythm – one which was more irresistible than his song.

NOTES

1   [TN: Here again, the next few paragraphs have already appeared in English. I make use of this translation, with a few alterations. Cf. 'Birth, love, politics,' in *Radical Philosophy*, pp. 20–2.]

2   Here I have in mind the critique of the predominant, heterosexual paradigm developed by Judith Butler in *Bodies that Matter* (New York: Routledge, 1993). On the other hand, I would like to indicate how, by posing the problem of '*who* comes after the Subject,' Jean-Luc Nancy rightly recognizes that the language of the *who* cannot leave the double gendering out of consideration.

Part IV

NARRATORS

11

SCHEHERAZADE TRAPPED IN THE TEXT

Memory is the Muse-derived element of the epic art in a broader sense
and encompasses its varieties. In the first place among these is the one
practiced by the storyteller. It starts the web, which all stories together
form in the end. One ties to the next, as the great storytellers, particularly the Oriental ones, have always readily shown. In each of them there
is a Scheherazade who thinks of a fresh story whenever her tale comes to
a stop.

Walter Benjamin,
'The Storyteller: Reflections on the Works of Nikolai Leskov'[1]

Devoting himself to a problem that would never have troubled Arendt, Roland
Barthes proclaims that 'as an institution the author is dead' – its 'biographical
person has disappeared.'[2] Soon after, by decree of other contemporary
philosophers, following the possible obsequies of the reader, the author 'died' in
favor of the unquestioned centrality of the *text*. The literary establishment was
not satisfied with this. On the contrary, the *renowned* theme of 'writing's
relationship with death,' that is, 'the relation which language maintains with
death,' has emerged as one of the stable pillars of contemporary thought.[3]

For Foucault, this is a productive relation that opens up the work of the text.
Along with death, in order to stop that which will stop it, language reflects on
itself as in a mirror, and reacts to the decree of its extinction by multiplying itself
infinitely through this specular game. The scene of the Phaecians would bear
witness to this, where 'the song of the rhapsod already sang of Ulysses before the
Odyssey and before Ulysses himself (since Ulysses listens to him), but the rhapsod
will sing of him indefinitely after his death (since for him, it is as if Ulysses were
already dead); and Ulysses, who is living, receives this song as a wife receives a
dead husband.' In short, the tale returns circularly to tell itself, in a kind of dance

with death; it produces itself through a potentially infinite narration on the threshold of that *end*, which attracts and generates the narration itself.

Still following Foucault, the example taken from the *Odyssey* nonetheless risks obscuring a crucial difference between the moderns and the ancients – which is, essentially, the difference between the centralization of writing and the form of oral narration. Contemporary philosophy, acting upon the death of the author, has indeed knowingly immersed itself in the mortal sign of writing – the true paradigm of the *text* – recognizing the way in which this is 'linked to sacrifice, even to the sacrifice of life.' The Homeric epic, by contrast, placed the hero at the center – turning his death into an occasion for the immortality of the tale – 'the narrative then redeemed this accepted death;' or, rather, the tale took death and immortalized the protagonist.[4] Foucault, unexpectedly sharing the Arendtian reading of the hero, thus comes to direct us towards a useful collaboration between the ancient tale and death. In the Homeric epic, the narration feeds on death. Beyond asking for a sacrifice of life, as happens with the moderns [modern narrators], the narration compensates the hero for his mortal fate. The tale owes its immortalizing function to this very death.

For Foucault, *The Arabian Nights* stands in clear opposition to the Greek epic, in so far as its motivation is not to die: 'one spoke, telling stories into the early morning, in order to forestall death, to postpone the day of reckoning that would silence the narrator, Scheherazade's narrative is an effort to keep death outside the circle of life.'[5] Unlike the Homeric narration, Scheherazade denies death the function of strengthening the immortalizing power of the tale. Unlike contemporary philosophers, she turns the tale into an even more powerful means to ward off death. There is, however, a curious affinity between Scheherazade's scene and what Foucault sees happening at the court of the Phaecians. In both, the tale proliferates and multiplies, as though in a game of mirrors. (But, one must add, the young Arab girl neither sings about death nor does her listener receive this song 'as the wife receives the dead husband.')

If we place the Foucauldian reading of the Homeric episode next to what Borges says about *The Arabian Nights*, this curious affinity becomes even stronger. Borges is not content to register the perseverance with which Scheherazade always recounts a new story each night in order to postpone her death until the following day; rather he interrupts the simplicity of this linear succession with one of his typical literary *fictions*. This happens, for example, when the protagonist of *The Garden of Forking Paths* remembers 'that night which is at the middle of the Thousand and One Nights when Scheherazade (through a magical oversight of the copyist) begins to relate word for word the story of the Thousand and One Nights, establishing the risk of coming once again to the night when she must repeat it, and thus on to infinity.' The narration, multiplying itself within itself, becomes 'infinite and circular.'[6] The key to this extraordinary

Borgesian fiction is obviously the distraction of the copyist. The game of infinite reduplication does not concern the narrator, but rather a technical error in the *tradition of the text*. The text, by now independent of Scheherazade – or, rather, the text with respect to which 'the death of the author' had already been decreed – becomes the true and only protagonist of this infinite circularity that indefinitely puts off death.

Borges' game is quite subtle, because the interpolated story of the copyist is what functions as a *frame*. As is well known, the book of *The Arabian Nights* is a compilation of fantastic stories within a story that acts as a frame. A heavily used device in the narrative of invention (think of the *Decameron*), the frame 'exhibits, flauntingly, the very act of narrating.'[7] The frame is therefore the tale that generates the tale, exhibiting without mystery its generative function. In *The Arabian Nights*, this consists in a story that opens and closes the internal proliferation of the stories.

As is well known, this is a story of the sultan Shahriyàr. Betrayed by his wife, the sultan kills her and extends his thirst for revenge to the entire feminine gender. He decides to marry a new virgin each night, in order to have the pleasure of then killing her at sunrise. The courageous Scheherazade enters the scene precisely in order to stop this slaughter. After offering herself as wife to the bloody king, before dawn she begins to tell him an engaging story, which is interrupted by the daylight. The suspension of the story, whose outcome he desires to know, thus suspends the death of the narrator as well. The story picks up again at sunset and the ritual begins again. Nights follow upon nights, and stories upon stories. Until, after the last story, Scheherazade is able to avoid death by showing the children (sons, it seems) born from the conjugal loves of the thousand and one nights. The first story is therefore taken up in the end, and happily concluded. It acted as a frame for all the other stories.

True to the standards of the classic model, the story of Scheherazade and the sultan, the frame-story, is not told by Scheherazade; rather, it is the story that legitimates the role of narrator that she assumes in relation to the other stories. If a frame is such because it generates and embraces the proliferation of tales, but does not confuse itself with them, then the literary invention of Borges works to upset the usual narrative order at a crucial point. Indeed, the distraction of the copyist puts the story which acts as a frame into the mouth of Scheherazade, turning it into one of the many stories from which it *should* distinguish itself. Obviously, the effect is rather disconcerting: 'None is more disturbing than that of the six hundred and second night, magical among all the nights. On that night, the king hears from the queen his own story. He hears the beginning of the story, which comprises all the others and also – monstrously – itself.'[8]

There are at least two disturbing elements: to the monstrosity of the tale, which encompasses all the others including itself, we might add the surprise of the sultan who hears his own story told to him. It thus seems that, following the fictions of Borges' inspiration, it has happened that we have met up once again with the paradox of Ulysses. The situation is truly curious and complex. Of course, it is the scene of the Phaecians that continues to unsettle things. There is a certain kinship between Foucault and the Arab tale, through the continual narration that wants to keep death far away and therefore maintains a relation with it. Borges, for his part, dwells heavily upon on the infinite circularity of the tale – going so far as to repropose the well-known situation in which someone hears another tell his own story. Within the perspective of the acclaimed centrality of the *textual* game, Scheherazade continues to be a mere function of the tale.

Obviously there is a more naïve way of looking at the figure of Scheherazade. In this extraordinary scene of misogyny – which sees the sultan strangle the unfaithful wife, and then immediately decapitate all of her servants, in order to then save himself for a long series of nuptial nights, all of which end with a morning strangling – Scheherazade is a special figure. Indeed, we come to know that 'she had read the books of literature, philosophy and medicine. She was learned and knew poetry by heart, had studied historical reports and was acquainted with the sayings of men and the maxims of Kings. She was intelligent, wise and refined. She had read and learned, and had a prodigious memory. Whatever she learned, she always remembered.'[9] There is thus, within the narrative construction, a clear two-sided game. On one side lies the sultan, as the symbol of a masculine position of misogyny and cruelty. On the other side lies Scheherazade, as the symbol of a feminine knowledge capable of giving the lie to the misogynist prejudice, and capable of overcoming its violent effects.

Nonetheless, the most interesting element does not consist in this somewhat anomalous victory of the feminine over the masculine, but rather in the type of knowledge that Scheherazade embodies: the womanly art of narration. In other words, the young girl – well read and equipped with a good memory – symptomatically affirms on Arabic soil the 'muse' that Homer invokes, or the myth of Calliope who, like every muse, is the daughter of Mnemosyne. We need not even return to the ancient epic in order to encounter the figure of the female *storyteller* – old witches and wise wet-nurses, grandmothers and storks, fates and sibyls, can be encountered at every stage of the literary imagination to attest to the sources and the feminine practices of narration.[10] Having entered into our narrative tradition at the beginning of the eighteenth century and having straight away become the *female narrator [narratrice] par excellence*, Scheherazade thus functions as a significant link between an East and a West that come together through the feminine matrix of the tale. Women tell stories: there is always a woman at the origin of the *enchanting* power of every story.

Alert to the feminine matrix of the tale, we can therefore go into detail regarding the story that acts as a frame. Perspicacious and courageous by nature, the young Arab girl reads, remembers and recounts. She is therefore not the author of the stories, but rather the one who transmits them. The art of choosing the occasions and the modes of the narration is nonetheless completely hers. No one, in fact, forces her to make the most of her talent; on the contrary, it is she herself who decides to risk her life in order to save other virgins from a certain death with her art. In addition to finding herself in a situation that requires her to tell stories in order to stay alive, Scheherazade lives in order to tell stories – and in order that other women live. Death, which looms at the end of every story, is challenged by an explicit choice. By decree of a champion of virility – which makes the maidens' sexual submission coincide with their murder – there is each day in the realm, 'a maiden married and a women dead,' according to an obsessive rhythm that consumes in a single day the virginity and the life of an ever new wife. Contrary to the law of the sultan, which makes death follow sex, the law of Scheherazade makes a story follow sex, disconnecting sex itself from death and from the rite of deflowering. Narration and conjugal love go together, step by step, for one thousand and one nights. The tale not only stops death, but also gains the time to generate life. Within the narrative scene of the relation, despite its terrifying side, eros and storytelling obey a single rhythm.

There is a detail of the greatest importance that usually gets overlooked in the analyses of *The Arabian Nights*. Scheherazade does not tell her first story to the sultan, but rather to her sister. Indeed, her sister had permission to sleep on a bed lower than the nuptial bed in the room of the couple. At the request of her sister, Scheherazade thus begins a tale before sunrise that enthralls the sultan until the sun comes up and which makes him postpone the death of the narrator until the next day. He is still not the explicit addressee of a tale that is requested by him, but rather only a listener knowingly seduced by the narrative art and her strategy of *suspension*.

It is in fact typical of every story to demand that the tale stop only at the end, when the story itself is finished and silence can speak. As Karen Blixen says, every good narrator knows that 'where the narrator is faithful, eternally unbendingly faithful to her story, there, at the end, silence will speak.'[11] The story is always suspended *at* its end. Evidently formed by the 'hard school' of oral narration, Scheherazade knows that the suspension of a tale belongs to the genuine art of storytelling. She therefore runs no real risk when faced with the bloodlust of her husband. The logic of the tale defeats the misogynist desire for revenge. Constitutively suspended at the end of the story, the development of the tale overcomes the desire of the listener up until its irresistible conclusion.

This conclusion, however, in *The Arabian Nights*, is at once the end of a story, and one that generates the beginning of another story. A masterpiece of its genre, the Arabic text is constructed like a game of Chinese boxes – where the characters of the stories told by Scheherazade likewise tell stories whose protagonists appear as narrators of subsequent stories, and so forth *ad infinitum*. Indeed, the number one-thousand-and-one, in medieval Arabic culture, represents infinity. The mechanism internal to the narrative plot is potentially capable of proliferating the tales infinitely. The interminable germination of the tales can thus inspire in Borges – and in his followers – the extraordinary fiction of the reader who finds himself trapped in the text. Here one could add, to the classic figure of the infinite-as-circularity, the form of a labyrinth with a thousand possible routes, but without exit. Everything is inside the tale and the tale is everything. It is not lives that produce stories; it is rather the stories that produce the characters who *believe* that they are alive. The tale is not limited to seducing the reader with its illusionist capacity, but creates for him/her the illusion of a real existence that is unaware of being a tale. Turning upon itself, the illusionist effect of the narration is therefore able to go well beyond what Plato himself could imagine.

There is still another possible meaning in this game of the infinite plot that interweaves the stories. From a certain point of view, *The Arabian Nights* in fact lends itself to be understood as something akin to Arendtian 'realism' on biography – since Arendt founds her theory of narration on the distinction between true stories and invented stories, in order to then specify that the tale is limited to the narration of the life-story that results from the actions of the one who really lived them. Even more surprising, therefore, is the hypothesis that such realism ends up being linked with what is perhaps the most famous example of the 'fantastic.' The point of convergence consists in the central role played by the plot [*intreccio*].[12]

Exposed, relational and contextual, the Arendtian self leaves behind a life-story that is constitutively interwoven with many other stories. 'The disclosure of the "who" through speech and the setting of a new beginning through action, always fall into an already existing web where their immediate consequences can be felt. Together, they start a new process that eventually emerges as the unique life-story of the newcomer, affecting uniquely the life-stories of all those with whom he comes into contact'.[13] The stories that result from the self-exhibiting of unique beings within a plural scene are already inextricably interwoven with one another. This is why Homer-the-*storyteller* is at the same time the first historian. Since it results from the interweaving of individual stories, the great History of humanity is nothing but the book of single stories – stories that Homer knows how to narrate, both in their uniqueness and in their interweaving. And because he puts into words the plot of the stories from which History results, Hannah Arendt assures us that the Homeric epic is more 'realistic' than modern historiography.

Moreover, like Scheherazade, Homer, too, emphasizes the interweaving/plot [*l'intreccio*] by telling of heroes who make themselves into narrators of stories, which in turn contain the other tales of later stories. Both Plato and Aristotle draw a famous literary theory from this. Rivers of critical ink have been spilled on this topic, and it is impossible to treat it exhaustively here. Limiting ourselves to a page from Plato's *Republic*, we can, however, summarily present the essential nucleus. The goal is to enquire after the strange bonds that seem to weave the 'realism' of the Arendtian type together with the archaic canons of the fantastic.

Liberally adapted to the Homeric episode that has accompanied us from the outset, Plato's argument consists in an elementary distinction. It underlines the way in which Homer's tale – which concerns the scene of the Phaecians, and the autobiographical tale – which flows from the mouth of Ulysses, are of different types. The first is a simple narration [*diegesis*], the second is an imitative narration [*mimesis*].[14] Put more simply, *diegesis* is an indirect discourse of the narrator, which tells how 'the Muse inspired the rhapsod to sing of the feats of heroes, a story whose fame then reached to the heavens,' etc.; while the *mimesis* consists in the Homeric imitation of the direct discourse of Ulysses, who, speaking in the first person, says: 'I am Odysseus, the son of Laertes, and I am known among men and gods,' etc.[15] Beyond the fortunes, even the recent ones, of this first sketch of narrative theory, a decisive fact becomes clear. Ever since the great epic tale, the *storyteller* essentially narrates stories in the course of which the protagonists of the stories themselves narrate their story in the first person. What is more, they in turn *produce* these stories, whether it is with the indirect discourse or the mimetic one, within the narration of others' stories. Not only do the stories intersect, but they reproduce each other. The structure of *The Arabian Nights* does not seem far from this. As Benjamin puts it, the musal element of the epic is the same as the great narrator Scheherazade.[16]

The Homeric epic, made even more interesting by this affinity with the Arab story, is thus capable of furnishing us with a few crucial ideas. First of all, as Hannah Arendt emphasizes, it rescues the identity of the hero from oblivion because it tells the story that follows his glorious feats and transmits their fame beyond death. Second, once again in perfect concordance with Arendt's reading, the epic puts into words the constitutive interweaving of the individual stories from which the great History results. Third, and this time departing from Arendt, the epic suggests that the time and place of the narration are *not* always and necessarily posthumous. By imitating direct discourse, *mimesis* indeed places the tale of the hero in the time and place of its happening. *Mis-en-scène* by the Homeric *mimesis*, Ulysses recounts his story to the Phaecians after he has heard it told by the rhapsod. *Mis-en-scène* by the tragedy – which is mimetic art in its purest state – Oedipus listens to others tell the story of his life. The *mise-en-scène* is obviously a fiction, a representation: in other words, a tale. Looking closely, its representing does, however, have a sense that goes beyond pure artifice. It consists in the implicit re-presentation of what we might call its *originary scene*.

This scene does not coincide with the artistic work, but with a spontaneous narrative practice, perhaps inscribed in the human condition itself, which generates the work and legitimates it. Put crudely, human beings tell each other their stories and bring back stories that they have heard being told, employing a narrative practice that goes back to the dawn of time. The constitutive scene of the tale completes a narratable self that desires the relation and belongs to a *real* context where human beings tell each other stories. Following Benjamin again, 'experience which is passed on from mouth to mouth is the source from which all storytellers have drawn.'[17] Hypothetically originary, or rather more ancient than the professional *storyteller* and capable of being the origin of his role, such a practice of narration through interweaving/plot [*intreccio*] is the true inspiration of the work. In its labor of representation, the work indeed limits itself to opening a literary scene that re-presents it in the form of a fiction.

Put simply, *mimesis* does not create, *it imitates*. Amazingly, it imitates even when it is *diegesis*, because it imitates a narrative practice that is really at work in human relations, where indirect discourse is already one of the modalities of storytelling that is interwoven with others. This is obviously still a part of different scenes of storytelling today – from gossip to the family feast, from the meetings of friends to conversations with strangers, and, especially, in friendship and love. To be sure, as Benjamin laments, the modern epoch abruptly distances itself from the ancient experience of narration, which configured itself as 'community.' Nevertheless, as especially women and lovers know, some scenes of narrative reciprocity resist the impact of modernity and renew, under different forms, the originary practice of storytelling. Their reality is diffused, and lives in the everyday.

Having come from Arendtian realism, intrigued by Scheherazade and invited by Homer, we are thus led to an even more material kind of realism; or better still, to the everydayness of certain experiences where the habit of narrating stories, one's own as well as others', is a fact. In order not to lose the thread of the argument, we will limit ourselves to drawing some conclusions, formulating a sort of literary 'theory.' This theory begins by claiming that narrative imitation by plot [*a intreccio*] responds directly to the practical context that engendered it.

Obviously this is a complex and marvelous imitation, which has standards, developments and inventions. It seduces, through the *imitative* impulse of its art, the very context that engenders it – a feature that annoyed Plato. Moreover, the work has its own history, or rather belongs to a history of literature that articulates it in genres and subsequent recountings. If our hypothesis is true, then Homer and Scheherazade, in so far as they are *storytellers* (albeit in different ways), are found at the beginning of this succession. By making the intersection of stories proliferate within the tale, according to ancient rhythms, their art responds to the relational character of the originary scene through a *mimesis* that is still close to practice. Their explicit admirer, Borges, lies – in a certain sense – at the end of this succession, because he overturns the very genesis of the foundation at its roots. In his story, in which the lives are swallowed up, the relations become exclusively textual, or contextual. The text denies the reality from which it had originally drawn its inspiration. The representation, instead of re-presenting reality, swallows the originary scene and erases it.

The genealogy of the narration, after having turned the everyday practice of storytelling into a refined art, thus leads – through a progressive slide into the autonomy of the work – to the omnipotence of the book. At the end of the succession, instead of being the 'narratable,' the existent becomes paradoxically a 'narrated,' which from time to time is under the illusion that it has an existence. It is therefore obvious that Scheherazade, in so far as she is an exotic, literary creature, falls more easily than others into the trap of the game. In Borges' game, everything is overturned. The infinite storytelling of Scheherazade, which would like to avoid death, now ends up frustrating its goal by turning life itself into an illusion. She tells, in the text, how *the body of the book* is the only thing that facilitates the love-making of *The Arabian Nights*, giving birth to three sons. In short, the tale proliferates and procreates. The stork, drawn on the paper, regularly reveals unforeseen outcomes.

Anyone who has had the good fortune of having a childhood full of stories, while believing for a time that babies were brought by the stork, nonetheless knows perfectly well that texts are not what give birth. In spite of everything, the existent exists and resists. Moreover, we know that, starting with the Platonic love that gave birth through discourse to discursive children, the fertile power of the *logos* is an old nemesis of the existent. With all due respect to Descartes, *cogito ergo sum* never brought anyone into the world.

As a rather British scholar calmly puts it: 'at a certain point, surely, we must accept that material reality exists, that it continually knocks up against us, that texts are not the only thing.'[18]

NOTES

1 Benjamin, *Illuminations*, p. 98.
2 Roland Barthes, *The Pleasure of the Text*, p. 30.
3 Michel Foucault, 'What is an author?' from *The Foucault Reader*, edited by Paul Rabinow (New York: Pantheon Books, 1984), p. 102.
4 *Ibid.*
5 *Ibid.*

6 Jorge Luis Borges, 'The Garden of Forking Paths,' from *Labyrinths*, edited by D. Yates and J. Irby (New York: New Directions Books, 1964), p. 25. The interpolation of the framing-story does not seem, however, to have sprung entirely from the imagination of Borges. The Catalan Ramón Llull (1233–1316) could be the source of the game. Cf. Robert Irwin, *The Arabian Nights: a Companion* (London: Penguin Books, 1994), p. 95.

7 Renato Cavallero, 'Sociologia e storie di vita: il "testo," il "tempo," e lo "spazio" ' in *Biografia, Storia e Società*, edited by Maria I. Macioti (Naples: Liguori, 1985), p. 61.

8 Borges, 'Partial magic in the *Quixote*,' in *Labyrinths*, ed. Yates and Irby, p. 195.

9 *The Arabian Nights*, trans. Husain Haddawy (New York: Norton, 1990), p. 11.

10 Marina Warner, *From the Beast to the Blonde*, p. 13.

11 Karen Blixen, 'The Blank Page.' A famous feminist reading of this extraordinary tale, which turns upon the relation between the sexual and the textual, can be found in Susan Gubar, ' "The Blank Page" and the issues of female creativity,' *Critical Inquiry*, **8** (1981), pp. 294–306.

12 [TN: The Italian word 'intreccio,' – 'plot,' – has the additional sense of 'interweaving,' upon which Cavarero plays.]

13 Arendt, *The Human Condition*, p. 184.

14 Plato, *The Republic*, p. 392d.

15 Homer, *The Odyssey*, p. 137; Book ix, vv. 19–20.

16 Benjamin, *Illuminations*, p. 83.

17 *Ibid.*, p. 84.

18 Liz Stanley, *The Auto/biographical I: the Theory and Practice of Feminist Auto/biography* (Manchester, New York: Manchester University Press, 1992) [distributed exclusively in the USA and Canada by St Martin's Press, p. 246].

12

KAREN BLIXEN, OR THE CLASSIC RULE OF STORYTELLING

> I wish you would write about What it is in people that makes them want
> a story. The telling of tales. Ordinary life of ordinary people, Simenon-
> like. One can't say how life is, how chance or fate determine people's
> lives, except by telling the tale. In general one can't say more than –
> 'yes, that is the way it goes' [...] We seem unable to live without events,
> without events, life becomes an indifferent flux and we [are] hardly able
> to tell one day from the next. Life itself is full of tales.
>
> Hannah Arendt, from a 'Letter to Mary McCarthy'[1]

As a self-proclaimed modern Scheherazade, Karen Blixen writes fascinating
stories, and adopts, in the middle of the twentieth century, an archaic form of
narration – the oral timbre of storytelling.[2] Her philosophy is condensed by
Hannah Arendt in the sentence: 'no one has a life worthy of consideration about
which one cannot tell a story.' The story, indeed, 'reveals the meaning of what
would otherwise remain an intolerable sequence of events.' And yet, reading
Karen Blixen, we can meet a man who has no story. This happens to Mr Clay,
the protagonist of the tale 'The Immortal Story.'

Mr Clay, 'an extraordinarily rich purveyor of tea,' makes his existence
coincide with his work. There is no world for him, beyond the sphere of his
business affairs and his merciless power as a major businessman. What he leaves
behind, therefore, is not a life-story, but rather the calculated figures of his
business transactions. In fact, when he is old and no longer able to move about,
he finds no other way to pass the time than to ask a young employee to read to
him the master books. From register to register, the nights pass with some relief
for the sick insomniac. From register to register, the monotonous reading of the
employee narrates to Mister Clay the *whats* [*cose*] that happened in his life; the
recorded figures of the business dealings that the businessman has left behind as

the only tangible form of his existence. Until the registers end. And there is nothing left to read.

This is the decisive turning-point. Mr Clay, indeed, knows that there are things to read. He knows that 'people can refer to things which have already happened outside of the master books,' and he also knows that these accounts are called stories. In his youth, he had even heard one or two stories told by a sailor who 'referred to things which had happened to him.' These stories were, thus, autobiographical stories – accounts of the things that happened to the narrator. Since he still recalls one, Mr Clay decides to narrate in turn to the employee, with the roles inverted.

He tells the story of the sailor: how the sailor happened to be stopped by a rich gentleman during a brief stay in the port of a large city. The gentleman, promising to pay him five guineas, took the sailor to his sumptuous house in order to offer him refreshments, wine and dinner. After which, the gentleman began to reveal to the sailor how he had a young wife, but no children to whom he could leave his enormous fortune ... The tale, at this point, seems ready to take an interesting turn. But then Mr Clay is forced to interrupt the tale, to catch his breath. The employee interrupts, and declares that he, surprisingly, knows the same story and can take his employer's place, and continue to tell it. In the mouth of the employee, therefore, the tale goes on. The old gentleman, rich and childless, led the sailor to his wife's bed, telling him 'you know my wish, now you do your best to grant it.' Five guineas richer, after a night of love-making, and without ever again encountering his benefactor, the young man returns to his boat and departs for other ports of call.

The strategy of narration by successive voices, or the renarration of the same story from different perspectives, is rather common in Blixen's work. Moreover, it is obvious that the whole story that we are here rereading is a story invented by Karen Blixen. (But was this not already the case for the Homeric Ulysses and for Sophocles' Oedipus?) Following Arendt, we have indeed decided to 'naïvely' assume the artistic invention to be the frame that offers speculative material to the theorem of the link between identity and narration.

In the case of Mr Clay, this theorem runs up against a truly extraordinary problem. Namely, that the story of the sailor has the peculiarity of never having happened to anyone. As the employee says; 'all the sailors tell it, and each one of them, since they would like it to have happened to themselves, tells it as if it really had happened to him. But it didn't.' In short, this is a clearly invented story, not an *account* [*resoconto*] of things which happened. The difference between the master books and this story, thus, is abyssal. Before his stunned employer, the employee goes even further – the story never happened and never *will* happen, and this is why it is told. If the tales of the prophets have the defect – according to Mr Clay – of predicting things which begin to happen only 'every

130

THE CLASSIC RULE OF STORYTELLING

thousand years,' the story of the sailor has an even greater defect. It not only never happened, but never will happen. The factual unreality of its content is part of the past, the present and the future: it does not belong to time.

Actually, this is only a problem for Mr Clay. Anyone, including the employee, could indeed be content with the distinction between true stories and invented stories. Nevertheless, this is not a simply invented story, but rather a story that is characterized by the extraordinary law of not being able to ever happen to anyone. The stubborn realism of Mr Clay – for whom every tale is an account of things that 'really' happened – cannot tolerate this. Moreover, he finds himself in a truly paradoxical situation – faced with a personal existence that has no life-story to correspond with it; he discovers that there is a life-story to which, in principle, no existence can correspond. The attraction between the two poles of this opposition is inevitable. As the protagonist of mere business events – events that are accounted for in calculated figures, Mr Clay in fact decides to translate into events the only life-story he knows. He will make these narrated events happen – he will give empirical material to the tale.

Since an old man stricken with gout would have a hard time performing the part of the sailor, this materialization will not produce the story of Mr Clay. Rather it will be a story in whose happening he will play the part, obviously, of the rich gentleman. And here the troubles begin, because Mr Clay is not married, and certainly has no young wife. A young girl must be procured – well, not all that young – one who will become the prized actress of the story. The law of unhappenability [*inaccadibilità*] wins out from the start, imposing itself upon the fiction. Everyone has to play a part, simply staging a script. The only one to whom the story could effectively happen is a young sailor, chosen from among those who disembark at the port. The challenge, as Mr Clay puts it, is to make the story into reality – until a sailor can at least narrate it, from beginning to end, as it really happened to him.

Having made all the necessary preparations, this sort of 'demonic comedy' has begun. Its hero is a Danish sailor who, though he recognizes the story which he has heard narrated many times, accepts the invitation of the old gentlemen entirely out of the need for the five guineas. Everything unfolds, more or less, according to the script – lest the authentic aim of the play fail utterly. After the night of love-making, the sailor – interrogated by the employee – indeed denies that what happened to him was identical to that old and famous story. Moreover, he thinks that it is not worth telling a story that everyone knows, and which no one would believe to be true. If the goal was to make someone who really lived it narrate the story, the whole *mise-en-scène* has therefore failed. The Dane will never recount the story. Rather, all the other sailors of the world will continue to tell it, since they know that this story has never happened and can never happen. In this way, the story confirms its un-materializable status [*immaterializzabilità*] and, because of this, reveals itself to be immortal.

There is great fun, and a quite refined art, in Karen Blixen's polysemic fabric [*tessuto*] of 'Immortal Stories.' One of its possible meanings is nonetheless clear: it consists in the desire of Mr Clay to make the story real. And it is a unique story since, while it is invented, it is without author, just like life-stories. It is an immemorial story, invented and recounted by ordinary people, a story just as old as the hard milieu of sailors who recognize in it their ironic desire to be its protagonist precisely because they know it is impossible. Mr Clay's desire is quite different. Unlike the young Dane and unlike the sailor, he has no story of his own. His is an extraordinary case in which the narratable identity is absent and gets replaced by the figures of the master books. Rooted in this total lack, or, rather, rooted in this isolated existence that seems to leave behind no life-story, his desire to have a story cannot help confusing this 'having' with 'possessing' and, thus with domination and production. The 'materialization' of the story is indeed for him a manifestation of omnipotence, of doing something that cannot be done. In the same way in which he has made his millions, he wants to generate the story, together with this son, who is not his, and who could result from the night of love-making with this woman who is not his wife. What he intends to realize with this undertaking is indeed 'a world created by his will and his command,' a theater of young and robust puppets, moved by his hand. It is not enough for him to take part in the staging of the story, through the fictitious role that he plays. Old Clay wants to *make* the story, removing it from its scandalous status as the invention of an immemorial origin. If the story has no author, it will at least have its materialization.

A crucial point clearly escapes his commercial greed. While it does not claim to have any empirical factuality, even an invented story narrates past things, or things that have already happened, for the present. To make a story [*una storia*] happen in the future is impossible by definition. In the case of this story, of the autobiographical genre, we find ourselves nonetheless in the presence of a peculiar characteristic. This story has the extraordinary quality of being infinitely repeatable. Every sailor tells it as if it were his own story, overcoming the rule which makes of every life-story – even an invented one – the unrepeatable story of someone. The act of telling a story is indeed infinitely repeatable – though the story itself is not; it is the unrepeatable story [*storia*] of someone. The story of the sailor is therefore everyone's story precisely because it is not the story of anyone. Its hero is a vacant place that can be infinitely filled in with a proper name. In wanting to make it happen, Mr Clay wants to stop the play of infinite replacement, by factually linking it to a proper name which makes it into the unrepeatable story of a single hero. The story should indeed transform itself into the story of the Danish sailor, Povl, coming thus to adhere perfectly to that status of unrepeatability that in real stories can *never* be overcome.

The economy of desire that Mr Clay inhabits is therefore truly strange. The characteristic of his persona is not having a narratable identity, and therefore he does not miss it. Indeed, he not only leads an existence that leaves behind no life-story, but he is also ignorant of the fact that others lead existences that leave behind a story. Incapable of conceiving of a narratable identity, and insensitive to the self-rendered familiar by the narrating structure of memory, he is even ignorant of the desire for narration that belongs to that self. What is more, everything here proceeds in the reverse fashion. What is already there, is, in fact, a narration – a famous one, which is infinitely repeated – and which recounts a story that never happens and can never happen. The desire of Mr Clay, far from going from the narratable self to the narration of his own story, goes from the narration to the impossible facts from which the story should result. Mr Clay, indeed, is first of all ignorant of the bonds that intertwine a life-story with a narratable self that desires narration.

Mr Clay desires instead that the only story that he has ever heard be an *account* of things that have happened. Just as figures correspond with transactions, for events there should be a corresponding story. Business affairs are tangible, therefore things that happen should be equally tangible. This assumption about events in terms of material tangibility reveals the strange nature of his desire. This is not the desire for a story, but the desire to overturn the epistemic status of every story, especially invented ones, for which events are intangible by definition.

In a certain sense, Mr Clay ends up figuring as the opposite of Teiresias. The blind soothsayer in fact knows the whole story, but cannot intervene in the things that occurred or in things that will occur. Mr Clay, on the other hand, knows the whole story and intervenes in order that the occurrences pass from narrative fiction into fact. He wants to materially translate an invented story into a true story, but he ignores the fact that both always come *after* the narrated events. His mistake is rather large but, in its vain unfolding, an unexpected convergence of the invented story and the life-story is produced in the same narrative 'truth.'

Indeed, the impossible task of translating this immortal story into a life-story obviously fails – but the unexpected result of this failure becomes translated, in the meantime, into the life-stories of the same characters. The Danish sailor, while refusing to recognize himself in the immortal story staged for him, reveals that he indeed has a personal and unrepeatable story. He was recently rescued from a shipwreck, he comes from a long line of sailors, and he dreams of acquiring a boat in order to sail back to the shores of his beloved homeland. Indeed, this is why he has accepted the offer of five guineas and has made himself an accomplice of Clay's absurd plan. The plan itself – the immortal story in which the sailor finds himself playing a role – crosses over into the sailor's life-story, or at least comes to be part of it. Even other minor characters find their life-stories intersecting with the mechanism inspired by Mr Clay's invented story. The most extraordinary result nevertheless concerns Clay himself. His encounter with the immortal story, and the absurd undertaking which follows it, come to constitute the only events of his entire life that leave behind a story. By trying to materialize the immortal story, he ends up leaving behind the trace of his unrepeatable uniqueness.

Thus, at the end even Mr Clay has his story. His personal identity, narrated by the tale, is, however, the result of an oblique desire. As the owner [*padrone*] of goods, he in fact wanted to *control* [*padroneggiare*] the irreversible status of an invented story. What resulted instead was a life-story of that very personal identity which he, like every human being, does not master. Indeed, this story has the characteristics of every life-story – it could not be foreseen, or mastered, or planned, because its hero is not its author. Of course, Karen Blixen is the author behind it all, and she narrates it in the pages of the book. But the ideal narrator, *the other* in the scene, is – in this context – the employee. From the beginning, since he is the only one with whom the old man has a relationship, no one better than he could have told us *who* Mr Clay is.

Of course, the great narrator Karen Blixen knows this too. 'Who are you, sir?' asks the woman in black to Cardinal Salviati at the beginning of one of Blixen's *Last Tales*.[3] This is a good narrative beginning; indeed, as Arendt says, it is the only question in which the *beginning* itself gets recognized.

'Who am I?' replies the Cardinal. His is a sort of automatic repetition of the question, which, however, grasps its essence perfectly. It concerns an 'identity to be confessed.' In this nod to confession, there is undoubtedly a professional touch, but not in a banal sense. In the discourses 'of his penitents,' the Cardinal has indeed always recognized, not the *confession* of an identity, but rather 'the variations of a single cry from the heart, of a single question: who am I?' In such circumstances, the confessor is therefore the interrogated: he is not asked to listen, but rather to respond regarding the identity of the one who interrogates him. And yet, he declares that he does not know how to respond. 'If only I could respond to this question, if only I could resolve this enigma, then the people who ask me would be saved.' The enigma of someone who asks another for the revelation of his/her own identity therefore seems, in this case, to encounter a stalemate.

The woman in black, however, does not give in. She too has often spoken of the urgency of the question 'who am I?' in her sorrowful interviews with the bishop. But now her question is different, reversed: she asks him 'who are you?' In this scene, equally rare, where the roles are inverted, the Cardinal finds himself forced to respond to his own enigma. He realizes then, not only that he has a certain interest in the question, but that he has always known its solution. It consists in responding *according to the classic rule of storytelling.*

In the mouth of the Cardinal, the story – his life-story – thus begins, according to the usual, charming style of Karen Blixen (which is fascinating, but which here we must pass over). Whatever the content of this story is, what is certain is that the classic rule holds – namely, that the question of *who* one is finds its response in the unfolding of the story. The Cardinal's answer, like that of every human being, does not turn out to be an 'identity to be confessed,' but rather an identity to be narrated. If, on the side of the answer, the identity coincides with the narration, then on the side of the question, it reveals a kind of ontological desire that springs from its own narratability. In the question: 'who am I?' there speaks a narratable self in search of the tale of its story. And it is only in the decisive recognition of that narratability that the tale can make itself into an answer.

The autobiographical tale of the Cardinal, solicited by the woman in black, therefore meets the enigma and solves it. The sequence seems rather simple. The question 'who are you?' – posed by the woman to the bishop – finds its natural echo, almost an automatic repetition, a rhetorical sequence, in the 'who am I?' of the interrogated. And the autobiographical tale is able to offer itself as the correct response to both formulations. And yet they are not on the same level, and they are not indifferent. It is indeed precisely the question 'who am I?' that sustains the autobiographical tale of the Cardinal, while the 'who are you?' functions here rather as an invitation or introduction. There is, in short, a fundamental and urgent question, which resounds in the heart of everyone as the self-interrogation about his/her own identity. It is a question that is often made explicit by the 'penitent,' who turns to others, as if others could respond. This is nonetheless a desire for narration, which finds its answer, not in the words of others, but rather in the autobiographical tale. In this context, if it were not for the role of listeners, the others end up being superfluous, or function as the rhetorical pole of the question 'who am I?' The woman in black, who has asked the Cardinal who he is, would thus have no other role than that of introducing the self-interrogation of the bishop and of listening to his story.

The stylistic choice of the Cardinal – as the narrator of this story – neverthe-less produces an effect that complicates the theory and makes us suspect that things are not so simple, even for Karen Blixen. The Cardinal indeed not only announces that he will tell *a* story that only at the end is revealed to be *his* story, but he also chooses to narrate it in the third person rather than the first person. Although it is an autobiography, the narration that results has neither the tone, nor the style, nor the synthesis, of an autobiography. It seems rather that the impersonal tale of the Cardinal puts him in the classic position of the narrator, in so far as he appears to be other than the narrated characters. In this way the autobiography takes on the aspect of a biography, and it even risks losing this character by narrating material that precedes the birth of the Cardinal, and which deals with the tragic fate of two twins, about whom, in the end, it is unknown whether the bishop has narrated his own story or the story of his twin. Our theory of the relation between identity and narration remains therefore strong, but there is much that attenuates its autobiographical mark.

On the other hand, it is curious that the Cardinal does not deal with the obvious consequences of his experience as a confessor. The question 'who am I?' posed to him by the penitent, insists on a crucial paradox, namely, that of obtaining a response *from him*. If the classic axiom, according to which such a response consists in the telling of a story, is right, then it is in the guise of a biographer that he invokes this axiom. Everyone wants a story – *their own* story – which the Cardinal narrates.

For Blixen, too, the theory of the link between identity and story seems to move from autobiography to biography, bringing into play the need for the *other*. According to this hypothesis, the Cardinal no longer has the secondary role of listener, but rather the essential role of narrator. If the solution to the enigma consists in an 'identity to be narrated,' then the other, as the narrator, is now fundamental. If, in the heart of everyone beats the question 'who am I?' and if it needs as a response one's own story narrated by another, then this other is no longer the rhetorical site of interrogation, but rather its decisive hinge.

The theory is now clear and coincides perfectly with the paradox of Ulysses. It lies in the coming to self-interrogation of a narratable identity, whose status of narratability must be recognized by another through the biographical tale. 'Who am I?' was the explicit question that the penitents addressed to the bishop; 'tell me my story,' was its intrinsic message.

We have read Karen Blixen with Arendt's eyes. In the brief comment that Arendt dedicates to this very story, a single detail is worth noting: the question of the woman in black becomes directly linked to the story of the Cardinal, without any gesture towards the autobiographical aspect of that very story. Arendt's strange reticence regarding the autobiographical nature of the tale can obviously be attributed to her known preference for biography. But there is perhaps something more. Blixen's tale comes indeed to repropose the paradox of Ulysses between a horizon that alludes to the narratable self and to its desire. In other words, unlike Arendt, Blixen introduces a narrative, contextual and relational scene where biography and autobiography explicitly link the story to the desire to hear it told.

'The Tale of the Cardinal' lends itself quite well to a kind of commentary on Homer's Ulysses who, unexpectedly meeting up with the narration of his story, recognizes his narratable identity as the 'emotional' reality of his desire. In Blixen's tale, nonetheless, this interweaving is more complex, and at once, more evident – at least, too evident to be ignored. The enigma of identity here has indeed two figures for a solution. The first is the one that the Cardinal adopts when he responds to the question 'who are you?' with an autobiographical tale. The second is the one that the penitents invoke when they ask for others to tell their stories. Especially in this second figuration – which repeats the paradox of Ulysses – narratable identity is linked to an explicit desire for narration from another's mouth. It is indeed the very desire for narration, rooted in the self, that sustains the question 'who am I?' that flows from the heart of the penitents.

For Karen Blixen, who is fascinated by the figure of the stork, the narratability of the self is obviously not intended as a potential, as a possible logic that the self finds at its disposition; but rather as a total, irresidual exposition of the self *to* its own story, which has a truer, more profound nucleus. The narratable self only constitutes itself fully through the tale of its story; or, through the design of a life that only the tale refigures. Even if in Blixen's writing this design often takes on the disquieting name of destiny, it nonetheless reveals itself only *after*, and as a type of *newness* [*novità*] with respect to the life that it (albeit unintentionally) embodies.

Indeed this happens to the young Calypso in 'Deluge at Norderney.' Her own story, told to her by Madamigella Malin, is heard by the protagonist as though it were 'a new story for her,' although it is 'a symbol,' or a beautified simulacrum of 'how the young girl had really lived.'[4] The self does not plan her destiny, nor does she follow it; rather, she finds it in the tale of others, recognizing with surprise the acts of her life.

For Blixen, who knows a thing or two about stories, the question which reveals the desire of the self on the narrative scene is therefore the question 'who am I?' addressed to another. It is helpful, once again, to distinguish the scenarios in order to avoid confusion. As Arendt puts it, the question 'who are you?' does not belong to the same scene as the question 'who am I?' but rather belongs to that of a shared, exhibitive space where the response is the action. The ambiguity that caused difficulty for the Cardinal and, consequently, made Arendt curiously reticent regarding the autobiographical mark of the tale, is thus due to the woman in black. Her question is out of context.

By asking 'who are you' within the scene of narration, she forces the answer to be autobiographical instead of biographical. Thus, the Cardinal is not wrong: he simply adapts to the inverse of the paradox of Ulysses, by adopting the style and the syntax of the biographical tale. If he had had the prudence to first ask 'who am I?' – addressing this question to the woman in black – he would have achieved a double result: first, of obtaining the narration of his story, although this is unlikely; and second, more importantly, of recognizing, in the strange question of the penitent, a narratable self that has come to the full expression of her desire.

This desire goes in search of a narrator because life-stories, like destinies, have no author. Only invented stories, it seems, have an author. Faithful to the archaic form of narrating, Karen Blixen herself prefers nevertheless to define herself as a *conteuse*; a woman who, like Scheherazade, does more than invent stories of which she is the author – she comes across them and tells them. 'In principle, it was a story,' says the Cardinal, mocking with surprising irreverence the reading of the sacred text. The irreverence is, however, only *apparent*.

The only author of all stories, in the opinion of the cleric, is in fact God himself.

NOTES

1 Hannah Arendt, *Between Friends: the Correspondence of Hannah Arendt and Mary McCarthy, 1949–1975* (edited and with an introduction by Carol Brightman), 1st edn (New York: Harcourt Brace, 1995), pp. 294–5.
2 Cf. Nadia Fusini, *Nomi* (Milan: Feltrinelli, 1986), p. 23.
3 Cf. Karen Blixen, 'The Cardinal's Tale' in *Last Tales*.
4 Karen Blixen, *Seven Gothic Stories* (New York: Modern Library, 1982).

13

THE WORLD IS FULL OF STORIES JUST WAITING TO BE TOLD

She wrote some stories about what must have been for her the lesson of the folly of her youth, namely the 'sin' of fulfilling a story – and inserting it into life through a preconstituted model instead of patiently waiting for the story to emerge, or revealing it in the imagination – insofar as it is distinct from creating fictions – and then trying to stay faithful to it.

Hannah Arendt, *Isak Dinesen*

Karen Blixen loved to compare herself to Scheherazade. In fact, in some scenes from *Out of Africa*, she adapts the role to herself perfectly. She and her lover, Denis Finch Hutton, sat down on cushions scattered on the ground, around a tapestry. *Entertaining him [Intrattenendolo]* with the suspension of the story, Karen narrated stories to Denis in to order to *keep him [trattenerlo]* close to her, and far from his adventures as a hunter. Eros and narration are thus modulated to the tempo of their secret rhythm. Unlike Scheherazade, it was not the threat of death that multiplied the tales, but rather love for the other – or, perhaps, that type of little death that one finds in the abandonment that follows departure. When death really took Denis, keeping him away forever, the art of narrating thus became useless as the continual entertainment [*in-trattenimento*] of the lover.

Pressured by debts, Karen Blixen was in those very same days also losing her Africa forever. The experience of abandonment could not have been more total. As we know, Blixen nonetheless knew how to adapt herself to the 'anecdotes of destiny.' At the dawn of her new life, in the little Danish house by the sea, she made herself into a professional narrator in order to entertain a wider number of listeners. As her brother says, after having read the first drafts of *Seven Gothic Stories*, her steps thus came to follow that course that would at last have brought her to see her stork.[1]

Occasionally glimpsed by her, and certainly seen by others, the design of Karen Blixen's life leaves behind the profile of a stork, or perhaps that of

Scheherazade. She writes stories but, as she keeps emphasizing, her art is that of the *storyteller*; that is, an art which belongs to the oral tradition of the tale. Unlike the novel, which constructs characters and is ready to sacrifice the tale to their psychological substance, Karen Blixen throws herself into telling stories that 'have no pity' for their protagonists.[2] According to the orality that has belonged to storytelling since ancient times, the story indeed does not content itself with introspection, and neither does it aspire to describe the *Bildung* of a soul like the famous *Bildungsroman*. The story, rather, narrates a destiny that proceeds quickly through events and occurrences. It is the destiny, totally unmasterable and unique for each human being, that Arendt calls *daimon*. As Blixen puts it, it alludes to the conviction that 'in the end, there is probably *something* for each individual which he cannot refuse ... "life" is its price.'[3]

Whether it is called *daimon* or destiny, or simply *something*, this is that unrepeatable design that each life traces with its course. It is not a role to be interpreted, or even less a hidden substance to be embodied, but rather the totally *apparent* figure of a unique existence that suggests a unity.

Like Scheherazade, the Danish narrator understands perfectly how the story makes its hero shine, and not the reverse. 'Ali Baba, who in himself is nothing but a wood-cutter, is the worthy hero of a great story.'[4] In other words, Ali Baba does not plan or foresee his story. As with many other heroes, the story happens to him without his having to worry about facing it, 'since it will be the story which foresees.'[5] As a good narrator, Scheherazade recounts the story of Ali Baba just as it happened, faithful to a contingency of events that cannot be explained by the logic of cause and effect. 'It is, indeed, already half of the art of narrating, letting each story be free, in the act of reproducing it, from every sort of explanation.'[6]

The modern art of the novel, on the other hand, loves explanations, and loves to look inside, to excavate appearances in order to discover the interiority of the subject.[7] By indulging in the psychological characteristics of the individual in order to make them closer to us, more like us, almost a friend – and making us interested in the individual more than his story – this shows itself quite evidently to be 'a human product.'[8] As the Cardinal says, 'in principle it was the story,' the tale of a story that is closest to the divine art, in the sense that no human being makes her own story, or plans it, or controls it, or decides it. Like destiny, the story results from uncontrollable events that cannot be explained, or brought back to an interior nucleus that would be their cause.

It is therefore not by chance that this divine source of the tale is drawn to the metaphor, often used by Blixen, of the puppeteer behind the scenes, who constructs destinies. As Arendt puts it, this ancient metaphor, already present in Plato, is indeed 'a symbol for the fact that real stories, in distinction from those we invent, have no author.'[9] In other words, only an omniscient divinity, that looks from above and hands out destinies like a great puppet-master, can symbolically play the role of the author. For Arendt, this is an imaginary role – life itself never fulfills a destiny, but rather consists in the unmasterable exposition of uniqueness, from which there results a story that the protagonist had never planned and that was always without an author.

Karen Blixen the narrator, who is less concerned with distinguishing real stories from invented ones, seems rather to have known the temptation to make every story into a destiny that life works to 'realize.' This is a rather powerful temptation, if it is true that, in her youth, 'the story which she had planned to play out in her life had been to follow the story of her father.'[10] After her 'planned' life played some cruel tricks on her, she knew that she had to learn the existential lesson inscribed in the narration. Whether true or invented, stories are always stories of *someone* whose uniqueness is put into the words of the tale. The task of the narrator is not to create them, but to make sure that the tale is faithful to its story.

The call to the divine art aligns Blixen once again with her beloved counterpart, Scheherazade. As the tradition of the *storyteller*, which goes back to the 'muse' invoked by Homer, has it – the one who tells stories is hardly preoccupied with the question of the *author* (unlike the philosophers of our time). At the center of the ancient art of telling stories lies the figure of the narrator, not that of the author. Scheherazade read a lot and knew how to tell stories. Karen Blixen, mediating the voice of her characters, continually alludes to the narrator as the one who knows a story, and knows how to tell it faithfully. It is almost as though the logic of occurring always makes this a given, the story is *already given* to the sublime art of the one who tells it. The chosen ones of this art therefore have no reason to worry about the role of the author, or about the power to invent a story that 'constructs' or 'reveals' a character. On the contrary, they insist on the central role of a story that seems to be autonomous, both from the will of the protagonist and from the one who narrates it.

Like all great storytellers, Karen Blixen knows that the narrative fiction alludes to a horizon of meaning in which, always and necessarily, the significance of each lived life comes into play. She has no difficulty in *passing* from the fable of the man by the pond, to the expression of her personal desire that her life too leave behind a stork. Unlike the paradigm of modern man, whose experience is that of 'the anonymity of the series, the impersonality of life,' she recognizes in each life an unrepeatable meaning and gives it the 'tellability' of a tale.[11] As many have noted, the gesture runs contrary to all the tendencies that twentieth-century culture inherits and transforms.

The writings of Karen Blixen thus open a narrative scene that ends up being anomalous with respect to the authors of classic *Bildungsroman*, and with respect to those who write 'stories of formation in which the formation does not happen:

in which the objective culture, rigid in its conventions and institutions, no longer contributes to the construction of a subject, but wounds it and disintegrates it.'[12] Put simply, Blixen's stories do not court the modern subject, or the strange fate of its post-modern dissolution. Rather, by telling of a uniqueness in which a destiny that outlines unforeseeable events comes to the fore, Blixen pursues that ' "desire for meaning," for imagination, for *re-enchantment*,' which persists, like an unconfessable secret, in the stubborn desire of the contemporary reader.[13]

Recent attempts, especially on the part of feminist criticism, to re-appropriate Blixen's texts through the post-modern perspective, end up being equally singular.

At first sight, this criticism seems appealing. Not only because the archaic form of oral narration, like Homer or Scheherazade, never proceeds in a linear way – intersecting and assembling, interrupting and deviating, without offering a centered narrative strategy that valorizes the fragment – but also because of the known tendency of Danish writers to often change their name. All of this obviously appears irresistible to the theory of multiple subjectivity.

In the circle of feminist criticism, the tale most often taken as testimony to Blixen's post-modernism is 'The Dreamers.' It tells the story of the singer Pellegrina Leoni who, after losing her voice in a tragic accident, fakes her death in order to assume many other identities. 'I no longer only want to be a single woman, from now on I want to be many women,' she says, 'I never again want to link my heart and my whole life in a single woman, to suffer so much.'[14] She thus invites her friend, Marcus Cocoza, to do the same – he indeed becomes 'the slave and the prisoner.' 'From now on you must be more than one, many people, too many to even think of,' Pellegrina tells him. And she maliciously adds, 'Is it not strange that no philosopher has ever thought of it, and that the idea came to me?'

For the post-modern approach, especially the feminist one, all of this is too rich to be turned down.[15] And yet, the actual progression of the story of Pellegrina should dampen this initial enthusiasm. We come to know, from the tale of her different lovers, how Pellegrina has impersonated 'many women' – a Roman prostitute, a Swiss revolutionary, and a Swedish dame – each time changing names, but nonetheless letting a common personality show through, which is, in effect, recognized by her lovers, who overhear her tales. The story of Pellegrina Leoni and her decision to be many women is told, to the lovers themselves, by Marcus Cocoza – the only one who followed her like a silent shadow, from beginning to end, and helped in all her metamorphoses.

The tale of Marcus Cocoza comes to the bed where Pellegrina, surrounded by those who love her, is dying. Indeed, it is the very moment of death that reveals the meaning of the story. In her delirium she recovers her first identity and sings an operatic aria, while her whole body 'vibrates like the string of an instrument.'

'Pellegrina Leoni is back' exclaims Marcus, turning to an imaginary public. And she echoes him 'Come unto her, now, all again ... It is I – I, forever, now.'[16]

The tale thus lends itself only superficially to a post-modern reading, and then ends up contradicting it. The tale narrates how Pellegrina can journey ['*pellegrinare*'] through many identities, in order to flee and forget that 'first' identity that caused her such enormous suffering. The first identity, that of the lyric singer, returns however in the end and closes the circle of the metamorphosis. The first, too, is nevertheless an identity that corresponds with a role, to a vocation, to a talent. In other words, this is not the identity that Arendt would call the *who* of Pellegrina, but rather that which names her *what*. Marcus Cocoza tells the story of *who* Pellegrina is – a story that is assembled through the stories told by her lovers, and which composes, in the end, a unique and unrepeatable destiny. The story results from intentional choices and from chance, from the extraordinary decision to be many women, and from unforeseeable circumstances. The many women whom the heroine has embodied belong, however, to a single story – that of Pellegrina.

Arendt rereads the 'philosophy' of Karen Blixen through the life of Pellegrina. Like the lyric singer, Blixen was always afraid of the trap of professional identity – of being identified with the writer, 'with the author whose own identity is inevitably reified by the public.'[17] She did not want to be a writer. To write stories was something that simply happened to her in life, since she had to earn a living and she only knew how to write and cook. Rather, she liked being a *conteuse*, a narrator who was interested in stories and in the ways of telling them.

Of course, being a *conteuse* is also a profession, if not a passion. Proclaiming herself to be a narrator, Karen Blixen risks therefore once again falling into the trap of professional identity, since it says *what* she is, and not *who* she is. According to Arendt, this identity – founded in an ability, an artistic talent, a gift – has nonetheless the great merit of adhering to the human world and its plural spectacle, by gathering the narrative threads that human lives leave behind.

The world is indeed 'full of stories, circumstances and curious situations which are just waiting to be told.'[18] More precisely, suggests Arendt from her unique perspective, the world is full of stories because it is full of lives. To be faithful to the story 'means being faithful to the life.'[19] This is not simply a metaphor. To live, in the sense of fully living from beginning to end – in perfect fidelity to life, just as the good narrator tells her story from beginning to end in perfect fidelity to the story – this represents only one side of the theory. The other side is represented by the conviction that one can only recount, or relive, through the imagination and put into words, 'what has in some way happened.'[20] For the stubborn realism of Arendt, therefore, Blixen's art does not consist in invention, in fiction, or in the fantastic vein that *creates* stories. It consists rather in the ability to look at the world as a stage on which many lives intersect, leaving behind their story.

Of course, Karen Blixen uses her own imagination. Nonetheless, the most admirable side of her art consists in respecting the relation of 'dependency' between lives, stories and storytelling that escapes Mr. Clay. Indeed, following Arendt, while a story results from every life, no life can result from a story. The figure of the stork that results from the footsteps of the man by the pond does not guide him. To plan one's own life as though it were a story, to make it conform to an idea, to live it like a novel, is merely an error that Karen Blixen herself committed in the years of her youth.

The uniqueness of the existent has no need of a form that plans or contains it. Rooted in the unmasterable flux of a constitutive exposition, she is saved from the bad habit of prefiguring herself, and from the vice of prefiguring the lives of others. The figure, the unity of the design, the profile of the stork – if it comes – only comes afterwards: as in the dream of a fable, or, perhaps, as a desire that is not exchanged for its dream.

NOTES

1 Cf. Judith Thurman, *Isak Dinesen: the Life of Karen Blixen* (London: Weidenfeld and Nicholson, 1982), pp. 255–6.
2 *Ibid.*, p. 285.
3 Karen Blixen, *Letters from Africa:1914–1931* (London: Weidenfeld and Nicolson, 1981), p. 351.
4 Karen Blixen, 'The First Tale of the Cardinal,' in *Last Tales*, p. 36.
5 *Ibid.*, p. 37.
6 Walter Benjamin, 'The Storyteller,' *Illuminations*.
7 Arendt, *The Human Condition*, pp. 71–4.
8 Karen Blixen [writing as 'Isak Dinesen'], 'The First Tale of the Cardinal,' in *Last Tales* (New York: Vintage Books, 1975), p. 36.
9 Arendt, *The Human Condition*, p. 185.
10 Arendt, *Isak Dinesen*, p. 170.
11 Nadia Fusini, *Nomi* (Milano: Feltrinelli, 1986), p. 25.
12 Cf. Franco Moretti, *Modern Epic: the World-System from Goethe to Garcia Marquez*, trans. Quintin Hoare (London; New York: Verso, 1996).
13 *Ibid.*, pp. 232, 234.
14 Karen Blixen [writing as 'Isak Dinesen'], with an introduction by Dorothy Canfield, *Seven Gothic Stories* (New York: Vintage Books, 1972), p. 332.
15 For example, see Susan Hardy Aiken, 'Writing (in) exile: Isak Dinesen and the poetics of displacement,' in *Women's Writing in Exile*, eds Mary Lynn Brow and Angela Ingram (Chapel Hill: University of North Carolina Press, 1989), pp. 114–30.
16 Karen Blixen, *Seven Gothic Tales*, p. 352.
17 Arendt, *Isak Dinesen*, p. 162.
18 *Ibid.*
19 *Ibid.*, p. 163.
20 *Ibid.*, p. 162.

INDEX

8233105R0

Made in the USA
Lexington, KY
20 January 2011